Protesting Power

WAR AND PEACE LIBRARY

Series Editor: Mark Selden

Protesting Power

War, Resistance, and Law

Francis A. Boyle

ROWMAN & LITTLEFIELD PUBLISHERS, INC.
Lanham • Boulder • New York • Toronto • Plymouth, UK

ROWMAN & LITTLEFIELD PUBLISHERS, INC.

Published in the United States of America
by Rowman & Littlefield Publishers, Inc.
A wholly owned subsidiary of The Rowman & Littlefield Publishing Group, Inc.
4501 Forbes Boulevard, Suite 200, Lanham, Maryland 20706
www.rowmanlittlefield.com

Estover Road, Plymouth PL6 7PY, United Kingdom

British Library Cataloguing in Publication Information Available

Library of Congress Cataloging-in-Publication Data

Boyle, Francis Anthony, 1950–
 Protesting power : war, resistance, and law / Francis A. Boyle.
  p. cm. — (War and peace library)
 Includes bibliographical references and index.
 ISBN-13: 978-0-7425-3891-7 (cloth : alk. paper)
 ISBN-10: 0-7425-3891-5 (cloth : alk. paper)
 ISBN-13: 978-0-7425-3892-4 (pbk. : alk. paper)
 ISBN-10: 0-7425-3892-3 (pbk. : alk. paper)
 1. Civil disobedience—United States. 2. Civil resistance. I. Title.
 KF4786.B69 2008
 342.7308'54—dc22

                                                    2007024394

Printed in the United States of America

$\otimes$[TM] The paper used in this publication meets the minimum requirements of American
National Standard for Information Sciences—Permanence of Paper for Printed Library
Materials, ANSI/NISO Z39.48-1992.

This book is dedicated to Virginia Monarque Boyle, who taught me everything worth knowing:

> And those who have chosen the portion of injustice, and tyranny, and violence, will pass into wolves, or into hawks and kites;—whither else can we suppose them to go?

—Plato, *Phaedo*

Contents

Introduction

About twenty-five years ago I received a telephone call asking me on very short notice to become involved in the defense of my first civil resister. Ardently believing the U.S. government was committing state crimes, Richard Sauder climbed the fence of a Minuteman missile silo near Warrensburg, Missouri, and then performed the Catholic ritual of exorcism over the missile. He faced six months in prison for this act and another six months for violating probation after having done the exact same thing at a Titan II missile silo in Arkansas.

My original reaction was that the U.S. government prosecutors should have better things to do with their time and resources than go after the Richard Sauders of the world. But as I pondered the matter at greater length, it made perfect sense for the government to prosecute a religious person who repeatedly denounced the Pentagon's beloved weapons of mass destruction (WMD) as the devil incarnate. Mr. Sauder was a serial prayer for peace. As the U.S. government saw it, he was a greater threat to its war system than a murderer, a robber, or a rapist. So of course he had to be prosecuted and persecuted.

Since I was given only a few days' notice to prepare for this case, I decided to consult a senior colleague of mine who had a reputation as a civil libertarian. "Why are you wasting your time with him?" he responded. "Obviously he's guilty!"

"That remains to be determined at trial—not by you or me," I tartly replied. That was the last time I ever asked that senior law professor for advice. I flew to Kansas City not knowing exactly what to expect.

Upon my arrival at the federal courthouse just before the trial, I was brought up to meet Mr. Sauder in a small holding cell just outside the courtroom. Mr. Sauder was kneeling on the bare floor, Bible in hand. When he finished his prayer, he rose, shook my hand, and introduced himself: "Why don't you join me in jail as a resister against nuclear weapons?"

Somewhat taken aback, I laughed uncertainly: "I am here to keep you out of jail!"

Not content with my answer, Sauder persisted, so I somewhat lamely responded: "We each have our own talents and gifts. Mine is being a lawyer and a law professor. It's my job to keep you and others like you out of jail. I cannot really do that while sitting in jail myself." At that point we hurriedly ended our conversation to walk down the hall for the opening of his criminal trial.

This was the classic case of Daniel going into the proverbial lion's den. Sauder had decided to defend himself as a matter of principle. In addition, the courtroom was packed with air force officers in their uniforms to make it perfectly clear to this federal judge that the Pentagon wanted Sauder's head on a platter. Of course, the judge was more than happy to oblige them.

During my testimony on behalf of Sauder, the judge repeatedly cut me off, interrupted me, shut me down, and admonished me. At one point I thought he was going to cite me for contempt of court and return me involuntarily to that small holding cell down the hall where I had first met Mr. Sauder.

Sauder then took the stand in his own defense: "Jesus said, 'Blessed are the peace makers.' He didn't say that about war makers."[1] Not surprisingly, the judge found Mr. Sauder guilty as charged.

Right after these kangaroo-court proceedings were over, I spoke with a former U.S. attorney who had advised Mr. Sauder free of charge: "You're lucky to get out of this town. I know that judge. He wanted to put you away in jail with Sauder!"

Flying home in freedom that evening, there was only one thought that constantly reverberated in my mind: "There has to be a better way!" So when I returned to my office, I began to figure out how to do precisely that.

Soon thereafter, I received a letter from Mr. Sauder informing me that the judge had sentenced him to five months and twenty-nine days in jail, one day less than the maximum, in addition to imposing six months for his probation violation. One year in prison for praying for peace. "You would think this was the Soviet Union," I said to myself as I read the disheartening but not unexpected news.

Furthermore, Mr. Sauder wrote that at the sentencing hearing the judge told him "that I need rehabilitation, my disrespect for the law demonstrates that I am not ready to be released into society, that I have acted recklessly and endangered the lives of others, that I need to need to spend more time in a jail setting, etc." Mr. Sauder asked for my opinion, so I immediately wrote back:

May 24, 1982

Mr. Richard Sauder
14th Floor/N-3
Jackson County Jail
415 E. 12 St.
Kansas City, MO 64106

Dear Richard:
　　Thank you very much for your letter. It was most appreciated. I am sorry to hear about the sentence the judge handed down to you. As a fellow who teaches international law and criminal law, I can only say that in my opinion the magistrate was dead wrong to state that you are in need of rehabilitation. I think that what the world needs today is more people like Richard Sauder who are willing to take a courageous stand against nuclear weapons in an effort to bring to the attention of America the immorality, illegality, and sheer insanity of our government's policies. I was honored to have done what little I did to mount a defense against your prosecution.
　　Please keep in touch.

　　　　　　　　　　　　　　Yours very truly,
　　　　　　　　　　　　　　Francis A. Boyle
　　　　　　　　　　　　　　Associate Professor of Law

　　This book keeps my promise to Richard Sauder. It distills twenty-five years of the knowledge, judgment, and experience that come from defending civil resisters who acted to prevent the commission of state crimes by the U.S. government as well as by several foreign states around the world. I have selected some of the most difficult, and seemingly impossible, cases that I have worked on during the past quarter century in the hope of providing some light in these dark days of the administration of President George W. Bush. It is an expression of hope in the power of the human spirit for doing good and resisting evil. As this book demonstrates, sometimes the human spirit for good triumphs. Sometimes it does not. But the power of the human spirit is never defeated.
　　While Mr. Sauder sat in jail for that year and repeatedly corresponded with me, others rose up to take his place and directly confronted the genocidal horrors of weapons of mass destruction deployed by the U.S. government. Others would rise up to oppose the history of criminal U.S. military interventions around the world in the post–Vietnam War era starting with the Reagan and Bush Sr. administrations, continuing through the Clinton administration, and now during the Bush Jr. administration. Today the American peace movement

is alive and well and fighting back against the Bush Jr. administration's military interventionism abroad and police-state tactics at home.

The GI resistance movement has gathered a full head of steam, with many members of the U.S. armed forces exercising their constitutional right to conscientious objection, while about eight thousand other GIs have simply gone AWOL when faced with the Bush Jr. administration's multifaceted international transgressions.[2] A counterrecruitment campaign designed to keep the youth of America out of the military is thriving as well. The Pledge of Resistance campaign has been reactivated from the days when it opposed the Reagan administration's *contra* war against Nicaragua. Finally, the national campaign to impeach President Bush, Vice President Cheney, and Attorney General Gonzales has entered the mainstream of American political discourse.[3]

A monumental struggle for the heart and soul of the United States of America and the future of the world is being waged by the peacemakers on one side, arrayed against the war makers on the other—to use the biblical reference that Mr. Sauder so bravely articulated in court twenty-five years ago. This book is intended to provide some hope as well as some nonviolent ammunition for the peacemakers of the world to use. This book demonstrates that civil resistance solidly grounded in international law, human rights, and the U.S. Constitution can be used to fight back and defeat the legal, constitutional, and humanitarian nihilism of the Bush administration and its neoconservative minions.

To be sure, civil resistance, international law, human rights, and the U.S. Constitution are no panacea for the numerous dilemmas of contemporary international relations and of domestic politics that confront the United States and the world at large in this new millennium. But considered together, they do provide one promising medium for extricating the United States from the deadly acts that have driven the American foreign-affairs and defense decision-making establishment throughout the post–Cold War epoch, especially during the second Bush administration. Civil resistance, international law, human rights, and the U.S. Constitution constitute the most hopeful alternatives to the Bush administration's Hobbesian vision of a U.S. empire abroad, an American police state at home, and incessant warfare to sustain them both along the lines of George Orwell's classic novel, *1984*.

In civil resistance, international law, human rights, and the U.S. Constitution, the peace movement has the four quintessential principles to counter these forces of militarism run amok. In my extensive experience over three decades, I have found that the vast majority of Americans readily agree with the proposition that their elected government officials should possess and promote the rule of law and human rights both at home and abroad. Traveling around the country for lectures, lawsuits, and debates, I have always experienced a very warm reception for these principles among people, regardless of their partisan political affiliations. I have repeatedly found that when properly and vigorously presented to the citizens of America, arguments based on international law, human rights, and the U.S. Constitution invariably triumph over a Hobbesian argument based on the application of power politics and the threat or use of military force. These principles are becoming even more relevant to the American people and Congress in the face of the second Bush administration's wanton, wholesale, and vicious attack on them—as evidenced by the massive, overwhelming repudiation of the Bush administration and its criminal war against Iraq by the American people in the November 2006 elections.

How many times have Americans heard the incessant refrain, especially during this Bush administration, that there are really only two alternative courses of conduct: either threaten—or actually use—U.S. military force in a particular situation, or allow the "enemies" of the U.S. government to prevail? Or as President Bush baldly told the rest of the world after the terrible tragedy of September 11: "Either you are with us, or you are with the terrorists."[4] There is, however, a third alternative to this deliberately false and misleading rhetorical dichotomy of Hobbesian power politics or a do-nothing policy of isolationism: an Aristotelian strategy of the mean that embraces the rules of international law, human rights, the U.S. Constitution, and civil resistance.

An enormous amount of work can and must continue to be done by the peace movement to explain to the American people both why and how these principles can be brought to bear upon and prevail in the daily conduct of U.S. foreign affairs and defense policies as well as domestic politics. Grassroots proselytization is the most effective long-term strategy. In the meantime, active civil resistance for the prevention of ongoing state crimes by U.S. government officials must become an integral component of this overall strategy. It is up to the peace movement to educate American citizens about why and how they must and can hold their policymakers fully accountable. Civil resistance to prevent state crimes by U.S. government officials is one effective way to accomplish that objective.

Notwithstanding all the serious crimes committed by successive U.S. administrations that I have amply documented here and elsewhere during the past three decades as a lawyer and professor, the truth of the matter is that the United States of America is still the oldest constitutional democracy in the world today. We the people of the United States must fight to keep it that way.

We the People of the United States, in Order to form a more perfect Union, establish Justice, insure domestic Tranquility, provide for the common defence, promote the general Welfare, and secure the Blessings of Liberty to ourselves and our Posterity, do ordain and establish this Constitution for the United States of America.

NOTES

1. John T. Dauner, *Arms Protester Convicted of Trespassing at Missile Site*, Kansas City Times, May 7, 1982.
2. Jeremy Brecher & Brendan Smith, *Lieutenant Watada's War Against the War*, Nation, June 12, 2006.
3. Francis A. Boyle, *A Guide to Impeaching President George W. Bush*, in *Destroying World Order* 158–72 (2004); John C. Bonifaz, *Warrior-King* (2003); Center for Constitutional Rights, *Articles of Impeachment against George W. Bush* (2006); Dave Lindorff & Barbara Olshansky, *The Case for Impeachment* (2006); Elizabeth Holtzman & Cynthia L. Cooper, *The Impeachment of George W. Bush* (2006).
4. President George W. Bush, Address to a Joint Session of Congress and the American People (Sept. 20, 2001) (transcript available at http://www.whitehouse.gov/news/releases/2001/09/20010920-8.html).

Chapter One

The Right to Engage in Civil Resistance to Prevent State Crimes

IN THE UNITED STATES DISTRICT COURT
FOR THE DISTRICT OF COLORADO
Criminal Case No. 02-CR-509 R B
UNITED STATES OF AMERICA,
Plaintiff,
v.
1. CAROL GILBERT,
2. JACKIE MARIE HUDSON,
3. ARDETH PLATTE,
Defendants.

DECLARATION OF FRANCIS A. BOYLE

Pursuant to 28 U.S.C. § 1746, Francis A. Boyle declares under penalty of perjury:

1. I am a professor of law at the University of Illinois, at Champaign, Illinois. I hold both a Juris Doctor magna cum laude (1976) from Harvard Law School, as well as an A.M. (1978) and Ph.D. (1983) in Political Science from Harvard University, specializing in international law and politics.

2. I am an expert in International Law and foreign policy. I have studied, read, and written extensively in these areas, and have been qualified as an expert witness in several courts across the country. I have also taught in the field of criminal law. My resume is attached to this declaration and incorporated by reference.

3. I offer this declaration in support of the Motions to Dismiss the charges of sabotage (18 U.S.C. § 2155) and malicious destruction of property (18 U.S.C. § 1361) and in establishing the content and application of the laws of war to elements of the offenses charged and in support of justification defenses including necessity and crime prevention.

4. I am aware that expert opinion on points of law is ordinarily not permitted in court. Opinion of published international legal scholars is an important exception to that rule. The Statute of the International Court of Justice provides that questions of international law shall be determined by resort, inter alia, to "the teachings of the most highly qualified publicists of the various nations. . ." Id., Art. 38(1)(d). An integral part of the United Nations Charter, which is a treaty and thus equivalent to a federal statute as Supreme Law of the Land, this rule of evidence is applicable in federal court. The Supreme Court expressed the same opinion in *The Paquete Habana*, 175 U.S. 677, 700 (1900). Cf. Fed. R. Crim. P. 26.1 (ordinary Rules of Evidence do not apply to determination of foreign law).

5. In the implementation of foreign policy, the current Administration has threatened to use nuclear weapons and was on October 6, 2002, actively threatening to use the Minuteman III, N-8 at issue in this case. Because this threat or use of 300 kilotons of heat, blast and radiation are uncontrollable and because the threat or use of this weapon is for a "first-strike," the Minuteman III, N-8, on October 6, 2002, was not merely unlawful, but actually criminal. This conclusion is elaborated in paragraphs 6-15 below.

6. The body of federal law which governs these matters includes rules and principles of international law. International law is not "higher" or separate law; it is part and parcel of the structure of federal law. The Supreme Court so held in the landmark decision in *The Paquete Habana*, 175 U.S. 677, 700 (1900). Thus international law must be considered along with Congressional statutes, Constitutional law, administrative law, federal common law, Rules of Court, military law, incorporated state law and any other pertinent body of law, whenever it applies according to the pertinent rules of supremacy, parallel construction, and choice of law.

7. International law, as part of U.S. law, includes the law of war. Under the fourth Hague Convention, various types of weapons are absolutely prohibited under all circumstances. For example, no nation may use a weapon which causes unnecessary suffering to human beings. Second, the use of poison or poison weapons is flatly prohibited by the Hague Regulations, by the Geneva Protocol of 1925, and by the U.S. Army *Field Manual 27-10* on the Law of Land Warfare (1956) and the U.S. Department of the Air Force Pamphlet on "International Law—The Conduct of Armed Conflict and Air Operations" (AFP 110-31, 1976). The United States is bound as a party to each of these. Third, a nation may not adopt methods or tactics of warfare that fail to distinguish between combatants and non-combatants. Because of the inevitable effects of the explosion of the Minuteman III, N-8, each of these rules prohibits its use. Other provisions of international law, moreover, prohibit destruction of the natural environment, another inevitable consequence of the explosion of any nuclear weapon including the Minuteman III, N-8.

8. The most recent and most authoritative summary of the current and binding laws of war as applied to any threat or use of nuclear weapons is found in the International Court of Justice Opinion, *Legality of the Threat or Use of Nuclear Weapons*, 8 July 1996. As further explained in my recent book *The Crim-*

inality of Deterrence, that the Defendants left at the Minuteman III, N-8 site, the Minuteman III is in a category of nuclear weapons that is, ipso facto, incapable of distinguishing between civilian and combatant, is uncontrollable in space or time and causes unnecessary suffering. Thus any threat or use of the Minuteman III, N-8 was illegal and criminal.

9. The Charter of the Nuremberg Tribunal made explicit that violations of the law of war are criminal and that individuals are punishable for committing war crimes. In addition, the Nuremberg Charter defined crimes against peace and crimes against humanity. The former basically consist of waging a war of aggression or a war in violation of a treaty or other international obligation. It is also important to note that the Nuremberg Charter articulates inchoate crimes as well, such as the planning or preparation and conspiracy to commit a crime against peace, a crime against humanity or a war crime.

10. These provisions apply equally in times of formal peace as in times of war.

11. The various scenarios developed by the United States Government for the use of nuclear weapons cannot be accomplished without violating international law, including the law of war. The plans for targeting of U.S. nuclear weapons are found in the Single Integrated Operational Plan ("SIOP"), which lists the targets to be destroyed in a number of nuclear and non-nuclear countries. To employ these weapons, as is currently planned, would clearly violate the Nuremberg Principles, in that the concept of a crime against humanity specifically prohibits such wanton destruction.

12. I am aware from my reading and study, including the Nuclear Posture Review (January 2002) and the National Security Strategy (September 2002) as well as fact sheets and reports published by the Air Force specifically related to the Minuteman III, that U.S. nuclear policy includes on-going threats of a "first-strike" made "believable" by maintaining the Minuteman III at a high-alert rate (above 98 percent), prepared for launch on short notice. I am further aware from my reading and study that a high degree of accuracy of the Minuteman III is crucial to a first strike.

13. Any first use of nuclear weapons would, for that reason alone, violate the United Nations Charter and the Hague Convention of 1907, prohibiting the opening of hostilities without a formal declaration of war. And any use of even one nuclear weapon such as the Minuteman III, N-8 in any circumstance whether in response or defense would violate the principles of necessity and proportionality because it cannot be used within the intransgressible rules and principles of humanitarian law.

14. Since the threat or use of the Minuteman III, N-8 is inherently criminal under international and U.S. law, anything used to facilitate its operation is an instrument of a crime.

15. The judgment of the Nuremberg International Military Tribunal meted out severe punishment in 1946 against individuals who, acting in full compliance with domestic law but in disregard of the limitations of international law, had committed war crimes as defined in its Charter. 6 F.R.D. 69 (1948). That Charter has been enacted as a law of the United States, 59 Stat. 5144 (1945). See also U.S. War Crimes Act, 18 U.S.C. § 2441. By implication, the Nuremberg

judgment privileges all citizens of nations engaged in war crimes to act in a measured but effective way to prevent the continuing commissions of those crimes. The same privilege is recognized by means of Article 38 of the Statute of the International Court of Justice, "General Principles of Law Recognized by All Civilized Nations," which has been adopted as a Treaty by the United States. In my opinion, such action certainly could include non-violent exposure, inspection and symbolic disarmament of sites of ongoing war crimes.

16. In the present day, there has been a breakdown in the Constitutional principle of checks and balances which implements the separation of powers; most notably neither Congress nor the courts have been willing to ensure that the Executive Branch act within the laws that limit methods and means of the threat or use of military force. The fact that Minuteman III missiles exist and that their use is actively threatened on high alert reflects the stubborn refusal of the U.S. to abide by its own fundamental laws of war and to proceed with negotiations for nuclear disarmament in all its aspects. In spite of years in which these Defendants have participated in citizens petitions, letters, referendums, civil cases, requests for criminal prosecution and the recent decisions on these questions with the full participation of the United States before the International Court of Justice, the U.S. flouts its responsibility to abide by the laws of war, laws to which we are fundamentally bound. Under these circumstances, where redress within traditional channels is refused and ineffective, domestic criminal law coincides with the "Nuremberg privilege" mentioned in the preceding paragraph to afford a justification for seeming violations of domestic criminal laws in an effort to prevent the war crimes outlined above.

17. In my opinion the charges brought against these defendants in these circumstances must be dismissed. The prosecution of this case can not go forward because the sabotage statute that has been promulgated pursuant to the war powers of Congress can only be and must be interpreted consistent with the laws of war. Any alleged "national-defense" and/or "national-defense materials" must be specified and defined within the laws of war. Clearly the Minuteman III, N-8 can never be used within the laws of war and its ongoing threat or use or any instrumentalities or property furthering its threat or use are illegal and criminal. Likewise, this prosecution for malicious destruction of property must be dismissed because the court may not apply the general protection of property statute in a way that ignores or abrogates the fundamental laws of war. In these circumstances, where the alleged "property" is part of an illegal and criminal threat of use of a weapon of mass destruction these defendants acted lawfully and reasonably to prevent the most egregious and fundamentally prohibited of all crimes, war crimes.

18. I declare under penalty of perjury that the foregoing is true and correct. I am prepared to testify under oath and answer questions on these and related matters.

Signed this 7th day of January, 2003, at Champaign, Illinois
Francis Anthony Boyle

For much of the past six decades, American governmental decision makers have tried to base their foreign policies on Hobbesian power politics as defined, for example, by Hans Morgenthau in his classic treatise *Politics among Nations* (1948), instead of on international law, international organizations, the U.S. Constitution, and human rights.[1] The net result has been a series of disasters for the United States, both at home and abroad, the inflicting of extreme hardship on other nations, and the subversion of the post–World War II international legal order that the United States championed and constructed at the 1945 San Francisco conference for establishing the United Nations.[2] This is because Hobbesian power politics contradict several of the most fundamental principles upon which the United States is supposed to have been founded: the inalienable rights of the individual, the self-determination of peoples, the sovereign equality and independence of states, noninterventionism, respect for international law, and the peaceful settlement of international disputes.

By comparison, a cardinal tenet of Morgenthau's "realist" or power-politics school of international political science is that international law and international organizations are "irrelevant" to conflict between states over matters of vital national interest, which are said to comprise those issues of high international politics concerning the very survival of nation-states and the human race itself. Considerations of international law do not and should not intrude into such areas; or if they do, it should only be to the extent that they serve as a source for the manufacture of ad hoc or ex post facto justification for decisions made on the basis of antinomian factors such as power politics and national interest. In the realist view of international relations, international law is devoid of any intrinsic significance within the utilitarian calculus of international political decision making. International law, morality, ethics, and even knowledge itself become mere components in the power equation, devoid of noninstrumental significance or prescriptive worth, and subject to compulsory service as tools of power when deemed necessary for the national interest of a state. There are no barriers to the acquisitive nature of the nation-state beyond its domestic limitations and constraints imposed by the international political milieu. Consequently, the analysis and conduct of international relations must concentrate exclusively on the dynamics of power politics and national interest.

According to the political realists, the nations of the world precariously survive in the Hobbesian state of nature, where life is "solitary, poor, nasty, brutish, and short."[3] Here there exists no law or justice, no conception of right or wrong, no morality, but only a struggle for survival in a state of war by every state against every state. The acquisition of power and aggrandizement at the expense of other states in a quest for unattainable absolute national security is the fundamental right, the fundamental law, and the fundamental fact of international politics. Sheer physical survival in a Hobbesian world of

power politics, *raison d'état*, totalitarianism, and nuclear weapons must be
the litmus test for the validity of people's political, philosophical, moral, and
legal presuppositions. International law therefore becomes irrelevant to those
matters that count for anything in international relations. And international
law will not become relevant to international politics in the foreseeable or
even distant future. According to the political realists, statesmen who disobey
the "iron law" of power politics at the behest of international law invite destruction at the hands of aggressors and thereby facilitate the destruction of
third parties that, in today's interdependent world, cannot realistically hope to
remain neutral in a serious conflict between major powers: "From that iron
law of international politics, that legal obligations must yield to the national
interest, no nation has ever been completely immune."[4]

Yet the reasons for this realist perception of international law are more the
product of metaphysical speculation than of solid empirical research.
Throughout the twentieth century, the promotion of international law, international organizations, human rights, and the U.S. Constitution has consistently provided the United States with the best means for reconciling the idealism of American values and aspirations with the realism of world politics
and historical conditions. Both well before and immediately after World War
I, as well as immediately after World War II, the United States established an
excellent track record for pioneering innovative rules of international law and
human rights as well as novel institutions for the peaceful settlement of international disputes. Succinctly put, this pre–World War I American legalist
approach to international politics sought to create an actual "regime" of international law and organizations that would prevent, reduce, and regulate the
transnational threat and use of force in international relations. In particular,
the pre–World War I American legalist war-prevention program for world
politics had the following concrete objectives: (1) the creation of a general
system for the obligatory arbitration of disputes between states, which resulted in the establishment of the Permanent Court of Arbitration that still
functions today at The Hague; (2) the establishment of the International Court
of Justice, which is still in operation today at The Hague; (3) the codification
of important areas of customary international law into positive treaty form;
(4) arms reduction, but only after, not before, the relaxation of international
tensions by means of these and other legalist techniques and institutions; and
(5) the institutionalization of the practice of convoking periodic peace con-
ferences for all states in the recognized international community. This last objective was attained and far exceeded by the creation of the League of Nations, the predecessor to today's United Nations.[5] The legalist program also
strengthened the well-established international legal institution of neutrality
and the humanitarian laws of armed conflict to further isolate the bulk of the

international community, and especially the United States, from some future war in Europe that might erupt, despite the enactment of these preventive legalist devices.

There is not space to discuss here all the institutions, procedures, and rules of the international-law regime concerning the threat and use of force as well as human rights that was set up by the U.S. government in reaction to the Second World War. Of course, its central component was the United Nations, including affiliated organizations and institutions in numerous functionalist areas, such as the World Health Organization (WHO), the Food and Agriculture Organization (FAO), the United Nations Educational, Scientific, and Cultural Organization (UNESCO), and the International Atomic Energy Agency (IAEA). To this list should also be added the UN-affiliated international economic institutions that the U.S. government established at the same time for the express purpose of dominating the international economic order, especially the International Monetary Fund (IMF), the World Bank, and the General Agreement on Tariffs and Trade (GATT), now succeeded by the World Trade Organization (WTO). In addition, so-called regional organizations were brought into affiliation with the United Nations by means of chapter 8 of the UN Charter: the Organization of American States (OAS), the League of Arab States, and the Organization of African Unity (OAU)—now the African Union—and perhaps someday the Association of Southeast Asian Nations (ASEAN) as well as the Organization for Security and Cooperation in Europe (OSCE) and the European Union (EU). And of course constituting an integral part of the post–World War II U.S. foreign-policy objective of "containment" of the Soviet Union were the collective self-defense arrangements organized under article 51 of the UN Charter such as the North Atlantic Treaty Organization (NATO), the Inter-American Treaty of Reciprocal Assistance (the Rio Pact), the Central Treaty Organization (CENTO) (also known as the Baghdad Pact), the Southeast Asia Treaty Organization (SEATO), and the Australia–New Zealand–United States Security Treaty (ANZUS). Finally, numerous bilateral self-defense treaties under article 51 were negotiated for the same purpose between the U.S. government and states along the periphery of the Soviet empire such as Japan, South Korea, the Philippines, Iran, Pakistan, and Taiwan.

In contrast to America's legalist, humanitarian, and constitutionalist approach to international relations, geopolitical practitioners of Hobbesian power politics such as Robert McNamara, Dean Rusk, Richard Nixon,[6] Henry Kissinger, Zbigniew Brzezinski, Alexander Haig, Jeane Kirkpatrick, George Shultz, James Baker, and the Bush Jr. neoconservatives demonstrate little appreciation for or knowledge of the requirements of the U.S. constitutional system of government, with its basic commitment to the rule of law, human rights, and democracy.[7] Fortunately, American citizens have never been willing to provide sustained popular support for a foreign policy that flagrantly violates elementary norms of international law and human rights. This is precisely because they have always considered themselves a democratic political society governed by an indispensable commitment to the rule of law and human rights in all aspects of national life, evidenced in part by the massive, overwhelming rejection of the Bush administration and its criminal war against Iraq in the November 2006 elections.

The interconnected transgressions of Vietnam and Watergate during the Nixon-Kissinger administration is a paradigmatic example of the spillover effects of Hobbesian international power politics into U.S. domestic politics.[8] The same phenomenon was evident in the Reagan administration's Iran-Contra scandal.[9] This shall likewise prove true for the second Bush administration's torture scandal: a cancer on the presidency and on this president.[10] The consequences of a foreign policy out of control, in short, not only have had devastating global repercussions for its victims but again and again have come home to haunt the American people.

Concerned citizens living in a popularly elected democracy with a constitutional commitment to the rule of law must use the rules of international law, human rights, and the U.S. Constitution as checks and balances against the natural abuses of power endemic to any form of government when it comes to the conduct of foreign affairs and defense policies. Otherwise, a U.S. government can too easily operate as if it does not really care about the expectations of other states and peoples for the minimal degree of respect and deference that they are entitled to in their relations with the U.S. government. When that attitude is translated into the conduct of American foreign policy, it then quite naturally becomes a prescription for disagreement, difficulties, and conflict with other states and peoples. The U.S. government thus places itself in a position where the primary means of achieving its objectives are the brute application of political, economic, and military coercion. Needless to say, these techniques involve very high costs, both internationally and domestically, in today's interdependent world.

By contrast, if in the formulation of American foreign-policy decision making serious attention is paid to the rules of international law, human rights, and the U.S. Constitution, decision makers will be taking into account the reasonable expectations of other states and peoples in defining their objectives (the ends) and accomplishing them (the means). It seems almost intuitively obvious that this process would make it far easier for the U.S. government to carry out its foreign affairs and defense policies as well as to achieve its ultimate goals. To be sure, U.S. objectives might have to be scaled down somewhat under international law (especially in light of the inalienable right of the self-determination of peoples); certain means to achieve American objectives might have to be discarded because of the requirements of international law (especially the general prohibition on the unilateral threat and use of military force); and human rights should generally be promoted both around the world and at home. Although the U.S. government might not be able to achieve all of its objectives under this anti-Hobbesian framework, this approach does leave room for the United States to achieve a very significant portion of its objectives and at the same time minimize countervailing costs and uphold human rights and the world order.

For these reasons, the rules of international law, human rights, and the U.S. Constitution provide useful criteria by which U.S. government decision makers can and should formulate their foreign-affairs and defense policies. This does not mean, however, that the rules of international law are so clear that all the U.S. government has to do is to apply them in order to achieve its objectives. Rather, the rules of international law typically tell U.S. government decision makers what they should *not* do. Similarly, in a more positive sense, the rules of international law, the principles of human rights, and the techniques of international organizations usually provide a guiding way to resolve some of the basic dilemmas that confront American foreign-policy decision makers in today's interdependent world. In any event, American citizens have in the past and will in the future vigorously demand that U.S. government decision makers adhere to the rules of international law, promote human rights, and obey the U.S. Constitution. For example, this book will explain how international law and the U.S. Constitution enabled a corporal in the U.S. Marine Corps to prevail in his court-martial for objecting as a matter of principle and conscience to participation in President George H. W. Bush's 1991 war against Iraq.

LEGAL NIHILISM

It is not the purpose of this book to comprehensively review the history[11] of violations of international law and human rights perpetrated by the U.S. government around the world, from the outbreak of the so-called Cold War until the time of its culmination in the criminal war against Vietnam initiated by the "best and the brightest" of the Kennedy administration and continued by the Johnson, Nixon, and Ford administrations.[12] With the American defeat in and withdrawal from Vietnam, and the election of Jimmy Carter as president in 1976, the United States was at least publicly committed to human rights, international law, international organizations, and the peaceful settlement of international disputes. To be sure, many scholars have argued that there was no fundamental discontinuity in the basic Hobbesian thrust of American foreign policy under the Carter administration except for the public rhetoric: for example, Carter's support for the brutal military dictatorship in El Salvador as well as for the mujahideen in Afghanistan that would return to haunt the United States on September 11, 2001.

In any event, from the Reagan administration's ascent to power in 1981, successive U.S. administrations have demonstrated little, if any, respect for international law, international organizations, and human rights, let alone appreciation of the requirements for maintaining global peace and security.[13] Rather, there has been a comprehensive assault on the integrity of the international legal order. The foreign policies of the Reagan and Bush Sr. administrations represented a gross deviation from those basic rules of international deportment and civilized behavior that the U.S. government had pioneered in promoting for the entire world community by means of the United Nations, the Nuremberg and Tokyo trials, the Convention on the Prevention and Punishment of the Crime of Genocide (the Genocide Convention), and the Universal Declaration of Human Rights. Even more seriously, in many instances, specific components of the Reagan and Bush Sr. administrations' foreign policies constituted ongoing criminal activity under well-recognized principles of both international law and U.S. domestic law, and in particular the Nuremberg Charter,[14] the Nuremberg Judgment,[15] and the Nuremberg Principles[16]—for example, the 1983 invasion of Grenada, the *contra* terror war against Nicaragra, support for Israel's 1982 invasion of Lebanon, and repeated acts of military aggression against Libya.[17] Many of the senior officials in the Reagan and Bush Sr. administrations hold high posts in the Bush Jr. administration, bearing responsibility for such dark episodes as those at Abu Ghraib, Bagram, Guantánamo Bay, and Fallujah, as well as "extraordinary renditions."[18]

Depending on the substantive issues involved, those international crimes typically included but were not limited to the Nuremberg offenses of crimes against peace, crimes against humanity, and war crimes as well as grave breaches of the Geneva Conventions and the 1907 Hague Regulations on land warfare, genocide, torture, assassinations, and now enforced disappearances. For example, the Reagan administration's 1983 invasion of Grenada was a clear-cut violation of UN Charter articles 2(3), 2(4), and 33 as well as of articles 18, 20, and 21 of the revised OAS Charter. There was no valid reason under international law for the invasion, and as a result, it constituted an act of aggression within the meaning of article 39 of the UN Charter. Similarly, the Reagan administration's policy of organizing and participating in military operations by *contra* groups for the purpose of overthrowing the legitimate government of Nicaragua also violated the terms of both the UN and OAS charters prohibiting the threat or use of force against the political independence of a state. The Reagan administration flouted its obligation to terminate immediately its support for the *contra* groups in accordance with the interim order of protection issued by the International Court of Justice on May 10, 1984.

In addition, various members of the Reagan, Bush Sr., and Bush Jr. administrations committed numerous inchoate crimes—begun but not yet completed—incidental to these substantive offenses that under the Nuremberg Charter, Judgment, and Principles were international crimes in their own right: planning, preparation, solicitation, incitement, conspiracy, complicity, attempt, aiding and abetting—for example, threatening and planning to attack militarily the above-mentioned states. Of course the great irony is that six decades ago at Nuremberg and Tokyo, the U.S. government participated in the prosecution, punishment, and execution of Nazi and Japanese government officials for committing some of the same types of heinous international crimes that members of the second Bush administration are currently inflicting on innocent people all around the world.[19] Many scholars have in good faith argued that the Nuremberg Tribunal and the Tokyo Tribunal were nothing more than exercises in so-called victor's justice, on the ground that the United States, Britain, and the Soviet Union refused consideration of their own war crimes. Be that as it may, UN General Assembly Resolution 95(I) of December 11, 1946, unanimously affirmed "the principles of international law recognized by the Charter of the Nuremberg Tribunal and the judgment of the Tribunal." In this way, international law constructed a regime that held governments and their leaders responsible for crimes against peace, crimes against humanity, and war crimes. Since then, the status of these Nuremberg Principles as peremptory norms of customary international law has never been seriously questioned by the world community of states.

According to basic principles of international criminal law, all high-level U.S. civilian officials and military officers in the American government who either knew or should have known that soldiers or civilians under their control committed or were about to commit international crimes and failed to take the measures necessary to stop them or to punish them, or both, were personally responsible for the commission of these international crimes.[20] This category of officialdom who actually knew or should have known of the commission of such substantive or inchoate international crimes under their jurisdiction and failed to do anything about them typically included the president, the vice president, the secretary of defense, the secretary of state, the director of the Central Intelligence Agency, the national security adviser, the attorney general, and the Pentagon's Joint Chiefs of Staff and its regional commanders in chief. These U.S. government officials and their immediate subordinates, among

others, were personally responsible for the commission—or at a minimum
were complicit in the commission—of crimes against peace, crimes against
humanity, and war crimes as specified by the Nuremberg Charter, Judgment,
and Principles.

U.S. DOMESTIC CIVIL RESISTANCE

I grew up in a family that rooted for the success of Martin Luther King Jr.'s
nationwide civil disobedience campaign, which was designed to achieve basic human equality for African Americans by applying the techniques of
satyagraha pioneered by Mahatma Gandhi in South Africa and India. Then in
the mid-1960s came the massive civil protests and demonstrations against the
Vietnam War. Of course at the time, I was only a student participant in some
of these demonstrations and so had no role to play in defending civil resisters
(I became an attorney in 1977). During that era, it was extremely difficult to
obtain acquittals in such civil-resistance cases prior to the monumental decision by the U.S. Supreme Court in *Mullaney v. Wilbur*, 421 U.S. 684 (1975),
which came down near the end of the Vietnam War. The critical significance
of this decision for defending civil-resistance acts designed to prevent U.S.
state crimes in the post–Vietnam War era will be discussed in the next chapter of this book.

There was a brief hiatus in mass civil protests after the end of the Vietnam
War in 1975, which was followed by the tenure of the comparatively benign
Carter administration from 1977 to 1981. But in direct reaction to the Reagan
and Bush Sr. administrations' wanton attacks upon the international and domestic legal orders as well as on human rights, tens of thousands of American citizens engaged in various forms of civil-resistance activities to protest
U.S. foreign policy. These citizen protests led to numerous arrests and prosecutions by federal, state, and local governmental authorities all over the country. Many individuals involved in these protests were prosecuted, convicted,
and sentenced in a particularly harsh and vindictive manner.

For example, the Reagan administration's offensive nuclear-weapons
buildup generated protests by numerous groups and individuals against U.S.
nuclear-weapons facilities, programs, and personalities around this country
and abroad. The Plowshares,[21] England's Greenham Common Women,
Greenpeace, and the Catholic nonviolent civil resistance group known as
Pax Christi were among the most prominent leaders of the antinuclear movement. In addition, much outstanding antinuclear work was performed by the
numerous groups and individuals who protested the production of plutonium
triggers for U.S. hydrogen bombs at the PUREX facility near the Hanford

reservation in Washington State and who protested at the U.S. government's nuclear-weapons test facility in Nevada, at the Rocky Flats nuclear facility in Colorado, and at the navy's extremely low frequency (ELF) facility near Ashland, Wisconsin. It was these American and worldwide antinuclear and antiwar movements, including importantly the contributions of civil resistance, that forced the pronuclear Reagan and Bush administrations to conclude the Intermediate-Range Nuclear Forces (INF) Treaty with the Soviet Union on December 8, 1987, and the Strategic Arms Reduction Treaty (START) on July 31, 1991, respectively. The imposition of a moratorium on nuclear tests by the Bush administration in 1992 that continues until today is a tribute to the courage and principles of these antinuclear civil resisters. But this long-standing moratorium on nuclear testing is now under serious and sustained threat by the second Bush administration.

The Reagan and Bush administrations' illegal military interventions into the Caribbean Basin (Grenada, Nicaragua, El Salvador, and Panama) were probably responsible for the greatest upsurge of civil-resistance activities during the 1980s.[22] For example, the Sanctuary movement involved approximately four hundred American church and synagogue communities that provided sanctuary to refugees fleeing the conflicts of Central America in fear for their lives.[23] In explicit violation of the requirements of both the 1967 Protocol to the UN Convention Relating to the Status of Refugees[24] and the U.S. Refugee Act of 1980,[25] the Reagan and Bush administrations refused to give these refugees political asylum so as not to undercut the pseudolegitimacy of the military dictatorships that ruled El Salvador and Guatemala with the active political, economic, and military support and training of the U.S. government. To sustain this policy, the Reagan and Bush administrations launched a vendetta against those who had organized the Sanctuary movement as an expression of their deeply held religious convictions. They were prosecuted and persecuted beyond the limits of the law, in violation of the protections afforded their activities by the First Amendment to the U.S. Constitution.

Next came the Pledge of Resistance movement, whose roughly 100,000 members took a vow that if the Reagan administration launched an invasion of Nicaragua, they would engage in nationwide civil resistance. The Pledge of Resistance movement called on its members on several occasions to demonstrate against repeated votes by the U.S. Congress to provide military and so-called humanitarian assistance to the *contra* mercenary bands that, at the Reagan administration's behest, had been illegally attacking both the people and the government of Nicaragua in violation of the UN Charter, the OAS Charter, the Geneva Conventions of 1949, and two World Court decisions from 1984 and 1986.[26] These resistance activities consisted of sit-ins and other forms of nonviolent protests conducted at federal military installations and the offices of U.S. congressional representatives and senators who had voted in favor of such aid. These individuals were motivated to protest in significant part by the conviction that the U.S. foreign policy toward Nicaragua violated fundamental principles of both international law, U.S. domestic law, and human rights—and they were right!

U.S. military intervention in the affairs of Latin American states was exacerbated during the tenure of the first Bush administration, beginning with its illegal invasion of Panama during December 1989, in which thousands of innocent Panamanian civilians were killed by American troops in violation of the UN Charter, the OAS Charter, and international humanitarian law.[27] The Bush administration continued and expanded U.S. military assistance to the military dictatorships that ruled El Salvador and Guatemala by means of a naked reign of terror, and drove from office the democratically elected Sandinista government in Nicaragua. The Bush administration then threatened a new round of U.S. military intervention in large numbers of Latin American states on the grounds of fighting its self-proclaimed and bogus "war" against drugs.[28]

This gross pattern of illegality in the Caribbean culminated in the Clinton administration's naked aggression against Haiti in 1994 and the subsequent military occupation of that heroic black republic. Then, following in the Hobbesian footsteps of his father, President George W. Bush mounted a second coup d'état against the democratically elected president of Haiti, Jean-Bertrand Aristide in 2004.[29] Haiti still remains in a state of U.S.-generated chaos at this writing. The second Bush administration also intervened militarily in Colombia's civil war and supported a coup d'état against the democratically elected government of Venezuela.

DEFENDING CIVIL RESISTANCE

Soon after the Reagan administration came to power in 1981, I began to give advice, counsel, and assistance to individuals and groups who had engaged in acts of civil resistance directed against several aspects of the U.S. government's foreign policy—among them, the nuclear freeze movement, the Sanctuary movement, Greenpeace, the Anti-Apartheid Movement, the Plowshares movement, the Pledge of Resistance campaign, Gulf War resisters, the South African divestment campaign. I also participated in the defense of individuals who were not part of formal movements but nevertheless resorted to civil resistance to protest the government's policies on nuclear weapons and nuclear deterrence, Central America and the Caribbean, Southern Africa, Europe, the Middle East, and so on.

In addition, I helped defend active-duty members of the U.S. armed forces who were persecuted and prosecuted by the U.S. Department of Defense because of their courageous acts of conscience and principle. For example, in the fall of 1990, I served as counsel for the successful defense of Corporal Jeff Paterson, a member of the U.S. Marine Corps and the first military resister to the Gulf War. Then I represented Lance Corporal David Mihaila in a successful effort to obtain his discharge from the Marine Corps as a conscientious objector during the Gulf War. Lance Corporal Mihaila was the clerk of the court for the *Paterson* court-martial proceedings and was motivated to apply for conscientious-objector status as a result of my oral argument for Corporal Paterson.[30]

In 1991 I served as counsel for the defense of Captain Yolanda Huet-Vaughn, a doctor who was court-martialed by the U.S. Army in part because of her refusal to administer experimental vaccines to U.S. soldiers designated to fight in the Gulf War, which she believed violated the Nuremberg Code on medical experimentation.[31] Later, I served as counsel for the defense of Lawrence Rockwood, a U.S. Army captain who was court-martialed for his heroic efforts to stop torture in Haiti after the Clinton administration illegally invaded that country in 1994. In 2004 I served as counsel for the defense of Staff Sergeant Camilo Mejia, the first military resister to the Iraq War, who was court-martialed as a conscientious objector for refusing to return for a second round of armed combat in Iraq.[32] Most recently, I served as counsel for the defense of First Lieutenant Ehren Watada, the first commissioned officer in the U.S. armed forces to be referred to a general court-martial for his principled refusal to serve in the war of aggression against Iraq.

Upon their incarcerations after military kangaroo-court proceedings, both Captain Huet-Vaughn and Staff Sergeant Mejia were designated as prisoners of conscience by Amnesty International. We Americans like to delude ourselves into believing that there are no prisoners of conscience or political prisoners held by the United States. In fact, there are many.[33] Both Captain Yolanda Huet-Vaughn and Staff Sergeant Camilo Mejia are America's equivalent of such prisoners of conscience as Václav Havel, Andrei Sakharov, Wei Jingsheng, and Aung San Suu Kyi. They are the archetypal American heroes whom we should be bringing into our schools and teaching our children to emulate instead of those wholesale purveyors of violence and bloodshed adulated by the U.S. government, America's power elite, and the mainstream corporate news media and its interlocked entertainment industry.

THE GOOD AMERICANS

One generation ago the peoples of the world asked themselves, where were the good Germans? Well, there *were* some good Germans. The Lutheran theologian and pastor Dietrich Bonhoeffer was the foremost exemplar of someone who led a life of principled opposition to the Nazi terror state even unto death.[34]

Today the peoples of the world are likewise asking themselves, where are the good Americans? Well, there are some good Americans. Notable among them are Richard Sauder, Jeff Paterson, David Mihaila, Yolanda Huet-Vaughn, Lawrence Rockwood, Camilo Mejia, Ehren Watada, the late Philip Berrigan, Elizabeth McAlister, Daniel Berrigan, Kathy Kelly, and other war resisters and protesters.[35] Or consider three Catholic Dominican sisters in Denver—Carol Gilbert, Jackie Hudson, and Ardeth Platte—who called themselves the Sacred Earth and Space Plowshares.[36] They faced arrest, prosecution, and served about two and one-half years in prison for protesting U.S. weapons of mass destruction (WMD), whose power for human extermination far exceeds even the wildest fantasies of Hitler and the Nazis.

Many more activists risk arrest for protesting illegal U.S. military interventions around the world. In 2004 the *Nuclear Resister* estimated that since the fall of 2002, there had been more than 9,500 antiwar-related arrests in the United States alone.[37] As my friend and colleague former U.S. attorney general Ramsey Clark once said: "Our jails are filling up with saints!"

Today the Bush administration is committing myriad actions in violation of the Nuremberg Charter, the Nuremberg Judgment, and the Nuremberg Principles: repeated wars of aggression, crimes against peace, crimes against humanity, and war crimes. American citizens possess the basic right under international law and U.S. domestic law, including the U.S. Constitution, to engage in acts of civil resistance to prevent, impede, thwart, or terminate these ongoing criminal activities perpetrated by U.S. government officials in their conduct of foreign affairs and military operations purportedly related to defense and counterterrorism.

This same right of civil resistance extends to all citizens of the world community. Everyone around the world has both the right and the duty under international law to resist ongoing criminal activities perpetrated by the Bush administration and its foreign accomplices in allied governments such as Tony Blair in Britain and John Howard in Australia. If not restrained, the Bush administration could very well precipitate a third world war.

PEOPLE POWER

The time for preventive action is now. Civil resistance is one important strategy. People power can overcome power politics. Popular movements have succeeded in toppling tyrannical, dictatorial, and authoritarian regimes in former Communist countries throughout Eastern Europe as well as in Asia, Latin America, and recently in the Middle East.[38] It is time for Americans to exercise people power here in the United States.

Despite the best efforts by the Bush administration to the contrary, American citizens still have First Amendment rights: freedom of speech, freedom of association, freedom of assembly, freedom to petition the government for the redress of these massive grievances, and civil resistance. If we fail to exercise these rights, as the saying goes, we will lose them.[39] We must act now, not only for the good of the peoples of the world but for humanity's future, that of our children, that of our nation as a democratic society committed to the rule of law and the U.S. Constitution as well as to human rights.

The Athenians lost their democracy to self-induced imperial warfare. The Romans lost their republic to a military coup d'état. And if we Americans do not act now, we could lose our republic to the Bush administration. The United States is not immune to the laws of history.[40]

CIVIL RESISTANCE UNDER THE FIRST AMENDMENT

Under the First Amendment, civil-resistance protesters are exercising their right "peaceably to assemble, and to petition the Government for a redress of grievances." The First Amendment does not require their assembly to be "lawful" in a positivist technical sense, only that it be peaceable. Certainly ongoing criminal activity committed by officials of the U.S. government itself is the type of grievance the American people should have a right to petition for the redress of by means of civil resistance. Therefore, we must recognize that the First Amendment includes within its scope the right of the American people to engage in acts of peaceable civil resistance specifically intended for the purpose of preventing or impeding ongoing criminal activity in the conduct of foreign policy on the part of this or any other U.S. administration.

The First Amendment also provides for and protects the free exercise of religion. In the course of involvement in a large number of civil-resistance cases for over two decades, I have observed that at the heart of many civil-resistance activities in America are religious people acting with the support of their local church or synagogue communities. These groups and individuals act out of a strong sense of religious and moral commitment.[41] Members of this country's mainstream religious groups such as Presbyterians, Congregationalists (UCC), Catholics, Episcopalians, Methodists, Friends, Unitarians, Lutherans, and Jews are among the major sources of organized opposition to the Bush administration's gross international lawlessness and criminality operating in America today.

THE CONSTITUTIONAL BREAKDOWN
IN SEPARATION OF POWERS

Despite the awesome apparatus of governmental repression arrayed against them, many principled Americans continue to plan or actively participate in civil-resistance activities directed against some aspect of the Bush administration's foreign policies. These activities represent the best hope for the future role of democratic government in the United States, with its historical commitment to the rule of law and human rights.

The U.S. federal courts are essentially powerless to prevent or impede the lawlessness of the Bush administration.[42] Even when given a rare opportunity to exercise some small degree of restraint on executive-branch excesses in foreign affairs, federal judges have generally deferred to presidential lawlessness under the so-called doctrines of political question, state secrets, standing, judicial restraint, or national security. For the most part, the members of the federal judiciary have almost completely abnegated any constructive role they might have played in support of the widespread public demand that American foreign policy be conducted in a manner consistent with the requirements of international law, U.S. constitutional law, and human rights. Yet in the face of these policies, large numbers of American citizens have decided to act on their own cognizance to demand that the Bush administration adhere to basic principles of international law, of U.S. domestic law, and of our own Constitution, in its conduct of foreign affairs.

CIVIL RESISTANCE IS NOT CIVIL DISOBEDIENCE

Civil-resistance activities designed to prevent or impede ongoing criminal activity by members of the Bush administration under well-recognized principles of international and U.S. domestic law represent one of the few constitutional avenues open to the American people to preserve their historical commitment to the rule of law and human rights. Civil resistance is essential if we are to prevent the Bush administration from moving even farther down the path of lawless violence in Southwest Asia and the Middle East, military interventionism in Latin America and Africa, and nuclear confrontation with Iran, North Korea,[43] Russia,[44] and perhaps one day, China.[45]

Such measures of "civil resistance" must be carefully distinguished from acts of "civil disobedience" as traditionally defined. In today's civil-resistance cases, what we witness are individuals attempting to prevent the ongoing commission of international crimes under well-recognized principles of international law and U.S. domestic law. This phenomenon is different from the classic civil-disobedience cases of the 1950s and 1960s, where African Americans and their supporters deliberately violated domestic laws for the express purpose of challenging and changing those laws. By contrast, today's civil resisters are acting for the express purpose of upholding the rule of law, the U.S. Constitution, international law, and human rights.

Civil resisters are constitutionally presumed innocent until proven guilty beyond a reasonable doubt to the satisfaction of a jury in accordance with all the substantive and procedural requirements of due process of law. Furthermore, people who engage in civil resistance have a constitutional right to rely on whatever statutory and common-law defenses are generally made available to every other criminal defendant in the jurisdiction concerned, for example, defense of self, defense of others, necessity, choice of evils, prevention of crime, execution of a public duty, citizen's arrest, prevention of a public catastrophe, measures otherwise authorized by law, absence of criminal intent. They are also entitled to receive the most vigorous defense that can be mounted on their behalf. After all, alleged murderers, robbers, and rapists are entitled to the presumption of innocence, a vigorous defense, and all the protections of due process of law. Society's standards and expectations must be no less for those who have engaged in civil-resistance activities designed to prevent the ongoing commission of international and domestic crimes by officials of the U.S. government. Today's civil resisters are the sheriffs. The Bush administration officials are the outlaws.

GOVERNMENT BY JURIES

The final arbiters of the technical legality of such acts of civil resistance are the American people themselves. Under the Sixth and Fourteenth Amendments to the U.S. Constitution, those individuals who have been charged for alleged prima facie breaches of positive law by engaging in acts of civil resistance are generally entitled to a trial by a jury of their own peers. Thus it is the American criminal jury system that shall prove to be the last bastion of democracy, the rule of law, human rights, and the U.S. Constitution against the Bush administration's pernicious assault on all of them. I would argue that under the conditions of political repression in the United States,[46] our criminal jury system remains a vital independent institution within the separation-of-powers structure created in the U.S. Constitution and its Bill of Rights by America's founders and framers.

Fortunately, the American jury system consists of common and everyday citizens. Most Americans are law abiding and peaceful and strongly believe that their government should be law abiding and peaceful as well. Thus, the fate of those prosecuted for civil resistance has been committed by the U.S. Constitution to the common sense of decency, justice, fairness, and peaceable inclinations so characteristic of the members of an American jury of their peers. For most U.S. citizens, invoking the rule of law, the Constitution, and human rights is as paradigmatically American as God, motherhood, and apple pie. It is high time for the peace movement and its lawyers to tap directly into this powerful reservoir that is so uniquely characteristic of the American people. When properly and vigorously presented to ordinary Americans, a legal argument will always beat a Hobbesian argument on almost any issue I can imagine.

In my experience, when American juries were made aware of the U.S. government's gross international criminal actions and state terrorism, they usually refused to convict those who had engaged in acts of civil resistance for the express purpose of stopping it. Invariably the jurors compared the minor nature of the crime for which the defendants were charged (typically trespass) against the monstrous nature of the international crimes committed, supported, condoned, or threatened by U.S. government officials (typically war crimes). The jurors usually concluded that the defendants were privileged to act as they did under basic principles of international law and U.S. domestic law to prevent the commission of international criminal activity by officials of the U.S. government.

By refusing to convict these civil resisters, the jurors ratified—without explicitly saying so—the argument that such civil resisters were merely engaged in an exercise of their First Amendment rights to peaceably assemble or to petition their government for a redress of grievances or to freely exercise their religion, or that they had no criminal intent to begin with.

It is for this reason that I believe we must carefully distinguish acts of "civil resistance" from acts of "civil disobedience." The former are not crimes, and the protestors who engage in them are not criminals—at least until they have been proven guilty beyond a reasonable doubt to the satisfaction of men and women sitting on a jury of their peers in accordance with all the constitutional requirements of due process of law, which are oftentimes denied to them by dictatorial judges. We must actively work to obtain their acquittal at trial by a jury of their peers, precisely because they courageously exercised their constitutional rights for the express purpose of restoring to the United States a democratic government with a commitment to the rule of law both at home and abroad as well as to human rights. These civil resisters have become the real American heroes for the twenty-first century.

I believe that most Americans are basically unaware of the gross violations of international law and human rights being perpetrated in their name by U.S. government officials on a day-to-day basis. Once informed, however, they are frequently outraged. In many of the civil-resistance cases I have worked on, after acquitting the defendants of some or all of the charges, jury members have been interviewed by the local news media. During such interviews, jury members have often said that they were "shocked" to discover that the U.S. government was committing gross violations of international law and that this had led them to acquit the defendants. Moreover, some of the jurors have said that they had been so "radicalized" by the trial that they thought they themselves should go out and start to protest to do something about the situation.

In any event, many of the jurors permitted to hear and consider our international-law arguments in defense of civil-resistance protesters invariably reached the conclusion that in light of the international criminal activities perpetrated by U.S. government officials, the defendants did what they had to do to stop such crimes. I believe that this is precisely the same type of reaction that most American people will have when properly informed and educated about the relevance of international law, human rights, and constitutionalism to the conduct of foreign policy by the U.S. government.

FIGHTING BACK IN COURT

Throughout many years of opposition to the Reagan administration's gross international lawlessness, I experienced many disappointments and failures in the defense of those who engaged in civil resistance. Too many brave and principled people were vindictively and unconstitutionally persecuted, prosecuted, punished, and incarcerated simply for opposing the ongoing commission of international and domestic crimes by the Reagan administration in its daily conduct of foreign affairs. Many of the very best and most admirable people produced by contemporary American society were treated as if they were common criminals, and sometimes prosecuted and punished more severely than murderers, robbers, and rapists.

But then in 1985 two criminal cases produced a major breakthrough and opened up a new era for the successful defense—using international law—of those engaged in civil resistance against the state criminality and terrorism of the Reagan administration: *People v. Jarka*[47] and *Chicago v. Streeter.*[48] In both cases, the defendants were acquitted by invoking the traditional common-law defense known as "necessity," which was incorporated into the Illinois Criminal Code. According to what was then chapter 38, sections 7–13 of the Illinois Revised Statutes (1983), conduct that would otherwise be an offense was justifiable by reason of "necessity" if the accused was without blame in occasioning or developing the situation and reasonably believed such conduct was necessary to avoid a public or private injury greater than the injury that might reasonably result from his or her own conduct.

In the *Jarka* case, the defendants were protesting U.S. military intervention in Central America and the Reagan administration's offensive nuclear-weapons buildup, in front of the Pentagon's Great Lakes Naval Training Center on November 14, 1984. The defendants were charged with the crimes of mob action and resisting arrest, despite the fact that they had merely linked arms and sat down in the middle of the road in front of the base. After a three-and-one-half-day trial in which defense attorneys produced eight expert witnesses on nuclear weapons, Central America, and international law, the defendants were acquitted of all charges on April 15, 1985.[49]

In *Jarka* the greater public and private injuries with respect to Central America were successfully argued to be Nuremberg crimes against peace, crimes against humanity, war crimes, grave breaches of the Geneva Conventions, and violations of the UN Charter, the OAS Charter, and the International Court of Justice's 1984 interim order of protection against the Reagan administration for Nicaragua. But the *Jarka* case was an even more significant precedent for the defense of antinuclear resisters under international law. To the best of my knowledge, for the first time ever in the annals of American jurisprudence, the judge in the *Jarka* case actually instructed the jury that the threat or use of nuclear weapons violated international law. To quote the exact language of this monumental instruction as read to the *Jarka* jury by Judge Alphonse F. Witt: "The use or threat of use of nuclear weapons is a war crime or an attempted war crime because such use would violate international law by causing unnecessary suffering, failing to distinguish between combatants and noncombatants and poisoning its targets by radiation."[50] Judge Witt's courageous instruction represented the successful culmination of four years of vigorous efforts by the members of the Lawyers Committee on Nuclear Policy (LCNP).[51]

The stunning victory in *Jarka* was immediately used as a precedent for establishing the defendants' right to the "necessity" defense with respect to international law in the *Streeter* trial, which was held just weeks later in Chicago. There was close cooperation between the respective teams of defense attorneys in *Jarka* and *Streeter*, and I served as counsel to both groups of attorneys on questions of international law. In the *Streeter* case, the defendants attempted to meet with the South African consul at his office in Chicago to discuss that country's policy of apartheid. When he refused to meet, the defendants in turn refused to leave the corridors of a building outside the consulate offices and were eventually arrested and prosecuted for violating a provision of Chicago's municipal code prohibiting "unlawful trespass." To substantiate their defense of necessity, the defense attorney team presented at trial several expert witnesses who testified to the effect that the government of South Africa had been committing international crimes as a result of its policy of apartheid and that the defendants acted reasonably in their efforts to prevent the continuation of these crimes. In this case too the jury acquitted the defendants of all charges.[52]

After these two acquittals, numerous attempts were made across the country by defense attorneys, and even defendants representing themselves in court, to invoke these cases as precedents for the defense of acts of civil resistance against the Reagan administration's illegal policies toward Nicaragua, El Salvador, South Africa, and nuclear weapons, among others. There were many such civil-resistance cases in which criminal charges were dismissed, or the defendants acquitted outright by juries or judges, because of *Jarka*-type defenses founded upon principles of international law. These successful courtroom battles using international law have been fought now for over two decades.[53] This book explains to civil resisters, their lawyers, their supporters, the U.S. peace movement, and all other concerned American citizens how to mount these legal battles of principle and conscience in court. The same strategies have been successfully applied by civil resisters and their lawyers and their supporters and peace movements in other countries.

GUERRILLA WARFARE IN COURT

It is crucial for preserving the future of our democratic system of constitutional government in the United States, with its historical commitment to the rule of law both at home and abroad as well as to human rights, that we conscientiously and systematically pursue trial strategies for the defense of such civil-resistance protesters under international law that will eventually result in a series of dismissed charges, acquittals, or at least hung juries. If properly publicized, each victory will encourage other private citizens to engage in similar civil-resistance activities. In the case of an acquittal, a jury would have already determined that the resisters' actions were not criminal behavior but rather lawful conduct under both international law and U.S. domestic law, including the First Amendment. In the case of a dismissal or hung jury, the presumption of innocence with respect to such activities would still remain undisturbed.

An extended series of acquittals or hung juries or dismissed charges in such civil-resistance cases will send a strong message that the ordinary people of America who make up juries will no longer tolerate their government's pursuit of patently illegal foreign policies that constitute ongoing criminal activity under well-recognized principles of international law and U.S. domestic law. Indeed, several years ago I was informed by more than one trial attorney that because of the success of such international-law defenses in their jurisdictions, there was no way prosecutors could obtain convictions for civil resistance protesting U.S. policies on nuclear weapons, Central America, or South Africa. In these jurisdictions, state and local government authorities were put into a quandary as to how they should proceed, while the civil-resistance protesters carried on with their activities.

For example, in one divestment case in which students protested a university's investments in South Africa, the trial judge granted our motion before trial to allow a "necessity" defense with respect to international law. Shortly thereafter the city's prosecutor announced that he was dropping criminal charges against the defendants, since the city would otherwise be placed in a position of having to defend the university's refusal to divest itself of stock in corporations doing business in apartheid South Africa—a burden the prosecutor's office was unwilling to accept. Eventually this university had to divest, because it was shorn of the coercive powers of the state to repress internal dissent and protest by its students—a direct result of this successful invocation of an international-law defense. The apartheid regime in South Africa was ultimately dismantled, in good part because of the successful worldwide divestment-disinvestment campaign that had been mounted against it from its organizational base here in the United States.

CONCLUSION

I once received an unsolicited telephone call from a woman who, in an unnecessarily self-deprecating tone of voice, identified herself as an ordinary middle-class, middle-aged housewife living in a typical suburb near Denver, Colorado, wanting to discuss the following matter with me: she and a group of similarly situated friends had an appointment in a few days with the director of the Rocky Flats nuclear arsenal, and at that time they planned to place him under citizen's arrest in his own office for the commission of crimes against international law. Unless and until the ordinary people of America rise up to challenge the elemental criminality and state terrorism of the Bush administration, in the streets, in the courts, at the ballot box, and in their communities, the future of the human race will be determined by those who now occupy positions of power and influence throughout the American political and social system. Only if ordinary people challenge U.S. policies will it become possible to curb the Bush administration's international lawlessness, criminality, and state terrorism.

The present danger is Hobbesian power politics. The only known antidotes are constitutionalism, international law, human rights, and civil resistance. At the dawn of the third millennium, our existential choice is that stark and compelling. We must apply this imperative regimen immediately, before humankind exterminates itself in an act of nuclear omnicide.

NOTES

1. *See* Francis A. Boyle, *World Politics and International Law* (1985).
2. Louis B. Sohn, *Cases on United Nations Law* (2d ed. 1967).
3. Thomas Hobbes, *Leviathan* 100 (Michael Oakeshott ed., 1962).
4. Hans Morgenthau, *In Defense of the National Interest* 144 (1951).
5. Francis A. Boyle, *Foundations of World Order* (1999).
6. Richard Nixon, *The Real War* (1980).
7. Robert A. Dahl, *How Democratic Is the American Constitution?* (2d ed. 2003). *But see* Greg Palast, *The Best Democracy That Money Can Buy* (2003); Michael Parenti, *Democracy for the Few* (6th ed. 1995).
8. Carl Bernstein & Bob Woodward, *All the President's Men* (1974); Leon Jaworski, *The Right and the Power* (1977); Bob Woodward & Carl Bernstein, *The Final Days* (1976).
9. Lawrence E. Walsh, *Firewall* (1997).
10. *See, e.g.*, John W. Dean, *Worse Than Watergate* (2004); John W. Dean, *Conservatives without Conscience* (2006).
11. *See* William Blum, *Killing Hope: U.S. Military and CIA Interventions since World War II* (1995); Noam Chomsky, *Pirates and Emperors, Old and New* (2002); Alexander Cockburn & Jeffrey St. Clair, *Imperial Crusades* (2004); *Covert Action: The Roots of Terrorism* (Ellen Ray & William H. Schaap eds., 2003); Frederick H. Gareau, *State Terrorism and the United States* (2004); Michael Mandel, *How America Gets Away With Murder* (2004); *War & State Terrorism* (Mark Selden & Alvin Y. So eds., 2004).
12. *See* Noam Chomsky, *Rethinking Camelot* (1993); David Halberstam, *The Best and the Brightest* (1969); Seymour M. Hersh, *The Dark Side of Camelot* (1997); Robert S. McNamara, *In Retrospect: The Tragedy and Lessons of Vietnam* (1995).
13. *See* Francis A. Boyle, *The American Society of International Law: 75 Years and Beyond*, 75 Am. Soc'y Int'l L. Proc. 270 (1981); Boyle et al., *Conclusions and Judgment of the Brussels Tribunal on the Reagan Administration's Foreign Policy (Sept. 30, 1984)*, N.Y. Times, Oct. 7, 1984, at 77, and in International Progress Organization, *The Reagan Administration's Foreign Policy* 459 (Hans Köchler ed., 1984).
14. Dietrich Schindler & Jiri Toman, *The Laws of Armed Conflicts* 911 (3d rev. ed. 1988).
15. *The Nurnberg Trial*, 6 F.R.D. 69 (1946). *See* Francis A. Boyle, *The Nuremberg Defence in Courts*, in International Peace Bureau, *The Right to Refuse Military*

Orders 73 (1994); Matthew Lippman, *Nuremberg: Forty Five Years Later*, 7 Conn. J. Int'l L. 1 (1991); Matthew Lippman, *The Other Nuremberg: American Prosecutions of Nazi War Criminals in Occupied Germany*, 3 Indiana Int'l & Comp. L. Rev. 1 (1992); *see also* Matthew Lippman, *The History, Development, and Decline of Crimes against Peace*, 36 George Wash. Int'l L. Rev. 957 (2004); M. Cherif Bassiouni, *World War I: "The War to End All Wars" and the Birth of a Handicapped International Criminal Justice System*, 30 Denver J. Int'l L. & Pol'y 244 (2002).

16. Schindler & Toman, *supra* note 14, at 923.

17. Francis A. Boyle, *The Future of International Law and American Foreign Policy* (1989); International Progress Organization, *supra* note 13.

18. Francis A. Boyle, *Destroying World Order* (2004).

19. *See* Joseph E. Persico, *Nuremberg* (1994).

20. Department of the Army, *Field Manual 27-10, The Law of Land Warfare*, ¶ 501 (1956).

21. *Swords into Plowshares* (Arthur J. Laffin & Anne Montgomery, eds., rev. ed. 1996); *Swords into Plowshares* (Arthur J. Laffin ed., 2003).

22. See Francis A. Boyle, *International Lawlessness in the Caribbean Basin*, in *World Politics and International Law* 266 (1985); Noam Chomsky, *Turning the Tide* (1985); Jack Nelson-Pallmeyer, *War Against the Poor* (1990); Jack Nelson-Pallmeyer, *School of Assassins* (rev. ed. 2001).

23. Francis A. Boyle, *The Sanctuary Movement and International Law*, American Branch, International Law Association, International Practitioner's Notebook, April 1985.

24. *See* Protocol Relating to the Status of Refugees, *opened for signature* Jan. 31, 1967, 19 U.S.T. 6223, T.I.A.S. No. 6577, 606 U.N.T.S. 267.

25. *See* Refugee Act of 1980, Pub. L. No. 96-212, 94 Stat. 102 (codified at 8 U.S.C. § 1101 (1982)).

26. *See* Francis A. Boyle, *Determining U.S. Responsibility for Contra Operations Under International Law*, 81 Am. J. Int'l L. 86 (1987); Francis A. Boyle, *Nicaragua Must Survive*, 6 U.I. ACDIS Bull., Winter 1985-86.

27. Francis A. Boyle, *The U.S. Invasion of Panama: Implications for International Law and Politics*, 1 East African J. Peace & Human Rights 80 (1993) (Uganda).

28. Alexander Cockburn & Jeffrey St. Clair, *Whiteout* (1998).

29. Mark Weisbrot, *Where Are U.S. Human Rights Groups? The Silence About Haiti's Torment*, Counterpunch, March 7, 2005, http://www.counterpunch.org/weisbrot 03072005.html.

30. Francis A. Boyle, *Foreword* to Rick Anderson, *Home Front: The Government's War on Soldiers* 13 (2004).

31. Boyle, *supra* note 18, at 65–91.

32. Interview by Mark Levine with Francis A. Boyle et al., *Torture and International Human Rights*, ZNET, Jan. 9, 2005, http://www.zmag.org/content/showarticle .cfm?ItemID=6987; *see also* Marjorie Cohn, *Navy Judge Finds War Protest Reasonable,* Truthout Report, May 13, 2005.

33. Verdict of the Special International Tribunal on the Violation of Human Rights of Political Prisoners and Prisoners of War in United States Prisons and Jails, Con-

ference at Hunter College, N.Y. (Dec. 7–10, 1990); Editorial El Coquí, *Can't Jail the Spirit* (3d ed.1992). See the latest edition of the *Nuclear Resister* for a current listing, and past editions for previous listings, of Prisoners of Conscience and Political Prisoners in the United States.

34. *See, e.g.*, Dietrich Bonhoeffer, *The Cost of Discipleship* (rev. ed. 1963); Dietrich Bonhoeffer, *Ethics* (Eberhard Bethge ed., 1955); Dietrich Bonhoeffer, *A Testament to Freedom* (Geffrey B. Kelly & F. Burton Nelson eds., 1995).

35. *See* Daniel Berrigan, *Lamentations* (2002); Daniel Berrigan, *Testimony* (2004); Philip Berrigan, *Fighting the Lamb's War* (1996); Murray Polner & Jim O'Grady, *Disarmed and Dangerous* (1997).

36. *United States v. Platte* 401 F.3d 1176 (10th Cir. 2005); Alicia Caldwell, *Nuns Won't Pay, May Do More Time*, Denver Post, March 3, 2005.

37. *Day by Day: A Continuing Chronicle of War Resistance*, Nuclear Resister, Oct. 15, 2004, at 8.

38. Adrian Karatnycky & Peter Ackerman, *How Freedom Is Won: From Civil Resistance to Durable Democracy* (2005); *see also* UNESCO, *Violations of Human Rights: Possible Rights of Recourse and Forms of Resistance* (1984).

39. William M. Kunstler, *The Emerging Police State* (2004); M. Wesley Swearingen, *FBI Secrets* (1995).

40. Francis A. Boyle, *Bush's Banana Republic*, Counterpunch, Oct. 11, 2002, http://www.counterpunch.org/boyle1011.html.

41. *See, e.g.*, Abraham J. Heschel, *The Prophets* (1962); Thomas Merton, *Peace in the Post-Christian Era* (2004); Thomas Merton, *Faith and Violence* (1968).

42. Arthur S. Miller, *Presidential Power* (1977); Arthur M. Schlesinger Jr., *The Imperial Presidency* (1989).

43. *See* Gavan McCormack, *Target North Korea* (2004).

44. Francis A. Boyle, *The Criminality of Nuclear Deterrence* (2002).

45. Samuel P. Huntington, *The Clash of Civilizations and the Remaking of World Order* (1996). *But see* Michael Parenti, *History as Mystery* (1999); Howard Zinn, *The Future of History* (1999).

46. Michael Parenti, *Superpatriotism* (2004).

47. *People v. Jarka*, No. 002170 (Cir. Ct., Lake County, Ill., Apr. 15, 1985).

48. *Chicago v. Streeter*, No. 85-108644 (Cir. Ct., Cook County, Ill., May 15, 1985).

49. For the trial materials, see Francis A. Boyle, *Defending Civil Resistance under International Law* 155–78 (1987).

50. *See id.* at 9–10.

51. Richard Falk et al., Nuclear Weapons and International Law, Occasional Paper No. 10, Center of International Studies, Princeton University (1981); Lawyers' Committee on Nuclear Policy, *Statement on the Illegality of Nuclear Weapons* (1981); Lawyers' Committee on Nuclear Policy, *Statement on the Illegality of Nuclear Warfare* (rev. ed. 1990); *see also* Elliott L. Meyrowitz, *Prohibition of Nuclear Weapons: The Relevance of International Law* (1990).

52. For the trial materials, see Boyle, *supra* note 49, at 216–81.

53. *See* Robert Aldridge & Virginia Stark, *Nuclear War, Citizen Intervention, and the Necessity Defense*, 26 Santa Clara L. Rev. 299 (1986); Arthur W. Campbell, *The*

Nuremberg Defense to Charges of Domestic Crime: A Non-Traditional Approach for Nuclear-Arms Protestors, 16 Cal. W. Int'l L.J. 93 (1986); Matthew Lippman, *Civil Resistance: The Dictates of Conscience and International Law Versus the American Judiciary*, 6 Fla. J. Int'l L. 5 (1990); Matthew Lippman, *First Strike Nuclear Weapons and the Justifiability of Civil Resistance Under International Law*, 2 Temp. Int'l & Comp. L.J. 155 (1989); Matthew Lippman, *Nuremberg and American Justice*, 5 Notre Dame J.L. Ethics & Pub. Pol'y 951 (1991); Matthew Lippman, *Reflections on Non-Violent Resistance and the Necessity Defense*, 11 Hous. J. Int'l L. 277 (1989); Matthew Lippman, *Revitalizing International Law in the Nuclear Age*, 13 Whittier L. Rev. 17 (1992); Matthew Lippman, *The Right of Civil Resistance Under International Law and the Domestic Necessity Defense*, 8 Dick. J. Int'l L. 349 (1990); David E. Neely, *Legal Necessity and Civil Disobedience: Preventing the Greater Harms of War and Apartheid*, 74 Ill. Bar J. 596 (1986).

Chapter Two

Defending Civil Resisters:
Philosophy, Strategy, and Tactics

During the past quarter century of defending civil resisters who courageously sought to prevent the commission of state crimes, I have worked on many cases all over the world. Obviously, there is no way in this one book that I could possibly advise on how to use in foreign countries the philosophy, strategy, and tactics articulated here. So unless otherwise expressly indicated to the contrary, my remarks and analyses set forth here shall be limited to defending civil resisters in the United States. Nevertheless, the philosophy, strategy, and tactics recommended in this book have been successfully employed in other countries with minor accommodations for the respective domestic constitutional and criminal systems. I would be happy to consult with non-American civil resisters and their attorneys on how to tailor a defense under international law to the unique circumstances of their national legal orders.

SHERIFFS VERSUS OUTLAWS

Everyone involved with defending and supporting civil resisters to prevent state crimes must start with the basic philosophical, moral, and legal conviction that under international law it is the civil resisters who are the sheriffs and the U.S. government officials committing state crimes who are the outlaws. Usually the civil resisters believe this in their bones—otherwise, they would not have acted against their own government at the risk of their freedom, health, safety, finances, and in some cases their lives. But this firm conviction becomes critical if and when civil resisters select a lawyer to defend them. Civil resisters must choose a lawyer who believes in them and in their cause.

For example, in one antinuclear protest case I worked on, the civil resisters thought they were fortunate to have retained the services of a prestigious corporate law firm of national stature. The problem was that the corporate-oriented status quo lawyers in that law firm working on their case could never abandon their inbred attitude that these civil resisters had done something wrong. That attitude became apparent during the course of the criminal proceedings and thus worked against the case of the civil resisters and hurt the cause that they believed in and had acted upon at risk of imprisonment. If civil resisters decide to be represented by an attorney, they must first find a lawyer who believes in them and in their cause. Of course, the above observations beg the fundamental question that immediately confronts all civil resisters: should they seek legal representation?

SHOULD CIVIL RESISTERS BE REPRESENTED BY A LAWYER?

Over the years, I have known some civil resisters who firmly believed as a matter of principle and conscience that they could not permit a lawyer to defend them in criminal proceedings. These civil resisters sought to emulate Socrates before the Athenian Assembly as portrayed in Plato's *Apology*, or Jesus Christ before Pontius Pilate as depicted in the Gospels of the New Testament. On the other hand, both Dr. Martin Luther King Jr. and Phillip Berrigan permitted themselves to be defended by lawyers against criminal charges in court. In my opinion, the basic question the civil resister should ask is, will my cause be advanced or retarded because I am or am not represented by a lawyer at trial? Almost invariably, that calculation weighs in favor of representation by an attorney who believes in you and in your cause.

Civil resisters must view the courtroom proceedings as a continuation of their original act of civil resistance. In that regard, there are three basic phases of civil resistance to prevent state crimes: (1) in the street; (2) in court; and if you lose, sometimes (3) in jail. Simply put, the purpose of this book is to keep civil resisters out of jail.

The courtroom phase of civil resistance is a continuation of the struggle that compelled the civil resister to act in the first place. Because of the intricacies of courtroom procedures, the above considerations almost invariably weigh in favor of civil resisters being represented at trial by a lawyer who believes in them and in their cause. Usually such lawyers will be able to figure out the best trial strategy to enable civil resisters to continue to fight most effectively for their cause in court. The successful defense of civil resisters typically requires a principled trial attorney working from the very outset of the case with an expert on international law to lay the proper foundation for getting the international legal considerations admitted into evidence before the jury. Conversely, it has been my experience over the years that civil resisters not represented by an attorney have a much more difficult time continuing their struggles of principle and conscience in court. If, on the other hand, their primary objective is to become martyrs like Socrates and Christ, then of course civil resisters do not need a lawyer. Most judges will be happy to oblige them. And during the past two decades, there have been numerous cases in which courageous and principled civil resisters obtained stunning acquittals from juries by means of invoking international law in court all by themselves without lawyers.

Civil resisters have the constitutional right to represent themselves in criminal proceedings pro se. But before they do so, they must ask themselves what harm might being convicted do to their cause. A criminal conviction might discourage other peaceable and law-abiding Americans from following their example in conducting civil resistance, whereas an acquittal, hung jury, or the dismissal of charges would establish a precedent for others to emulate. Civil resisters could accomplish a great deal of good for their cause by allowing a trial attorney and an international-law expert to defend them in court.

That being said, I have worked on cases where the civil resisters represented themselves at trial, and I am willing to do so again provided that I am convinced that the civil resister is dedicated to this course of action as a matter of principle and conscience. Some of the most admirable people I have ever known have insisted on representing themselves at trial. My only regret is that they would not allow a trial attorney working in tandem with me to do all we possibly could to obtain their acquittal. It is a monumental tragedy for all citizens in the United States and for the people of the world when such courageous and principled human beings are sent to jail.

FIND A LAWYER WHO BELIEVES
IN YOU AND IN YOUR CAUSE

If you choose to be represented by counsel, the most important consideration is locating a lawyer who believes in you and in the cause for which you acted. This axiom holds true no matter how inexperienced that attorney might be. For example, in one Plowshares case I worked on involving damage to a nuclear-weapons installation, the only local attorney we could find willing to defend the civil resister—who was facing up to forty years in prison—was a sociology professor at a community college who had never tried a case in her life. But she held a valid license to practice law in that state. Because she believed in her client and in his cause, she put on an astounding defense that achieved a result even better than that of a high-profile criminal defense attorney in a different Plowshares case also involving damage to a nuclear-weapons facility that I was working on at the same time half a continent away. To be sure, this second attorney believed in his client and in her cause as well and thus was able to cut down her criminal exposure from twenty years for sabotage to five years for destruction of U.S. government property. But this completely inexperienced attorney secured a thirty-three-month sentence for her Plowshares civil resister. Truly amazing what determined lawyers can do!

Ideally, civil resisters want to find a lawyer who possesses almost as much courage, integrity, and principle as they do. Despite the negative public perception of the legal profession, there are many lawyers who fulfill those criteria. Usually, however, such lawyers do not work for the big corporate law firms and are oftentimes solo practitioners. If a local attorney does not come to mind, start your search at the national office for the National Lawyers Guild in New York City.

TAKE THE INTERNATIONAL-LAW ARGUMENTS SERIOUSLY

Most regrettably, in my extensive dealings with criminal defense attorneys on civil-resistance cases, I have sometimes received the distinct impression that many of them do not take the international-law arguments very seriously. Invariably, the international-law arguments are at the very bottom of the list of grounds on which they intend to defend their clients. In order of priority, attorneys usually strongly prefer any type of argument based on the U.S. Constitution (e.g., the First Amendment, the Fourth Amendment, the Fifth Amendment, the Fourteenth Amendment), then traditional substantive and procedural criminal-law defenses, and finally, principles of international law. It is quite understandable why they should seek to defend their clients on the strongest grounds possible. And of course this means that if a traditional defense is available under well-recognized principles of constitutional law or criminal law, then it should be resorted to, with the express permission of their clients.

Yet in their search for such traditional defenses, trial attorneys oftentimes ignore or shortchange the international-law arguments. Generally they seem to treat the latter as if they were throw-away arguments that would be nice if they could be successful, but are not really critical or even central to their "real" defense, precisely because in their opinion they probably will not be successful. Such a subliminal attitude usually produces a self-fulfilling prophecy.

I believe this unwarranted assumption constitutes a grievous strategic error. If properly prepared and presented, international-law arguments can be just as effective as constitutional arguments. In many cases, principles of international law will be the only defense available to civil resisters.

In fact, civil resisters will want their attorneys to set up international-law arguments on their behalf because that is exactly why they protested in the first place. As a general proposition, their lawyers should honor their wishes and not try to talk them out of it. Rather, it will be up to their lawyers to fashion the international-law arguments in the context and the contours of traditional defenses under U.S. constitutional law and domestic criminal law. This book is designed to show how to do that.

Furthermore, a lawyer's effective reliance upon international law right from the very outset of the proceedings will give a defendant a strategic advantage over government prosecutors, because prosecutors generally know nothing about international law. Prosecutors usually try to persuade the judge to keep the jury from hearing the international-law arguments and expert-witness testimony on that subject in the first place, by filing a motion *in limine* to that effect before trial.

I have routinely witnessed the entire momentum of a civil-resistance criminal trial turn around in favor of the defendants once the jurors get to hear the international-law arguments. In some cases we were able to ambush prosecutors at trial by keeping our international-law arguments under wraps until after the government had closed its case. For example, in one antiapartheid civil-resistance case involving a special U.S. federal anti-terrorism felony charge where the resister was facing several years in prison, all of a sudden what appeared to be a "slam dunk" conviction by an assistant U.S. attorney turned into a hung jury in the U.S. District Court for Washington, D.C. Afterward, while we were making our way out of the courtroom, the prosecutor publicly berated me. Walking away from him contemptuously, I fired back: "Counsel, you get no sympathy from me because you used a cannon to shoot a fly."

It is my opinion that if the international-law arguments for the criminality of the U.S. government's foreign policies around the world are presented to a jury consisting of twelve ordinary men and women who consider themselves to be peaceful and law abiding, there is almost no way the government will be able to convict such civil resisters. Either the jury will acquit them outright or end up as a hung jury, or better yet, the charges will be dismissed before or during trial. The real task, then, is for lawyers to reorient their thoughts toward the effectiveness of the international-law arguments.

CONTACT AN INTERNATIONAL-LAW EXPERT RIGHT AWAY

It is vital that a lawyer in a civil-resistance case contact an international-law expert immediately. It never ceases to amaze me the number of phone calls I receive from criminal defense attorneys one or two days before the trial date asking me for advice on international law as it relates to the defense of their clients, or to appear as an expert witness at trial, or both. On the one hand, I know that litigators work by the seat of their pants and oftentimes do not have the opportunity to worry about such matters until the eve of trial. On the other hand, litigators are often slow to approach international-law experts because they do not really take the international-law arguments very seriously. There is little if anything an international-law expert can do for you twenty-four to forty-eight hours before trial, though I have done my best under such difficult circumstances in many cases.

The effectiveness of international-law arguments will increase directly in proportion to how early an expert is brought into the case. Consultation with an international-law professor immediately after agreeing to represent civil resisters is invaluable in terms of developing a proper theory or theories of defense, drafting any motions and briefs that must be submitted to the court before trial, determining and obtaining other necessary expert witnesses, laying the proper foundation necessary for the admission of international law and the expert's testimony into evidence before the jury at trial, and preparing appropriate jury instructions. By contrast, it has been my general experience that if the international-law expert is brought into the case on the very eve of trial, the odds in favor of successfully mounting a defense based on international law are significantly diminished. Such lackadaisical behavior is oftentimes characteristic of trial attorneys who do not really take the international-law arguments seriously, despite the fact that their clients took international-law seriously enough to risk prosecution and incarceration in the first place.

Most civil resisters want their day in court to articulate and defend publicly the reasons for their protest. It is up to their lawyers to honor and carry out their wishes. Win, lose, or draw, a lawyer wants his or her clients coming out of the trial feeling that they have had their proverbial day in court, and their say in front of a jury of their peers when available and before their community assembled in the courtroom and elsewhere by means of the attendant news media.

Occasionally, however, it is up to their lawyers to persuade civil resisters to escape on a legal technicality so that they can live to fight another day. Sometimes it is best for civil resisters and their lawyers to pocket these technical victories and publicly proclaim them to be positive contributions to their causes. Given the odds against civil resisters in court, even a technical legal victory can be valuable, especially when joined to an effective public education campaign and media strategy.

THIS IS NOT A CIVIL-DISOBEDIENCE CASE

Whenever a defense attorney contacts me to serve as an expert on international law, one of the most important preliminary conceptual tasks I have is to convince that defense attorney that this is not a civil-disobedience case but rather a civil-resistance case. Many attorneys automatically adopt a defeatist attitude toward such civil-resistance cases because they subconsciously assume that these are similar to the civil-disobedience cases that arose out of the civil rights movement conducted by African Americans and their supporters during the 1950s and 1960s. But by doing this, they subliminally endorse the status quo–oriented teaching by the U.S. establishment that civil-disobedience defendants should be prepared to accept their guilt and punishment.

To be sure, a generation ago, African Americans who engaged in civil disobedience sincerely believed that they had violated criminal laws in the name of a higher moral law. By comparison, today's civil resisters sincerely believe that they haven't violated any criminal laws; from their perspective, it must be U.S. government officials on trial and going to jail for violating the criminal laws of both the United States and the international community.

Individuals who engage in civil-resistance activities to prevent criminal aspects of American foreign policy are not engaged in civil-disobedience activities as classically defined. In such modern civil-resistance cases, individuals are attempting to prevent the ongoing commission of international crimes under well-recognized principles of international law and U.S. domestic constitutional and criminal law by U.S. government officials. This is a phenomenon very different from the classic civil-disobedience cases where individuals were purposely violating U.S. domestic law for the express purpose of changing that law. In these modern cases, the laws and the U.S. Constitution are on the side of the civil resisters and against the U.S. government officials.

Civil resisters disobeyed nothing—to the contrary, they obeyed international law and the U.S. Constitution. By contrast, U.S. government officials disobeyed fundamental principles of international law and thus committed both international and domestic crimes as well as violations of the U.S. Constitution. The civil resisters are the sheriffs enforcing international law, U.S. criminal law, and the U.S. Constitution against the outlaws working for the U.S. government.

Furthermore, civil resisters did not act in the name of a "higher law." Rather, international law is an integral part of U.S. constitutional and domestic law. Treaties and international executive agreements such as the UN Charter and the Nuremberg Charter are "the supreme law of the Land" under Article VI of the U.S. Constitution. And customary international laws such as the laws of war are part of federal common law and the common law of every state of the American union. All American criminal statutes must be interpreted to be consistent and compliant with international law.

The distinction between civil resistance and civil disobedience must be made crystal clear to the civil resisters, to their lawyers, to their supporters, to the news media, to the judge, to the jury, and to the members of the surrounding community. Indeed, one of the most difficult tasks civil resisters and their lawyers will have is getting them all to comprehend and understand the fundamental importance of maintaining this basic distinction between civil resistance and civil disobedience. Therefore, you must never refer to your case as one of civil disobedience, since such a characterization assumes the guilt of the civil resisters. Indeed, you must always object if the government prosecutor, the judge, or the news media refer to this as a case of civil disobedience instead of civil resistance. In particular, lawyers must emphatically explain to their clients that it is critical to employ the term "civil resistance" instead of "civil disobedience" in public and in court.

In one antinuclear protest case that I worked upon, an experienced criminal defense attorney perplexedly presented the following conundrum to me: he could not understand why government prosecutors routinely offered him plea bargains with respect to the murderers, robbers, and rapists he represented, but when it came to his current clients of ministers, priests, and nuns praying for peace in a park, the U.S. attorney's office strove to nail them to the wall—no mercy! I responded that the answer was quite simple: murderers, robbers, and rapists do not present threats to the system. But ministers, priests, and nuns praying for peace in a park across the road from a major U.S. military installation constitute a definitive threat to the system and are perceived to be such by its establishment.

PRESERVE THE RIGHT TO A JURY TRIAL

One of the most important things for a defense lawyer to remember from the very outset of a case is the need to preserve the defendant's right to a jury trial. Of course, this assumes that the civil resister has a constitutional right to a trial by jury under either the U.S. Constitution or the applicable state constitution. Generally speaking, in the United States a criminal defendant has a constitutional right to a trial by a jury if he or she faces more than six months of incarceration.[1] I should point out that the federal government has been quite devious in this matter, oftentimes charging those engaged in civil-resistance activities with "petty" offenses carrying penalties of less than six months in jail. This tactic usually precludes a jury trial and leaves civil resisters with only a bench trial before a federal magistrate instead of a judge.

Sometimes, however, this prosecution tactic has constituted a victory for international law, indicating that these federal prosecutors feared they might lose their cases before a jury because of the international-law arguments. In my experience, members of a jury are generally far more sensitive and receptive to the international-law arguments than federal judges or magistrates. The latter are part of the system and are card-carrying members of its establishment, whereas according to the preamble to the U.S. Constitution, members of a jury are supposed to represent "We the People of the United States."

If the government has been foolish enough to indict the civil resisters for a crime that will give them a right to a jury trial, you should be very cautious about engaging in any type of preliminary procedural maneuvering that might defeat that right. Once again, the litigator will prefer a good constitutional argument to strike one or more of the charges against his or her clients before trial. But if successful, this tactic might result in the removal from the case of the one charge that gives the civil resisters the right to a jury trial.

For example, in one antinuclear protest case, the defendants had prayed on a U.S. federal enclave, despite a ban-and-bar order prohibiting their reentry, and were charged with a variety of crimes under the federal criminal code and the federal Assimilative Crimes Act. Their attorney filed a motion to dismiss the most serious charge against them, arguing that the ban-and-bar order was "void for vagueness" and thus that prosecution on those grounds would have been a violation of due process of law—a good constitutional argument. Although agreeing with his analysis on that substantive point, I observed that if he were successful on this motion, his clients might lose their right to a jury trial because this was the only serious offense for which they were indicted. Realistically, he did not believe he had any chance to persuade the federal judge to acquit his clients on the grounds of international law during a bench trial.

I suggested that he withdraw his motion before the judge on the grounds that he intended to make international-law arguments with respect to all charges in the indictment. Less than one week later, the government dropped all charges against these civil resisters. Of course, we were never told the exact reason why the charges were dropped. But I have always suspected that the government prosecutors feared acquittal if the case went to trial before a jury.

STAY OUT OF U.S. FEDERAL COURTS IF AT ALL POSSIBLE!

In a state or municipal prosecution, civil resisters are often entitled to a trial by jury under the applicable state constitution, no matter how insignificant the criminal charge against them. Civil resisters should always demand a jury trial when they have the right to one. It has been my experience that state and municipal court judges are far more receptive to allowing international-law arguments to be presented to the jury than their federal judicial counterparts.

The attitude of state and local judges seems to be that the defendants are entitled to their day in court and therefore to put on whatever type of defense they want so long as it fits within a liberal interpretation of the state's rules of evidence and does not exceedingly prolong the proceedings. Oftentimes state and local judges are elected by the community whose members are on trial, and local public opinion may influence them. For many state and local judges, justice must be done and must be seen to have been done in their respective communities, unlike for many of their U.S. federal judicial counterparts. Many state and local judges feel more accountable to the members of their communities, which includes the defendant civil resisters themselves.

Not so for many federal district judges who believe that they are a law unto themselves and accountable to no one including the Almighty. Federal judges are nominated by the president and confirmed by the U.S. Senate. They serve for life on good behavior and are rarely removed from office by means of impeachment.

As of early 2007, about two-thirds of all sitting federal judges were nominated by Presidents Ronald Reagan, George H. W. Bush, or George W. Bush.[2] Many of these judges were drawn from the ranks of the extreme right-wing Federalist Society of lawyers and law professors.[3] Such judges will typically subject civil resisters to kangaroo-court proceedings.

For these reasons, protesters have often designed their civil-resistance actions to avoid standing in prima facie violation of federal law. For example, in one case, instead of entering a federal installation to protest, the protesters sat down on the state road outside the installation and impeded ingress and egress. As a result, when they were arrested, prosecuted, and tried, it was before local judges who were more sensitive to the concerns of their constituents that justice not only be done but also appear to have been done.

Of course there is no guarantee against the particularly harsh and vindictive Orwellian U.S. Department of "Justice" taking over the prosecution from state or local authorities, or even their prosecuting civil resisters in federal court after the civil resisters have been acquitted in state or municipal court. Despite the ban on double jeopardy set forth in the Fifth Amendment to the U.S. Constitution, the U.S. Supreme Court has interpreted this clause to permit criminal prosecutions by both state authorities and federal authorities for the same conduct, on the bogus grounds that they are deemed to be different "sovereigns" entitled to bring one prosecution each.[4] Two governmental bites at the one apple of civil resistance.

On the other hand, in some of the civil-resistance cases I have worked on, the federal government pressured state and local authorities to do their dirty work for them by prosecuting civil resisters in state or local courts. It always helps defense counsel to figure out the political dynamics behind the prosecution and persecution of such civil resisters. If the pressure to prosecute the civil resisters is coming from the federal government, then it can be counteracted by civil resisters and their supporters mounting a community education campaign to pressure local prosecutors to back off and let the federal prosecutors do their own dirty work. From another perspective, why should state and local taxpayers finance such prosecutions and persecutions on behalf of the federal government? For these reasons, in some localities, state and local prosecutors ultimately decided to exclude themselves from the prosecution and persecution of civil resisters. We fought them to a draw!

THIS IS NOT A SHOW TRIAL

So long as you have a jury trial, there is always a good chance of winning the case. On the other hand, even if it is a bench trial before a federal judge or magistrate where you might not have much of a chance of winning, there might be extremely good reasons for rejecting a plea bargain (if one is offered) and going ahead with the trial anyway. Here the first consideration would be the educational value of such a trial in the community where the civil-resistance activities took place. Greater public awareness of the issues produced by courtroom-generated publicity could create a significantly changed environment in the local community that is more conducive to achieving the civil resisters' overall objectives. Even a particularly harsh and vindictive persecution of civil resisters in court could end up helping their cause by engendering public sympathy and support. This is precisely what happened during the federal government's persecution of the founders of the Sanctuary movement in Tucson. As the early Christian apologist Tertullian so astutely observed: "The blood of martyrs is the seed of the Church." This same axiom has proved true for the now-worldwide Plowshares movement against nuclear weapons.

Electing to go forward with the trial, however, does not mean that you should approach it as a "show trial." As a matter of principle, I refuse to participate as an expert witness in courtroom proceedings that the attorney describes to me as a "show trial." An attorney who is resigned to losing a show trial does not need my help to do so. By contrast, I have been more than happy to work on cases with an almost nonexistent probability of victory, so long as the civil resisters and their attorneys have thought through a coherent strategy of what they intend to accomplish by going through with the trial instead of plea-bargaining, do whatever is necessary to win the case if at all possible, and educate the community by means of the trial. Your overall objective must always be to win the case by using principles of international law at trial to the best of your ability, no matter how difficult the circumstances or how insignificant the chances of victory. Occasionally, we have been pleasantly surprised by winning such cases for one reason or another. As you go into a trial, things can always break your way. A criminal trial is always a throw of the dice by the government prosecutors.

THIS IS NOT A NUREMBERG DEFENSE

Oftentimes, civil resisters will call their protests a Nuremberg action, which is a perfectly correct and acceptable nomenclature when they invoke the Nuremberg Charter, the Nuremberg Judgment, and the Nuremberg Principles as the basic authority for their civil-resistance actions. But then civil resisters and their lawyers will mistakenly state in public that they plan to put on a Nuremberg defense in court. There are two basic problems with that strategy. First, many judges in the United States have already arbitrarily rejected a "Nuremberg defense" in such civil-resistance cases. Saying that you are going to mount a "Nuremberg defense" in court provides the judge with a ready-made pretext to shut down any defense based on principles of international law.

Even more importantly, however, invoking a "Nuremberg defense" on behalf of civil resisters seeking to prevent state crimes is a perverse misnomer. The original Nuremberg defense was mounted by lawyers for the Nazi defendants before the Nuremberg Tribunal who argued that they were just carrying out the orders of their superiors. The Nuremberg Charter, Judgment, and Principles emphatically rejected the Nazis' Nuremberg defense and the related "führer principle."

As to the Nuremberg defense, in 1950 the United Nation's International Law Commission succinctly stated in its Nuremberg Principle IV: "The fact that a person acted pursuant to an order of his Government or of a superior does not relieve him from responsibility under international law, provided a moral choice was in fact possible to him." As for the führer principle, Nuremberg Principle III retorted: "The fact that a person who committed an act which constitutes a crime under international law acted as Head of State or responsible Government official does not relieve him from responsibility under international law." By comparison, today under President George W. Bush, America now seems to be operating under the principle that the president and his subordinates can do no wrong, are entitled to absolute obedience, and are above the rule of law and the Constitution.

Prospective civil resisters and their supporters should disseminate and propagate the seven Nuremberg Principles as widely as possible in their communities before any trial, to educate the potential jury pool.[5] But civil resisters and their attorneys do not want to state in public or in court that they plan to put on the same type of Nuremberg defense that the Nazi defendants unsuccessfully tried to do before the Nuremberg Tribunal. On the other hand, civil resisters and their attorneys should try to work into their defense the Nuremberg Charter, the Nuremberg Judgment, and the Nuremberg Principles. The rest of this book will explain how to do that.

THIS IS NOT AN INTERNATIONAL-LAW DEFENSE

In my dealings with criminal defense attorneys, it never ceases to perplex me that when I ask them on what grounds they intend to defend their clients, they go through a laundry list of one or two constitutional-law arguments, then two or three traditional criminal-law defenses, and then tack on at the end what they call a "general defense under international law." Such a recitation simply indicates to me that they really have not thought through the problem of mounting a defense using principles of international law for those involved in civil-resistance activities directed against criminal components of American foreign policy. My personal opinion is that it would be a tactical mistake to argue in court for the existence of a separate and independent defense under general international law. Indeed, sometimes you will only confuse the judge if you try to argue that there is something known as a "general international-law defense" that is separate and apart from the traditional common-law, statutory, procedural, and constitutional-law defenses already recognized in your jurisdiction.

RELATE INTERNATIONAL LAW TO TRADITIONAL DEFENSES

To the contrary, principles of international law must be related to and incorporated within those traditional common-law, statutory, procedural, and constitutional defenses that are already available in a particular jurisdiction. These substantive criminal-law defenses typically include but are not limited to defense of self, defense of others, defense of property, compulsion, duress, necessity, choice of evils, prevention of a crime, prevention of a public catastrophe, mistake of fact, mistake of law, citizen's arrest, measures otherwise authorized by law, reliance upon governmental authority, absence of criminal intent, and so on.

Criminal defense attorneys should draw up an exhaustive list of all such statutory and common-law defenses recognized in their jurisdiction, together with a brief analysis of the elements of each defense as defined. You will be surprised to discover the number and types of obscure, exotic, and generally helpful defenses you might be able to use to mount a defense for civil resisters by using principles of international law. For example, in Illinois we found a late-nineteenth-century case recognizing a common-law right to prevent the commission of a crime. As explained below, we then related it to the defense of our antinuclear civil resisters by using principles of international law.

Once you have compiled this comprehensive list of defenses recognized in your jurisdiction, submit it to the international-law expert for evaluation. The expert should be able to tell you how principles of international law can be related to one or more of the defenses and the most effective manner in which to do so. For example, with respect to defending those who have engaged in acts of civil resistance directed against U.S. nuclear-weapons policies, principles of international law would be relevant to establishing the defenses of compulsion, necessity, choice of evils, prevention of a crime, prevention of a public catastrophe, citizen's arrest, and measures otherwise authorized by law, among others. Similarly, with respect to defending civil resisters who were protesting to stop attacks by the U.S.-supported bands of *contra* mercenaries against innocent civilians and private property in Nicaragua during the Reagan administration, principles of international law proved relevant to establishing the defenses of defense of others, defense of property, prevention of crime, and necessity.

No point would be served here by an extended analysis of how international-law considerations actually should be related to these traditional criminal-law defenses, since the precise elements of each defense depend on the relevant state or federal law under which the civil resisters are being prosecuted. Trial attorneys representing civil-resistance protesters are simply advised to submit this detailed and comprehensive analysis of available statutory and common-law defenses to their international-law expert for advice on how this should be done most effectively. Without the careful establishment of this interconnection long before trial, the odds are fairly good that the judge will never allow the international legal principles or expert testimony to be brought to the consideration of the jury, since the proper legal and evidentiary foundation will not have been laid for their admission. As judges often say when they improperly deny defense counsels' requests to allow international-law experts to testify in civil-resistance prosecutions: "International law has nothing at all to do with this case!" It is incumbent upon defense counsel right from the very outset of criminal proceedings to patiently educate the judge and later the jury why international law has *everything* to do with this case.

Your basic objective will be to develop a theory or theories of defense that will persuade the judge to allow your introduction of international-law evidence at trial before the jury, including your expert's testimony. This can be most effectively accomplished by relating principles of international law to elements of the defense. For example, in the previous Illinois case invoking a common-law right to prevent the commission of crime, we argued that the international-law evidence and an expert should be admitted on the grounds that it was relevant to establishing the crimes the defendants were trying to prevent through civil resistance.

Depending on the jurisdiction, each common-law or statutory defense could have two or three elements, and evidence of international-law violations should be related to each element of all defenses mounted to whatever extent possible, in order to get the evidence admitted. The decisive factor has always been getting the international-law evidence considered by the jury under whatever theory of defense is possible. When jurors have the opportunity to consider principles of international law in civil-resistance cases, the odds of an acquittal or a hung jury are remarkably high, though not always certain. The usual response to the international-law evidence and expert-witness testimony by the jurors has been that they did not know that the U.S. government was committing international crimes; that they are appalled to have learned this for the first time; and that the civil resisters did what they had to do in order to stop it.

PAY ATTENTION TO THE BURDEN OF PROOF

In this regard, you should pay special attention to the evidentiary rules for the allocation of the burden of proof with respect to the affirmative defenses. For example, chapter 720 of the Illinois Compiled Statutes 5/3-2 (2005) provides generally that to raise an affirmative defense, the defendant must present "some evidence" for that defense. Once the defendant raises the issue involved in an affirmative defense (other than insanity) with "some evidence," the burden of proof shifts to the prosecution to prove the defendant guilty by disproving the affirmative defense as well as by proving all the other elements of the offense charged, beyond a reasonable doubt.

In a jurisdiction following this Illinois burden-of-proof rule for such affirmative defenses—which is fairly common—you can argue to the judge that evidence as to the principles of international law, including expert-witness testimony, constitutes "some evidence" with respect to an element or elements of whatever affirmative defense you are relying on. Under the terms of this burden-of-proof rule, the judge must allow your introduction of "some evidence" of the international-law violations, including your expert, to be admitted at trial for consideration by the jury. Otherwise, to refuse your request would impermissibly deny the civil resisters their statutory right to this affirmative defense and thus constitute an unconstitutional violation of due process of law under the Fifth and Fourteenth Amendments to the U.S. Constitution and analogous provisions of the applicable state constitution.

DISTINGUISH ELEMENTS OF AN AFFIRMATIVE DEFENSE FROM ELEMENTS OF THE OFFENSE CHARGED

According to the U.S. Supreme Court in *Patterson v. New York*, 432 U.S. 197 (1977), it is constitutionally permissible for a state to put the burden of proof on the defendant to establish by a fair preponderance of the evidence that he or she is entitled to claim the benefit of an affirmative defense. Not all jurisdictions do so, however. Some jurisdictions follow the Illinois practice that if the defendant raises the issue involved in an affirmative defense (other than insanity) by "some evidence," then the prosecution must sustain the burden of proving the defendant guilty beyond a reasonable doubt as to that issue "together with all the other elements of the offense" charged.

Notice that the Illinois statute also requires that the prosecution prove all elements of the offense charged beyond a reasonable doubt. According to the U.S. Supreme Court in *Mullaney v. Wilbur*, 421 U.S. 684 (1975), the prosecution has the burden of proof with respect to establishing the existence of all elements of the crime charged beyond a reasonable doubt. This fundamental requirement of due process of law is in addition to the Illinois statutory requirement that the prosecution disprove any affirmative defense beyond a reasonable doubt so long as "some evidence" related to it has been presented at trial. Hence, special care must be taken to distinguish elements of an affirmative defense from elements of the offense charged, the latter of which the prosecution must always prove beyond a reasonable doubt, even if the defendant produces "no evidence" on them. This basic requirement of U.S. constitutional law should permit the submission of international-law considerations and expert-witness testimony to the jury with respect to any element of the crime charged against a civil resister.

RELATE INTERNATIONAL-LAW PRINCIPLES
TO THE ABSENCE OF CRIMINAL INTENT

As a general proposition, for a defendant to be found guilty of a crime in the United States, the jury must find beyond a reasonable doubt that at the time the defendant committed the act (the *actus reus*), the defendant possessed the criminal intent *(mens rea)* required by the applicable statute or under common law. In every civil-resistance case I have worked on, the resisters have never denied that they did what they did—that is, that they committed the "guilty act." Indeed, they are proud of what they did and readily admit it before, during, and after the trial. For that reason, in civil-resistance cases the defense will oftentimes argue that the resisters did not possess the required criminal intent *(mens rea)* at the time they protested.

Hence, you should offer international-law evidence and an expert not only for the purpose of establishing any affirmative defenses but also for the purpose of creating "reasonable doubt" as to whether the state has proved all elements of the offense charged, including—and especially—criminal intent. Here a simple example would be the introduction of international-law evidence and an expert for the purpose of corroborating the defendant's intent at the time of the civil-resistance action, for example, that the defendant acted because of a reasonable good-faith belief that his or her conduct was authorized by international law to prevent the commission of international and domestic crimes by U.S. government officials. The prosecution must prove beyond a reasonable doubt that the civil resister possessed the required criminal intent when he or she protested. So you have a constitutional right to create reasonable doubt as to criminal intent by introducing into evidence before the jury considerations of international law, including an expert witness. For the judge to deny the admission of international-law evidence and an expert witness relevant to this element of the offense charged that establishes the absence of the required concurrent criminal intent would constitute an unconstitutional violation of due process of law.

DISTINGUISH THE SPECIFIC-INTENT CRIMES
FROM THE GENERAL-INTENT CRIMES

Many civil-resistance protesters have been charged with "specific-intent crimes." In addition to the general criminal-intent requirement that the defendant acted intentionally or voluntarily, specific-intent crimes require an additional mental element—for example, that the defendant also acted knowingly, willfully, maliciously, for an unlawful purpose, or without authority. A trial attorney must carefully establish whether any of the crimes for which the defendants have been charged are specific-intent crimes. Indeed, sometimes in civil-resistance cases the criminal indictment will add in specific-intent language that goes beyond the literal text of the statute under which civil resisters were charged. These specific-intent crimes should be distinguished quite clearly and consistently from the other offenses requiring only a general criminal intent as well as from any affirmative defenses that you have chosen to rely on.

As stated above, *Mullaney v. Wilbur* requires that the state prove all elements of a crime charged beyond a reasonable doubt. In the case of a specific-intent crime, this requirement would include the need to prove beyond a reasonable doubt not only the defendant's general criminal intent but also the defendant's specific criminal intent necessary to constitute the crime charged. For example, in another Plowshares case, the defendants were charged with felonious "depredation" of U.S. government property for inflicting some inconsequential damage at a U.S. nuclear-weapons installation and faced two years in prison. Acting on my advice, in pretrial papers filed with the federal district court, the defense counsel took the position that "depredation" was a specific-intent offense that required the government to prove beyond a reasonable doubt that the civil resisters had acted maliciously and that the defense therefore had the right to call an international-law expert to testify before the jury at trial that the resisters had acted with a reasonable good-faith belief that their conduct was permissible under international law to prevent the commission of international crimes by means of that particular nuclear-weapons system. After reviewing these papers, the U.S. attorney's office dropped the "depredation" count and fell back on the lesser included offense of trespass, with a maximum of less than six months of incarceration in prison, and thus deprived us of a jury trial.

I have always suspected the U.S. attorney did not want the international-law evidence of the criminality of that particular nuclear-weapons system to be considered by a jury by means of expert-witness testimony in open court, calculating that the civil resisters could very well get an outright acquittal or hung jury and in any event, that such testimony would produce scads of adverse publicity for that particular nuclear-weapons system in the surrounding community. Eventually, and predictably, a federal magistrate convicted these antinuclear civil resisters of trespass after a bench trial. But facing six months of incarceration for a misdemeanor is a lot better than facing two years for a felony!

This litigation strategy is analogous to criminal trials in which psychiatrists have been permitted to testify as to the defendant's mental condition in so-called diminished-capacity cases.[6] As a criminal defense, diminished capacity was derived from the common-law defense of voluntary intoxication, which, although not traditionally recognized as a defense to general-intent crimes, was nevertheless permitted as a defense to negate a specific-intent element in a specific-intent crime. For example, in the case of common-law larceny, a voluntarily intoxicated defendant was permitted to argue to the jury that he was so intoxicated that he could not have formulated an intention to permanently deprive the owner of the property at the time of the theft, which is the specific-intent element of that crime. This rationale was subsequently extended to permit criminal defendants to argue that although their mental incapacity, disease, or defect was not substantial enough to fulfill the requirements for the legal definition of insanity and thus to negate general criminal intent, expert psychiatric testimony about their mental condition should be admitted and considered by the jury with respect to the issue of whether it negated the existence of a specific-intent element necessary to constitute the crime charged.

If the judge allows the international legal considerations and expert-witness testimony to go to the jury with respect to the question of whether the civil resister actually possessed the specific intent necessary to constitute the crime, the defense can always argue that the government has not proved beyond a reasonable doubt that the defendant acted with the specific intent required, because of his or her reasonable belief—as corroborated by the international-law expert—that both international law and U.S. domestic law prohibited the U.S. government's commission of Nuremberg crimes against peace, Nuremberg crimes against humanity, Nuremberg war crimes, genocide, grave breaches of the Geneva Conventions, and the inchoate crimes incidental thereto such as planning, preparation, conspiracy, attempt, aiding and abetting, solicitation, and complicity. The civil-resistance protester might stand a good chance of obtaining an acquittal or at least a hung jury because the resister, the expert, and the attorney have all created "reasonable doubt" as to the existence of the specific criminal intent necessary to constitute the crime charged.

TRESPASS AND INTERNATIONAL LAW

The crime of trespass is usually a specific-intent offense. Generally, the prosecution must prove beyond a reasonable doubt not only that the civil resister voluntarily entered upon the premises but also that he or she did so for an unlawful purpose. Defense counsel should argue, for example, that although the civil resister might have voluntarily entered a nuclear-weapons facility, he or she did not do so for an unlawful purpose but was instead acting for the express purpose of upholding the requirements of international law, U.S. domestic criminal law, and the U.S. Constitution, in order to prevent the commission of international crimes by U.S. government officials there and elsewhere. This argument would then provide the basis upon which the testimony of an expert witness on international law could be introduced into evidence for consideration by the jury. Certainly the defense has the constitutional right to create "reasonable doubt" as to the defendant's alleged specific intent of "without authority" required to constitute the crime of trespass.

The expert's testimony as to the total criminality of the specific nuclear-weapons system being resisted under international law would be relevant to the question of the defendant's specific intent—in this case, establishing the lawfulness of the purpose for which the civil resister voluntarily entered the nuclear-weapons facility. All that would be required is for the civil resister to state that he or she generally believed that something known as international law—the Nuremberg Charter, Judgment, and Principles; the Genocide Convention; the Geneva Conventions; the Hague Regulations; the UN Charter; the 1996 World Court advisory opinion—prohibited the threat or use of nuclear weapons of mass destruction in general and of this particular nuclear-weapons system in particular, and therefore that he or she was acting to uphold the requirements of international law by preventing the commission of ongoing crimes by U.S. government officials when he or she entered the nuclear-weapons facility. The testimony of the expert witness should be admitted into evidence and considered by the jury for the purpose of corroborating the reasonableness of the defendant's good-faith belief as to the requirements of international law.

SABOTAGE AND INTERNATIONAL LAW

In another Plowshares case I worked on, the civil resister faced two counts of sabotage, with twenty years on each count for a total of forty years of incarceration, because of substantial damage he had inflicted upon a nuclear-weapons facility. During his direct examination at trial, he stated in part that he had read a book of mine arguing that nuclear-weapons systems and all their essential accouterments are criminal under international law and that my analysis had compelled him to do something about the situation. When his direct examination was over, his defense counsel argued to the judge that they had a right to put me on the stand in front of the jury and examine me as to the basis of my opinion upon which he had relied when he acted. The judge agreed, and I testified for about two and one-half hours before the jurors. The jury acquitted this antinuclear civil resister on one count of sabotage but convicted him on the second count, and eventually he received a thirty-three-month sentence. In another Plowshares case I later worked on, the antinuclear civil resisters left another book of mine at the scene of their protest and later testified at trial that its arguments had in part compelled them to resist the Minuteman III ICBM—an inventive way to get the international-law arguments introduced into evidence at trial as physical evidence.

RELATE INTERNATIONAL LAW TO THE FACTS NECESSARY TO CONSTITUTE THE CRIME CHARGED

The U.S. Supreme Court ruled in *In re Winship*, 397 U.S. 358 (1970), that in criminal cases the government must prove beyond a reasonable doubt all facts necessary to constitute the crime charged against the defendants. Over the years, in civil-resistance cases we have used *Winship* to argue that the defense has the right to introduce into evidence at trial principles of international law and an expert thereon to create reasonable doubt as to the facts necessary to constitute a variety of crimes charged against civil resisters, for example: What is "property" within the meaning of the offense of destruction thereof? What is the "national defense material" that must be destroyed for the crime of sabotage? What is a "lawful order" that must be violated for the military crime of failure to obey such? What is "terrorism" under a special U.S. federal antiterrorism statute?

The defense must carefully consider whether and how international law relates to any fact necessary to constitute the offense charged. If international law is relevant to any of the facts of the offense, then defense counsel must argue to the judge that the defense has a constitutional right to create a reasonable doubt as to that fact by submitting international-law principles and an expert thereon for consideration by the jury. And later on to the jury, defense counsel must argue that certainly the international-law expert has created reasonable doubt as to the specific fact at issue that warrants an acquittal. To paraphrase what I once told a military judge in a court-martial proceeding on behalf of a most courageous and principled military civil resister after about three and one-half hours of testimony: "Your Honor, whether or not you fully agree with what I have said here today, I submit that I have created a reasonable doubt." About sixteen days later, that military civil resister was discharged from the military.

SHOULD YOU USE THE NECESSITY DEFENSE?

You are almost wasting your time trying to use the necessity defense in a federal district court. In civil-resistance cases prosecuted in federal courts, judges have bent over backward to interpret the necessity defense out of existence. Indeed, these days even raising the necessity defense in a civil-resistance case in a federal court might undermine your ability to relate international-law principles to other valid theories of defense you might have developed for your clients.

On the other hand, many state and local judges will still give civil resisters a fair shake and a clear shot at establishing a necessity defense. Necessity is an extremely powerful defense for civil resisters.[7] But necessity is a complicated affirmative defense to put on, since it usually requires four or five elements and the defendant must submit at least "some evidence" for each element to even raise the necessity defense before the jury: (1) serious threatened harm to the public; (2) exigency of the harm; (3) action of lesser harm to prevent the threatened harm; (4) no reasonable legal alternative; and sometimes (5) effectiveness of the action. That task will usually require an international-law expert, together with several factual experts.

By comparison, in many of the specific-intent defenses I have worked on in antinuclear civil-resistance cases, we have basically needed only two experts: a legal expert on international law and an expert on the characteristics of the nuclear-weapons system involved. In some antinuclear cases where we did not have a nuclear-weapons expert, I have been qualified as a factual expert as well as a legal expert and so testified before the jury on both areas of expertise. But it would be extremely difficult to put on a necessity defense without multiple experts.

Who is brought in as an expert and what the expert will testify about should be carefully thought through well in advance of trial. In addition, the experts' willingness to appear at trial and the contents of their respective testimonies should be assessed personally by the attorney and not simply delegated to the defendants and their supporters. Of course, the logistics of the experts' travel schedules can be taken care of by the civil resisters and their supporters. But if the latter call me first, I always ask to speak with their attorney of record before committing my valuable time *pro bono publico* to come out to trial and testify on their behalf. Generally, I need to know personally from the attorney of record how, where, and when I fit into the defense strategy before I agree to become part of it.

INTERNATIONAL LAW IS PART OF U.S. DOMESTIC LAW

To better relate principles of international law to the defense theory or theories, the trial attorney must patiently explain to the judge, and later to the jury, that U.S. domestic law expressly incorporates international law by means of Article VI of the U.S. Constitution (the supremacy clause), with respect to treaties, as well as the famous decision of the U.S. Supreme Court in *The Paquete Habana*, 175 U.S. 677 (1900), with respect to customary international law.[8] Furthermore, in *United States v. Belmont*, 301 U.S. 324 (1937), and *United States v. Pink*, 315 U.S. 203 (1942), the U.S. Supreme Court held that other types of international executive agreements concluded by the U.S. government that have not received the formal advice and consent of the U.S. Senate are nevertheless entitled to the benefits of the supremacy clause. Defense counsel should argue that international treaties and executive agreements must be accorded the benefit of the supremacy clause with respect to state criminal-law statutes, and of the "last in time prevails" rule with respect to federal criminal statutes if appropriate.[9] In other words, if the treaty or executive agreement was enacted into law after the statute, it should supersede the statute, or at least the jury is entitled to decide this issue of supersession.

Likewise, counsel can also argue that since customary international law is a part of both federal common law and state common law,[10] federal and state criminal statutes must be construed in a manner consistent and compliant with the requirements of international law. Therefore, the testimony of an expert witness on this subject should be admitted into evidence at trial for consideration by the jury for this purpose. A similar argument can be made with respect to relevant international treaties and executive agreements to the effect that the jury should be permitted to consider expert testimony on their contents in order to interpret federal and state criminal statutes in a manner that would be consistent and compliant with international law and thus the U.S. Constitution.

The point of this exercise is to get the judge and later the jury to understand that international law is not simply some amorphous collection of rules adopted by some nebulous foreign entity, but rather is a living body of law that has been fully subscribed to by the U.S. government and, even more importantly, expressly incorporated into constitutional law, both federal and state. Moreover, it should be argued that the president of the United States has taken an oath as required by Article II, Section 1, Clause 7 of the U.S. Constitution to "preserve, protect and defend the Constitution of the United States," which expressly includes international treaties and agreements by virtue of Article VI.[11] Similarly, Article II, Section 3 of the U.S. Constitution requires the president to "take Care that the Laws be faithfully executed." These admonitions clearly include international treaties and executive agreements as well as customary international law.

President Bush has grievously violated his oath and his constitutional obligation to "take Care that the Laws be faithfully executed," including therein U.S. international treaties and executive agreements as well as customary international law. In this regard, the December 9, 2005, issue of *Capitol Hill Blue* reported that in a meeting in the Oval Office with Republican congressional leaders who had serious constitutional concerns about renewing the USA Patriot Act, President Bush angrily screamed out about the U.S. Constitution, "It's just a goddamned piece of paper!"[12] Civil resisters have acted to prevent the president and subordinate executive-branch officials from committing international crimes and U.S. domestic crimes in violation of the U.S. Constitution and thus to uphold and enforce the U.S. Constitution itself against these criminals. Once again, defense counsel should have a constitutional right to put on such international-law evidence and an expert witness to that effect before the jury.

INTERNATIONAL LAW AND THE FIRST AMENDMENT

Other provisions of the U.S. Constitution can also be invoked to establish yet another line of argument in favor of admitting expert testimony on the requirements of international law. According to the First Amendment to the U.S. Constitution, "Congress shall make no law . . . abridging . . . the right of the people . . . to petition the Government for a redress of grievances." That is exactly what civil resisters do when they protest, and so one can argue that they engage in constitutionally protected conduct under the First Amendment.

Civil resisters have a constitutional right "to petition the Government for a redress of grievances" against the president and other military and civilian officials of the executive branch of the federal government. In civil-resistance cases, these "grievances" stem from the government's violation of the basic rules of international law, U.S. domestic criminal law, and the U.S. Constitution. Your international-law expert's testimony should be admitted for the purpose of establishing precisely what these "grievances" are—"grievances" related to international and domestic crimes being committed by the government—that your clients were petitioning for redress of when they engaged in their civil-resistance activities. And be sure to check for analogous provisions in the state constitution when defending civil resisters in state or municipal courts.

WHY YOUR INTERNATIONAL-LAW EXPERT
SHOULD BE ENTITLED TO TESTIFY AT TRIAL

According to Rule 702 of the Federal Rules of Evidence (FRE),

> if scientific, technical, or other specialized knowledge will assist the trier of fact to understand the evidence or to determine a fact in issue, a witness qualified as an expert by knowledge, skill, experience, training, or education may testify thereto in the form of an opinion or otherwise, if (1) the testimony is based upon

sufficient facts or data, (2) the testimony is the product of reliable principles and methods, and (3) the witness has applied the principles and methods reliably to the facts of the case.

Many states follow a similar rule in their respective state codes of evidence.

Under this standard, any law professor who teaches a course on international law at an accredited American law school can be qualified as an expert on this subject for your civil-resistance trial. In addition, the second professionally recognized manner for someone to become an expert on international law is by obtaining a Ph.D. in political science, specializing in international law. So be sure to begin your search for an expert on international law at your local law schools and political science departments. Before your expert testifies at trial, he or she should feel free to review the sample testimonies that I have prepared for publication here and elsewhere in order to prepare his or her own testimony, as others have done.

WHY INTERNATIONAL LAW IS DIFFERENT

Sometimes, however, judges will respond that the testimony of an international-law expert is not necessary to inform either the court or the jury about the requirements of international law, since those tasks can be performed by submitting a trial memorandum to the judge and through appropriate jury instructions—as is oftentimes done in a case with respect to other questions of law at issue. The proper response to this question as to why international law should be treated differently is a bit complicated. But succinctly stated, the reasons for such differential treatment for international law are justified on the following grounds.

The Statute of the International Court of Justice (ICJ)—popularly known as the World Court—is an integral part of the UN Charter, which is a treaty that has received the advice and consent of the U.S. Senate. So the United States is legally bound by the ICJ Statute. The ICJ must be distinguished from the International Criminal Court, whose statute the Bush Jr. administration repudiated—for obvious reasons. But the ICJ Statute is entitled to the benefits of the supremacy clause of the U.S. Constitution, and is thus binding on any state or federal court in the United States whenever questions of international law are presented. ICJ Statute article 38(1) specifically designates the universally recognized sources of international law to be applied by the World Court itself:

    a. international conventions, whether general or particular, establishing rules expressly recognized by the contesting states;

b. international custom, as evidence of a general practice accepted as law;
c. the general principles of law recognized by civilized nations;
d. subject to the provisions of Article 59, judicial decisions and the teachings of the most highly qualified publicists of the various nations, as subsidiary means for the determination of rules of law.

ICJ Statute article 38(1) essentially creates an evidentiary and procedural rule for the determination of the rules of international law. It is applied not only by the International Court of Justice but also by any international or domestic tribunal seeking to determine the rules of international law. In the United States, both state courts and federal courts have routinely invoked the article 38(1) evidentiary and procedural rule to determine the rules of international law when confronted with such questions.

Article 38(1)(d) specifically states that "the teachings of the most highly qualified publicists of the various nations" are a "subsidiary means for the determination of rules of law." In other words, the teachings, publications, and opinions of international-law professors are explicitly recognized as being an authoritative source for the determination of the rules of international law. This characterization has been universally agreed upon by all states party to the UN Charter and ICJ Statute, including the United States. Hence this evidentiary and procedural rule attributing special importance to the "teachings" of international-law professors binds all U.S. federal courts and state courts under the terms of the supremacy clause of the U.S. Constitution.

Furthermore, article 38(1)(d) attributes just as much significance to the "teachings" of an international-law professor as to a judicial decision as a subsidiary means for the determination of the rules of international law. You should certainly point out to the judge that this equivalence in the degree of authoritativeness for international-law-professor "teachings" with judicial decisions is not true for any other area of the law. Indeed, it has always been the case that when it comes to determining the rules of international law, international tribunals and U.S. domestic courts have attached great weight, respect, and deference to the opinions of international-law experts.

Finally, and most persuasively, in the aforementioned case of *The Paquete Habana*, 175 U.S. 677, 700 (1900), the U.S. Supreme Court expressly ruled as follows:

International law is part of our law, and must be ascertained and administered by the courts of justice of appropriate jurisdiction as often as questions of right depending upon it are duly presented for their determination. For this purpose, where there is no treaty and no controlling executive or legislative act or judicial decision, resort must be had to the customs and usages of civilized nations, and, as evidence of these, to the works of jurists and commentators who by years of labor, research, and experience have made themselves peculiarly well acquainted with the subjects of which they treat. Such works are resorted to by judicial tribunals, not for the speculations of their authors concerning what the law ought to be, but for trustworthy evidence of what the law really is.

This, then, provides the reasons a judge should permit your international-law expert to testify at trial, even though this might not be the practice with respect to other areas of the law. The rule enunciated in FRE Rule 702 must be interpreted by reference to ICJ Statute article 38(1)(d) and *Paquete Habana* to permit an international-law expert to testify at trial.

WHAT IF YOUR INTERNATIONAL-LAW EXPERT IS NOT PERMITTED TO TESTIFY?

Sometimes the judge might rule that your international-law expert will not be allowed to testify. Such a ruling, however, does not mean that you cannot put on your defenses and international-law evidence at trial anyway. If your expert is not allowed to testify, simply have the civil resisters bring out considerations of international law in their own words during your direct examination of them at trial. Your clients' testimony can be easily prepared by having them sit down and read the relevant chapters of this book and other materials concerning the type of civil-resistance activities they have engaged in. You should attempt to get introduced into evidence as many of these substantive legal principles that you believe your clients can reasonably present during your direct examination of them at trial. Obviously, there is no way your clients can speak very technically about these complicated matters of international law, domestic criminal law, and U.S. constitutional law. But they can certainly get across to a jury of their peers the major international-law violations that have been committed by U.S. government officials in pursuit of whatever governmental policies your clients were protesting. Cases have been won this way.

LAY THE PROPER FOUNDATION FOR THE ADMISSION OF YOUR EXPERT'S TESTIMONY

When the case finally goes to trial, it will be extremely important for you to call at least one defendant to testify as a witness on the stand before your expert witness in order to lay some foundation testimony with respect to international law. This should be easy enough to do. Generally, most individuals who have engaged in civil-resistance activities have heard of something known as international law—the Nuremberg Charter, Judgment, and Principles; the Genocide Convention; the Geneva Conventions; the Hague Regulations; the UN Charter; the World Court. Moreover, it is probably the case that your defendants believed that their activities were either permitted or even required by principles of international law or the numerous treaties and conventions mentioned above.

All that is necessary, therefore, is for one defendant to take the stand and testify that he or she generally believed something known as international law prohibited the threat or use of nuclear weapons, the U.S. invasions of Iraq and Afghanistan, U.S. military interventionism around the world, the Bush administration's self-styled "global war on terrorism," and that he or she was therefore acting to uphold the principles of international law when protesting. This testimony provides the basis on which the testimony of an expert witness on international law could be introduced into evidence for consideration by the jury. The testimony of the expert witness should be admitted for the purpose of corroborating the defendant's reasonable and good-faith belief as to the requirements of international law.

PRIVILEGE VERSUS OBLIGATION

Your clients may have acted in the sincere belief that under international law, they were *obligated* to do something about the situation.[13] Nevertheless, it will be much easier for you to argue only that they were *privileged* to act under principles of international law. This privilege is referred to as the Nuremberg privilege, which was mentioned in the declaration reprinted at the beginning of chapter 1.

I cannot understand why defense counsel would insist on arguing for the existence of a duty to act when the establishment of a privilege to act would be just as effective and much easier to prove. Of course it might be true that your jurisdiction actually recognizes a defense based upon "other *obligations* of law." If so, then you should certainly present the "duty" argument with respect to that defense. Otherwise, no point will be served by making your job any more difficult than it already is going to be.

QUALIFYING YOUR EXPERT WITNESS

Long before your expert witness on international law appears in the courtroom, you should have submitted to him or her a list of questions that you will be asking during the course of your direct examination. The first group of questions should deal with qualifications as an expert. One of the cardinal rules that I am sure is well known to litigators is not to agree with the prosecution to stipulate to the formal qualifications of your expert. Usually it is the case that an international-law professor possesses numerous degrees, impressive qualifications, prestigious committee assignments, distinguished public-service activities, and so on. For that reason, it is extremely important for you to take time on the stand to go through the complete academic and professional background of your expert witness.

The purpose of this exercise is to convince the jury that your expert witness is not motivated by any type of political considerations or personal animosities but is simply appearing as an objective and detached scholar who is genuinely concerned about the gravity of the U.S. government's violations of international law and its commission of international crimes. The best evidence for this is the fact that normally the expert will receive no fee for the testimony, just reimbursement for out-of-pocket expenses. You should certainly emphasize this last point for the jury at the end of your direct examination to qualify your expert.

In this regard, I should also point out that it likely will prove to be very difficult for the prosecution to locate an international-law professor who is willing to testify as an expert on the prosecution's behalf for no fee and who is not currently or has never been employed by the U.S. government. In the unlikely event that you are confronted with an international-law expert on the prosecution's side, be sure to impeach that person's credibility in front of the judge and the jury by extensively inquiring into his or her economic, political, and career connections with the U.S. government and whether he or she has received any form of compensation for the testimony and from whom. I regret to report that the number of international-law professors in the United States who could pass such questions with flying colors are few and far between. If you conduct such a stringent cross-examination of an opposing expert before qualification, you should have a good chance of winning any "battle of the experts" in the collective mind of your jury. Most American professors of international law are, have been, or want to be in cahoots with the U.S. Department of State, U.S. Department of Justice, the Pentagon, the CIA, the National Security Council, or the White House. Just the nature of the beast.

PREPARE THE TESTIMONY OF YOUR EXPERT WITNESS

The great bulk of the proposed questions you should submit to your expert witness before trial will deal with the substantive issues of international law

involved in the case. The expert witness will be able to point out any substantive problems with the questions as stated, any difficulties in phraseol-
ogy, a proper sequence for asking the questions, any potential for damaging
cross-examination on certain issues, and any questions that you left out that
should be put in. You can use the sample direct examinations published in
this book and elsewhere as a basis for developing the international-law expert's testimony in your own case, subject of course to any modifications,
amendments, or additions the expert believes necessary or desirable. As a
matter of fact, other international-law experts have reviewed my materials
before giving their own expert-witness testimony at trial. So it is not essential that I be the one to testify. Indeed, a local international-law expert
would exert a more persuasive impact on the judge and the jury than an expert flown in from out of town.

THE EXPERT WITNESS SHOULD PRESENT
THE TESTIMONY AS IF IT WERE A SEMINAR

Once on the witness stand, the expert witness should assume that he or she is
there for the purpose of educating a group of men and women who are basically well-intentioned, law-abiding, patriotic, and peaceable Americans, but
who are probably not very well informed about the underlying substantive issues involved in the case. The expert should proceed to testify with the objective of educating the jury on the nature of the international crimes being
committed by U.S. government officials so that the jury members can come
to understand and sympathize with the sentiments that compelled the civil resisters to act in their comparatively restrained manner. To do this, the expert
witness should conduct the testimony as if it were a private seminar or tuto-
rial for the members of the jury on whatever the substantive legal issues are
from the civil resister's point of view.

Consequently, when the lawyer directs questions toward the expert, the expert should look at the jury, not the lawyer, while answering. The expert
should adopt a colloquial form of speech. The expert should not use technical terms of art; or, if the expert finds it absolutely necessary to do so, he or
she should first apologize for sounding "so much like a professor," and then
proceed to explain any such terms to the jury. Likewise, the expert should repeat concepts and definitions as often as necessary for the jury to clearly understand their meanings.

If the expert uses a term that is too technical and without adequate explanation, you should interrupt and ask the expert to define or further explain the term. Moreover, you should tell the expert beforehand that you are

going to do this whenever you feel that he or she has lost contact with the jury for any reason, that the expert should expect this to occur, and that he or she should not show any irritation on the stand over such interruptions. As is true in the classroom, the demonstration of patience, sincerity, simplicity, and respect by the professor for his or her student-jurors will produce the most rewarding results.

The expert witness must also remember that unlike in a seminar, he or she has a relatively short period of time in which to educate the jury about the defendant's point of view on a very complex subject. I would recommend that you allow at least one hour for the expert's substantive testimony, not including time for qualification. If you believe your direct examination will take longer than that, then you should schedule the expert testimony so that it can be broken up by lunch, to avoid taxing the jury's attention span. Even an outstanding group of bright and dedicated law students can rarely focus on complicated classroom lectures in a meaningful way for more than eighty minutes at a time.

Before trial, you should obtain authentic copies of any treaties, conventions, documents, or other sources of international law that the expert will be referring to during direct examination as well as the aforementioned provisions of the U.S. Constitution. These copies should be prepared as exhibits for formal introduction into evidence during the course of the expert's testimony. When the expert is about to discuss a particular treaty, agreement, convention, resolution, you should first pick up the prepared copy of the document, ask the expert witness to identify it, and then move that it be introduced into evidence as an exhibit. That way the jury will have such documents on hand when they retire to consider their verdict.

ESTABLISH A PATTERN OF ONGOING CRIMINAL ACTIVITY BY U.S. GOVERNMENT OFFICIALS

I cannot emphasize enough the importance of establishing a pattern of ongoing criminal activity by the U.S. government. The ordinary man or woman sitting on the jury believes that the U.S. government is essentially peaceable and law abiding. So it is up to you to convince them that this just is not true, by means of the evidence and expert testimony that will be adduced at trial. You must argue not simply that the U.S. government is committing violations of international law but also that these violations constitute ongoing criminal activity that creates personal criminal responsibility for officials of the U.S. government under well-recognized principles of international law and U.S. domestic criminal law as fully subscribed to by the U.S. government itself.

Depending on the substantive issues involved, these international crimes could include, but are not necessarily limited to, Nuremberg crimes against peace, crimes against humanity, war crimes, grave breaches of the Geneva Conventions, genocide, torture, enforced disappearances, and assassinations, as well as the inchoate crimes incidental thereto—planning, preparation, solicitation, incitement, conspiracy, complicity, attempt, and aiding and abetting. Here it would be worthwhile for your expert witness to explain to the jury the historical origins of the Nuremberg Charter, Judgment, and Principles as a direct reaction to the genocidal horrors inflicted by the Nazi regime of Adolf Hitler before and during the Second World War as well as the leading role played by the U.S. government in the establishment of the Nuremberg Tribunal to prosecute the Nazi leaders for these heinous crimes. Of course the great irony is that today's U.S. government officials are committing or planning and conspiring to commit international crimes for which their predecessors successfully sought to put Nazi government officials to death! It would be nice to have your expert mention that fact to the jury.

As if that were not enough, your expert should also explain to the jury that the U.S. Army's *Field Manual 27-10, The Law of Land Warfare* (1956) prescribes the appropriate standards of international criminal law applicable to such situations that have long been recognized as valid by the U.S. government itself. According to paragraph 498 of the field manual, any person, whether a member of the armed forces or a civilian, who commits an act that constitutes a crime under international law is responsible for it and liable to punishment. Such offenses in connection with warfare comprise crimes against peace, crimes against humanity, and war crimes.

Paragraph 499 defines the term "war crime" as the technical expression for a violation of the laws of war by any person or persons, whether military or civilian. Every violation of the laws of war is a war crime. Pursuant to paragraph 500, conspiracy, direct incitement, and attempts to commit as well as complicity in the commission of international crimes are similarly punishable as international crimes in their own right.

Paragraph 501 of the manual recognizes the existence of and sets forth the standard for vicarious criminal responsibility on the part of commanders for acts of subordinates. Any U.S. government official, whether civilian or military, who had actual knowledge or should have had knowledge through reports received by him or her or through other means that troops or other persons subject to his or her control (e.g., the CIA) were about to commit or had committed international crimes and who failed to take the necessary and reasonable steps to ensure compliance with international criminal law or to punish violators thereof is similarly guilty of an international crime. This test of vicarious criminal responsibility is based on the seminal decision of the U.S. Supreme Court in *In re Yamashita*, 327 U.S. 1 (1946).

Paragraph 509 denies an alleged war criminal the defense of superior orders, whether military or civil, unless the individual did not know and could not reasonably have been expected to know that the act ordered was unlawful, though superior orders may be considered in mitigation of punishment. Furthermore, paragraph 510 denies the defense of "act of state" to such alleged war criminals by providing that the fact that a person who committed an act that constitutes a war crime acted as the head of state or as a responsible government official does not relieve him or her from responsibility for that act. On these as in other matters, *Field Manual 27-10* generally incorporated the terms of the Nuremberg Charter, Judgment, and Principles.

Hence, according to the U.S. Army's field manual itself, all high-level civilian officials and military officers in the U.S. government who either knew or should have known that civilians or soldiers under their control committed or were about to commit international crimes and failed to take measures necessary to stop them or to punish them or both are likewise personally responsible for the commission of international crimes. Such U.S. government officials, among others, are personally responsible for commission and complicity in the commission of crimes against peace, crimes against humanity, and war crimes as specified by the army field manual and the Nuremberg Charter, Judgment, and Principles.

Sixty years ago at Nuremberg, representatives of the U.S. government participated in the prosecution and the execution or incarceration of Nazi government officials for committing some of the same types of heinous international crimes that officials of the U.S. government are today committing against innocent people around the world. Consequently, the American people must reaffirm the country's commitment to the Nuremberg Charter, Judgment, and Principles by holding government officials fully accountable under international law and U.S. domestic law for the commission of such grievous international crimes. We must not permit any aspect of our foreign affairs and defense policies to be conducted by acknowledged "war criminals" according to the U.S. government's own official and longstanding definition of that term. The American people must insist upon the impeachment, dismissal, resignation, indictment, prosecution, and long-term incarceration of all U.S. government officials guilty of such international crimes. That is precisely what your clients were doing when they engaged in their civil resistance activities.

This approach to conducting the direct examination of your international-law expert shifts the focus of the jury's attention away from an exposition of abstract principles of international law to a discourse on the criminal nature of the government's conduct. This latter point should prove to be a gut-level issue that the peaceable and law-abiding members of an American jury can readily understand, abhor, condemn, and oppose by acquitting the civil resisters. Such expert testimony will then set the stage for presenting to the jury your defenses of necessity, choice of evils, prevention of crime, prevention of a catastrophe, measures otherwise authorized by law, absence of general or specific criminal intent, during the subsequent course of the trial. The main point you want to drive home to the jury is that your clients were privileged to act as they did to prevent the ongoing commission of internationally recognized criminal activity by officials of the U.S. government. When you compare the minor nature of the crime for which the defendants have been charged with the monstrous nature of the international crimes being committed, supported, condoned, or threatened by U.S. government officials, jurors will likely conclude that the defendants are entitled to whatever defenses you are claiming. I believe that the American people are basically unaware of the gross violations of international criminal law being perpetrated in their name by their own U.S. government officials on a day-to-day basis, and that once they are informed, they will be outraged and do something to stop the elementally lawless and criminal behavior of U.S. government officials around the world. Sometimes even the jaded judges have been appalled.

SPECIAL ADVICE FOR PRO SE CIVIL RESISTERS

I know from prior experience that there will always be a few civil resisters who will affirmatively decide as a matter of principle and conscience to represent themselves at trial. So the following brief comments are specifically directed toward these pro se civil resisters. At trial, pro se civil resisters will usually have an opportunity to explain what they did and why they did it in their testimony in chief. You should prepare this statement with a great deal of care and consult sample direct testimonies I have already prepared with respect to the particular issue at trial in your case. You can use that testimony to prepare your own courtroom statement.

During the course of your testimony in chief, you should attempt to present *some* of the international-law arguments discussed in the relevant chapters of this book and elsewhere. This does not mean that you should simply commit my sample testimony to memory and repeat it by rote in front of the jury. Rather, you should make a good-faith effort to convey to the jury the meaning and content of some of the most important international-law principles that compelled you to protest; typically, these would include the Nuremberg Charter, Judgment, and Principles; the Genocide Convention; the Geneva Conventions; the Hague Regulations of 1907; the UN Charter; the Universal Declaration of Human Rights; and Article VI of the U.S. Constitution making treaties and executive agreements "the supreme Law of the Land."

If there is more than one defendant, the defendants can divide my sample testimony among themselves so that all the basic international-law arguments are covered by at least one resister. Please remember, however, that you must not attempt to sound as if you are experts on international law. Rather, you are simply explaining the relevance of international law to your protest in simple words to the members of the jury, as one group of concerned human beings and American citizens to another group of the same. Considerations of international law were a decisive factor that compelled you to resist the commission of international crimes by U.S. government officials.

Your objective should be to attempt to convince at least one juror that your protest was compelled by a reasonable good-faith belief that such conduct was justified by basic principles of international law that have been fully subscribed to by the U.S. government itself. The hope is that that one juror will be prepared to hold out for your acquittal. If you are convincing enough, you should at least be able to produce a hung jury in those jurisdictions where unanimity is required for conviction. In one case I worked on, this tactic by a pro se defendant resulted in an outright verdict of acquittal with respect to a less serious charge. Of course this same tactic can also be used by civil resisters being represented by an attorney at trial.

LAST-DITCH STAND

Finally, in the event that the judge has stripped you of all your defenses, rejected your expert witnesses, and then gone so far as to indicate that he or she will not even allow you to mention principles of "international law" during the course of your direct examination or testimony in chief, then you might wish to consider pursuing the following strategy as a last-ditch stand: when it comes time for the civil resisters to take the witness stand, each could stand up in open court and politely but firmly renew the request to have two experts (one on the facts, the other on the law—both mentioned by name) testify, assert that otherwise he or she has nothing more to say at this time, and then respectfully sit down. At that point the judge will find himself or herself in the difficult position of risking a reversal on appeal for denying the defendants' constitutional right to put on a defense if the judge does not accede to this renewed and reasonable request for only two experts. The judge will also look pretty unfair in the eyes of the jury if there is one.

When faced with such a joint strategy pursued by ten antinuclear protesters in sequential order, a U.S. federal district judge realized that he could very
well be overruled on appeal for committing reversible error if he did not allow the defendants to produce at least one expert on U.S. nuclear-weapons
policies and another expert on international law. So after originally denying
the defense request for these two expert witnesses, he relented, reversed himself, and gave defense counsel full scope to conduct extensive direct examinations of Admiral Eugene Carroll from the Center for Defense Information
and me. Although the judge, sitting in a bench trial without a jury, subsequently convicted these courageous and principled antinuclear civil resisters,
they all left the courtroom feeling satisfied that they had had their day in
court. Nevertheless, some quick thinking by defense counsel prevented this
federal judge from inflicting his planned kangaroo-court proceedings on these
admirable civil resisters.

SHOULD YOU APPEAL?

When civil resisters are convicted, they and their attorneys are confronted
with the question of whether they should appeal. Of course the civil resisters
have to decide this question for themselves as a matter of conscience and
principle. But generally, I have counseled civil resisters asking my opinion on
this question against an appeal unless they are facing several years in prison.

Since the original Plowshares Eight action in 1980, civil resisters, their
lawyers, and their supporters have been fighting guerrilla warfare in court-
rooms all over the United States and elsewhere in the world. So long as there
is not an adverse precedent by an appellate court, we can make these international-law arguments to every state, local, and federal judge in the country on
behalf of civil resisters. Personally, I would like to see it stay that way.

Given the incredibly repressive legal and political environment here in the
United States since September 11, 2001, there is a very high likelihood that
civil resisters will lose an appeal and in the process of doing so, set an adverse
precedent that would make it extremely difficult, if not impossible, for subsequent civil resisters and their lawyers in that particular jurisdiction to use international law to defend themselves against criminal charges in the future. I
respectfully submit that civil resisters should want to keep the appellate court
records as clean as possible from adverse precedents so that later civil resisters
would have a clear shot at defending themselves in court by using international law. In any event, there is absolutely no point in appealing a conviction
involving a minor penalty or insubstantial incarceration when there is always
the prospect of more serious criminal charges involving several years in

prison being brought against civil resisters sometime in the future, such as another Plowshares action. If an appeal is to be mounted, then let it be undertaken by civil resisters facing several years in prison. Do not spoil it for them!

Furthermore, if you did not have proper advice and counsel at the trial level, mounting an appeal would be dangerous. In one antinuclear case, the defendants faced an adverse appellate precedent set by a group of previous pro se resisters who went into court without an attorney, were convicted, and then appealed, setting an adverse appellate precedent for everyone else in that particular jurisdiction, including our defendants. Please do not do that! Think about the good of the civil-resistance community and the peace movement before you decide to appeal.

CONCLUSION

This brings the analysis back to the discussion at the very beginning of this chapter about why civil resisters should permit themselves to be represented by an attorney who believes in them and in their cause. Quite obviously, in the limited space of this brief chapter I cannot even begin to deal with all the problems that will arise in the defense of those who have engaged in civil-resistance activities to prevent the commission of state crimes by U.S. government officials. If after having digested the contents of this book you still have any questions, please feel free to contact me.

If you have any advice, comments, criticisms, or suggestions about the philosophy, strategy, tactics, and materials in this book, please communicate them directly to me. Finally, in return for my assistance, I would appreciate being kept informed of the progress you make on your case and its ultimate disposition and receiving any court pleadings that you and the prosecution might file. That way I can continue to serve as a central repository and resource center for all those who nobly engage in civil-resistance activities designed to terminate the U.S. government's brutal and malicious attack on the integrity of the international legal order, the U.S. domestic legal order, and the sacrosanct words of the U.S. Constitution.

Today is *our* Nuremberg moment!

NOTES

1. Louis Fisher, *American Constitutional Law* 665 (5th ed. 2003).
2. Patrick Martin & Joseph Kay, *Republicans Launch Power Grab in U.S. Senate*, World Socialist Web Site, May 23, 2005, http://www.wsws.org/articles/2005/may 2005/fili-m23.shtml.

3. George E. Curry & Trevor W. Coleman, *Hijacking Justice*, Emerge, October 1999, at 42; Jerry M. Landay, *The Conservative Cabal That's Transforming American Law*, Washington Monthly, March 2000, at 19; People for the American Way, *The Federalist Society: From Obscurity to Power* (August 2001), available at http://www.pfaw.org/pfaw/dfiles/file_148.pdf; Institute for Democracy Studies, *The Federalist Society and the Challenge to a Democratic Jurisprudence* (2001).

4. Fisher, *supra* note 1, at 676–77.

5. In 1950, the International Law Commission of the United Nations adopted the Principles of International Law Recognized in the Charter of the Nuremberg Tribunal and in the Judgment of the Tribunal:

Principle I

Any person who commits an act which constitutes a crime under international law is responsible therefore and liable to punishment.

Principle II

The fact that internal law does not impose a penalty for an act which constitutes a crime under international law does not relieve the person who committed the act from responsibility under international law.

Principle III

The fact that a person who committed an act which constitutes a crime under international law acted as Head of State or responsible Government official does not relieve him from responsibility under international law.

Principle IV

The fact that a person acted pursuant to order of his Government or of a superior does not relieve him from responsibility under international law, provided a moral choice was in fact possible to him.

Principle V

Any person charged with a crime under international law has the right to a fair trial on the facts and law.

Principle VI

The crimes hereinafter set out are punishable as crimes under international law:

(a) Crimes against peace:
   (i) Planning, preparation, initiation or waging of a war of aggression or a war in violation of international treaties, agreements or assurances;
   (ii) Participation in a common plan or conspiracy for the accomplishment of any of the acts mentioned under (i).

(b) War crimes:
   Violations of the laws or customs of war which include, but are not limited to, murder, ill-treatment or deportation to slave-labour or for any other purpose of civilian population of or in occupied territory, murder or ill-treatment of prisoners of war, of persons on the seas, killing of hostages, plunder of public or private property, wanton destruction of cites, towns, or villages, or devastation not justified by military necessity.

(c) Crimes against humanity:

Murder, extermination, enslavement, deportation and other inhuman acts done against any civilian population, or persecutions on political, racial or religious grounds, when such acts are done or such persecutions are carried on in execution of or in connexion with any crime against peace or any war crimes.

Principle VII

Complicity in the commission of a crime against peace, a war crime, or a crime against humanity as set forth in Principle VI is a crime under international law.

6. Wayne R. LaFave, *Principles of Criminal Law* § 8.2, at 338–46 (2003).

7. William P. Quigley, *The Necessity Defense in Civil Disobedience Cases: Bring in the Jury*, 38 New Eng. L. Rev. 3 (2003).

8. *See* Jordan J. Paust, *International Law as Law of the United States* (2d ed. 2003); Louis Henkin, *Foreign Affairs and the U.S. Constitution* (2d ed. 1996).

9. *Diggs v. Schultz*, 470 F.2d 461 (D.C. Cir. 1973), *cert. denied* 411 U.S. 931 (1974).

10. Harold Hongju Koh, *Is International Law Really State Law?* 111 Harv. L. Rev. 1824 (1998).

11. Robert F. Blomquist, *The Presidential Oath, the American National Interest, and a Call for Presiprudence*, 73 U.M.K.C. L. Rev. 1 (2004).

12. Doug Thompson, *Bush on the Constitution: "It's just a goddamned piece of paper,"* Capitol Hill Blue, Dec. 9, 2005.

13. *See* Jordan J. Paust, *The Other Side of Right: Private Duties Under Human Rights Law*, 5 Harv. Hum. Rts. J. 51 (1992).

Chapter Three

Trident II on Trial

STATE OF WISCONSIN CIRCUIT COURT, ASHLAND COUNTY

STATE OF WISCONSIN, *Plaintiff,* *v.* *DONNA E. HOWARD-* *HASTINGS* *AND TOM H. HOWARD-* *HASTINGS,* *Defendants.*	*DECLARATION OF DR.* *FRANCIS BOYLE,* *IN SUPPORT OF* *DEFENDANTS'* *OPPOSITION* *TO STATE'S MOTION IN* *LIMINE* *Case Nos. 96 CF 052* *and 051*

VERIFIED DECLARATION OF DR. FRANCIS A. BOYLE

INTRODUCTION

I, Francis A. Boyle, declare and state as follows:

1. I am a Professor of International Law at the University of Illinois in Champaign. I've held the Professorship since 1978. I have a Bachelor's degree in Political Science from the University of Chicago; a Master's degree in Political Science from Harvard; a Doctorate of Law from Harvard Law School; and a Ph.D. in Political Science from Harvard, specializing in the relationship between international law and international politics.

2. I have studied and written extensively regarding the legality of U.S. nuclear weapons systems and "defense" policies. I have read almost everything that has been published in the public record on the subject of the planning and preparation for nuclear war by the United States—including material regarding nuclear weapons targeting plans—and I have published a great number of articles on these subjects. See my curriculum vitae, attached.

3. I have been asked by attorneys John Bachman, Katya Komisaruk and Kary Love to prepare this declaration.

4. I have reviewed specific information and professional literature regarding the Navy's Project ELF (Extremely Low Frequency) submarine transmitter system, and have familiarized myself with its operation. I provided expert testimony at length in a case virtually identical to the case at bar. *Wisconsin v. Ostensen*, 150 Wis. 2d 656 (1968); trial transcript, Vol. II of III, pp. 133-204.

5. Based upon my review and analysis of these and other materials, the particular statutes with which the defendants are charged, and the facts of the case, international law is not only relevant to the various defenses available, but dispositive.

PROJECT ELF

6. The Project ELF transmitters send secret one-way orders to submerged, nuclear-armed ballistic missile submarines around the world. ELF transmissions are so slow and so limited, however—one three-letter message takes 15 minutes—that the ELF system has no function as a "deterrent" to nuclear war. It is incapable of announcing to submarines that an attack has been made upon the United States. The Navy's Vice Admiral Kaufman has testified that ELF would not survive an atomic exchange. Department of Defense Appropriations for 1979, Hearings Before a Subcommittee of the House Appropriations Committee, 4 April 1978, Pt. 4, p. 491.

7. For a first strike by the United States, however, ELF plays a vital role in secretly bringing all submarines into communication to coordinate targeting and timing. Using ELF, the Pentagon can give the appropriate coded signals to all submarines without tipping its hand. Congressional hearing transcripts are replete with testimony saying ELF is a call-up system before hostilities break out.

8. ELF is a "bell ringer," signaling submarines to put their antennae near the surface, to pick up much more rapid satellite communications. Defense Advanced Research Project Agency (DARPA) Director Dr. Robert Cooper has testified that submarines were being equipped with extreme high frequency (EHF) receivers. Dr. Cooper testified, "That combination of ELF bell-ringer and EHF capability should provide appropriate communication to our submarines in the latter part of [censored]." Department of Defense Authorization and Oversight, Fiscal Year 1984 Hearings before the House Armed Services Committee, 18 April 1984, Pt. 5, p. 991. The Navy uses the faster EHF for sending targeting instructions to nuclear-armed submarines because avoiding detection would be a moot point at the moment of launch. The submarines must approach the surface anyway because missiles cannot be launched from great depths. Since ELF is not a survivable system, Dr. Cooper's testimony is an admission that ELF is the triggering signal for a first strike.

A) International Law

9. The operation of Project ELF raises several international and U.S. law concerns relating to the potential and actual uses of nuclear weapons by the United

States. With regard to international law, the Constitution of the United States, Art. VI, sec. 2 provides that "all treaties made, or which shall be made, under the authority of the United States, shall be the supreme law of the land, and the judges of every state shall be bound thereby, anything in the Constitution or the law of any state to the contrary notwithstanding." The U.S. Supreme Court has established unequivocally that treaties to which the United States is a party apply to and are enforceable in all United States courts. *The Paquete Habana*, 175 U.S. 677, 700 (1900).

10. The function of Project ELF communications is to coordinate a "first strike," or "counterforce," nuclear attack. Such a surprise attack, or even planning such an attack, violates international and domestic law. A preemptive nuclear strike by one country against another is a crime against peace and therefore is absolutely prohibited for any reason whatsoever. Article 2(4) of the United Nations Charter prohibits both the threat and the use of force except in cases of legitimate self-defense as recognized by Article 51 thereof. The United Nations Charter is U.S. law, since the United States is a signatory party to the treaty which established the United Nations and is therefore bound by it.

11. Furthermore, retaliation, or response-in-kind, to a nuclear attack made upon the United States, would also be illegal because the effects of nuclear weapons cannot be limited to combatants, or to belligerent states, and because the effects of nuclear weapons cannot be limited in time or distinguished from those of banned weapons. Because of the inevitable, uncontrollable and indiscriminate effects of nuclear weapons, ELF's use as a "bell ringer" for a nuclear attack would constitute an act of aggression and wanton destruction, a war crime, a crime against humanity and a crime against peace, all prohibited by the judgment of the Nuremberg Tribunal. Consequently, even if the United States were to be attacked first, the use of nuclear weapons in combat is absolutely prohibited under all circumstances by both conventional and customary international law. It would violate, in addition, the November 24, 1961, U.N. General Assembly Resolution 1653 (XVI), that: "any State using nuclear or thermonuclear weapons is to be considered as violating the Charter of the United Nations, as acting contrary to the law of humanity, and as committing a crime against [hu]mankind and civilization."

12. Additionally, Project ELF functions as an operational threat to wage nuclear war. This ongoing threat itself also raises profound questions regarding international and domestic law violations. This is because of what are known as "inchoate" crimes: that is, not simply the substantive offense is illegal, but also the planning for, preparation of, conspiracy to commit, incitement to commit and the aiding and abetting of the substantive offense. (See defendants' "Criminal Indictment" attached.)

13. Because ELF's function and purpose is to prepare and enable the commission of a nuclear attack, its operation constitutes the above inchoate crimes, namely, the planning, preparation and conspiracy to commit crimes against peace, crimes against humanity, war crimes and genocide, as well as grave breaches of the Four Geneva Conventions of 1949, Additional Protocol I of

1977, and the Hague Regulations of 1907. Consequently, all first-strike nuclear weapons as well as their command, control and communications systems — such as Project ELF — are illegal.

B) Domestic Law

14. In addition to violations of international law, nuclear weapons and their concomitant systems, including Project ELF, are violative of the Neutrality Act, 18 USC 956(a). This Act was legislated in 1794 and it created liability for violation of the provision of Article I, section 8 of the U.S. Constitution, which reserves to Congress the power to decide when to go to war. The Neutrality Act makes clear that no individual or entity, even the president, can initiate war without Congress's approval.

15. The Neutrality Act is violated when two or more persons conspire to injure or destroy the property of a foreign government with which the United States is at peace. As with any conspiracy, there must be an agreement to commit the specified offense, and then an act in furtherance. That is, it is not necessary that the parties to the conspiracy actually destroy another government's property — it is enough that they planned to do so and took at least one step toward this goal. In the case of Project ELF, there was an agreement to set up a system which can devastate countries upon which we have no declared war, and steps were taken to set up this system. Therefore ELF is a crime-in-progress under the Neutrality Act. To find a violation of the Act,

> [i]t does not wait for the project to be consummated by any formal array or organization of forces, or declaration of war, but strikes at the inception of purpose, in the incipient step taken with a view to the enterprise, by their engaging men, munitions of war, means of transportation, or funds for its maintenance. *United States v. Ybanez*, 53 F. 536, 538 (C.C., W.D. Tex. 1892). [Emphasis supplied.]

Moreover, the Neutrality Act prohibits any type of military enterprise, not necessarily preparation for invasion. The goal, clearly, is to prohibit the unauthorized attack while it is still being prepared, rather than after the fact.

16. The Neutrality Act has delineated a separation of powers. In 1793, the Supreme Court Chief Justice John Jay held that no one, not even the president has the right to "lift up the sword of the United States. Congress alone have power to declare war." *Henfield's Case*, 11 F.Cas. 1099, 1108-09 (C.C.D. Pa. 1793) (No. 6, 360); see also *United States v. Smith*, 27 F.Cas. 1192 (C.C.D.N.Y. 1806) (No. 16, 342). The authority to initiate a nuclear attack has not been delegated and cannot be delegated to the military, neither its nuclear chain of command, nor Project ELF.

CONCLUSION

17. In light of the fact that nuclear weapons and their command, control and communications systems contradict fundamental norms of international and domestic law, all citizens of the world possess the basic right under international

law—which is part of U.S. law—and under the principle of crime prevention, to engage in nonviolent civil resistance activities for the purpose of preventing or terminating the ongoing commission of crimes, including the operation of Project ELF.

18. My opinions are based on information in the public domain, and are based on a reasonable certainty, consistent with relevant standards in my field.

I declare and verify under penalty of perjury that the foregoing is true and correct to the best of my knowledge.

Date: 6 September 1996
FRANCIS A. BOYLE
Professor of International Law
University of Illinois
Champaign, IL

Attachments:
1) Francis A. Boyle, Curriculum Vitae.
2) Criminal Indictment, 22 April 1996, by Donna and Tom Howard Hastings, defendants.

The Trident II strategic nuclear missile submarine is the most hideous and nefarious weapon of mass destruction (WMD) ever devised in the cosmically brief history of human disingenuity. Each Trident II strategic nuclear missile submarine can accommodate twenty-four Delta V missiles.[1] Each Delta V missile can carry up to twelve multiple independently targetable reentry vehicles (MIRVs). Each one of these reentry vehicles can accommodate a thermonuclear warhead of 300 to 475 kilotons. For the sake of comparison, note that in 1945 President Harry Truman criminally exterminated about 140,000 human beings at Hiroshima and then about 70,000 human beings at Nagasaki by means of two low-yield atomic bombs of 15 and 21 kilotons respectively.[2]

Currently the United States deploys fourteen Trident II submarines. And courtesy of the United States, the United Kingdom deploys four Trident II submarines.[3] Worse yet, in the post-9/11 world, the U.S. Trident IIs are now on a "modified alert status."[4]

Furthermore, each Trident II warhead is given near-pinpoint accuracy by the NAVSTAR satellite communications system.[5] For that reason, the U.S. and U.K. Trident II strategic nuclear submarine forces are ideal for launching an offensive, first-strike strategic nuclear-weapons attack of genocidal, near-omnicidal dimensions. Historically, the sole means by which the U.S. Navy communicated with Trident II strategic nuclear submarines sailing at patrol depth was the extremely low frequency (ELF) system. For that reason, in August 1987 George Ostensen decided to engage in his Plowshares civil-resistance action directed against the ELF facility near Ashland, Wisconsin, as explained below by his attorney of record, Susan Hedman. He was charged with two counts of "sabotage" and faced forty years in prison for his action of courage, integrity, and principle.

To the best of my knowledge, *Ostensen* was only the second case in the United States in which anyone had been able to obtain an outright verdict of acquittal from a jury on one count of sabotage for a Plowshares action directed against an American nuclear-weapons facility. It was a unique achievement, and a tribute to the vision, fortitude, and rectitude of George Ostensen. Therefore, I have included below the transcript of my *Ostensen* testimony to provide a basic idea of how we obtained this remarkable result by exposing the criminality of Trident II to the judge and the jury. The transcript has been edited for style, length, and typographical errors, but it provides a blow-by-blow account of what actually happened in the courtroom when we put on trial the Trident II nuclear-weapons system under well-recognized principles of international law and U.S. domestic law.

Over the years, I have used this transcript to help defend many Plowshares antinuclear civil resisters from some pretty serious criminal charges (e.g., felonious depredation of government property, felonious destruction of government property, sabotage). This track record includes obtaining two additional outright verdicts of acquittal from a jury on charges of sabotage in 1996 for another Plowshares action directed against the same ELF/Trident II facility in Wisconsin by Tom and Donna Howard-Hastings (the declaration quoted at the beginning of this chapter was submitted in that case).[6] Despite interference by the judge—who was the prosecutor in George Ostensen's trial several years earlier—we were able to convince the jury that the ELF/Trident II was an offensive first-strike strategic nuclear-weapons system of mass extermination that was criminal under well-recognized principles of international law and U.S. domestic law.

The arguments and transcript that we had developed and generated in the *Ostensen* case were also later used as the blueprint for obtaining the October 21, 1999, directed verdict of acquittal by a Scottish sheriff (i.e., judge) in favor of three Trident Ploughshares 2000 antinuclear resisters at Greenock, Scotland, on four charges each for criminal damage to Britain's Trident II nuclear-weapons facility.[7] This spectacular victory over Trident II was a real fillip to the worldwide antinuclear movement, coming just after the U.S. Senate rejected ratification of the Comprehensive Test Ban Treaty on October 13, 1999. The long-standing, massive, and continual acts of civil resistance mounted by the Trident Ploughshares 2000 movement against U.K. Trident II facilities in Scotland continue apace with active support from the Scottish National Party. As I stated to the U.K. news media right after my court testimony at Greenock: "Why don't the English put their nukes in Brighton?"[8]

Meanwhile, in a stunning victory for antinuclear civil resistance in the United States, the U.S. Navy announced that it would permanently shutdown and dismantle its Project ELF system in Wisconsin and Michigan as of September 30, 2004.[9] Then in early November 2004, a federal magistrate sitting in Madison, Wisconsin, found the last six antinuclear civil resisters guilty of trespassing during a previous May demonstration at the ELF site, but did not fine them: "The ELF battle is over. You're not coming back and there's no reason to fine you. It doesn't matter anymore."[10] Civil resistance had triumphed over the Trident II!

Notwithstanding these and other antinuclear victories in the United States and the United Kingdom, the Trident II nuclear-weapons system will bedevil humankind well into the twenty-first century.[11] Humanity must eliminate Trident II before Trident II obliterates humanity!

Ploughshares Protester Convicted on One Charge, Acquitted on Another
by
Susan Hedman

Peace activist George Ostensen began serving a thirty-three-month prison sentence for a conviction stemming from a protest at a naval communications site near Clam Lake, Wisconsin.

Ostensen's August 1987 action was the twenty-fifth in a series of twenty-six Plowshares disarmament actions since 1980. Ostensen cut down transmission line poles and damaged electrical boxes, forcing the navy to shut down the Project ELF facility for twenty-nine hours.

Because Wisconsin retains jurisdiction over the land on which the ELF facility is located, Ostensen was charged under Wisconsin law. He faced two counts of sabotage under an obscure McCarthy-era sabotage statute that requires proof of intentional damage to property with reasonable grounds to believe that the damage will interfere with preparation for defense by the United States.

Ostensen was represented at trial by attorney Susan Hedman. The defense team included Lawyers Commission on Nuclear Policy (LCNP) consultative council member Ramsey Clark, the former U.S. attorney general; LCNP board and council member Francis Boyle, professor of law at the University of Illinois; and attorney Brady Williamson of Madison, Wisconsin. Ashland County circuit court judge William Chase presided at the three-day jury trial, which began on January 7, 1988.

The ELF system that Ostensen damaged generates very-low-frequency radio signals used for one-way communication with nuclear submarines. According to the U.S. Navy, ELF is the only system that allows continuous contact with submarines while they are at patrol depth and cruising speed.

Peace advocates argue that ELF is designed to support a first strike. Because ELF is stationary, it would not survive a nuclear attack. Even the Pentagon concedes this point. It follows that ELF does not provide greater U.S. capability to assure retaliation if attacked, because it must be used before it is destroyed. The "go" message that would be relayed by the ELF system can be for only one of two purposes: either to launch a first strike or to order a "launch on warning."[12]

Submarines are already the most survivable leg of the U.S. strategic nuclear triad (missiles, bombers, and submarines). ELF serves no useful role in assuring their retaliatory capability. However, as Ostensen pointed out, ELF would be very effective in supporting a first-strike strategy, by coordinating the targeting and timing of an attack by submerged submarines.

In his testimony, Ostensen stressed that he believed that the ELF-Trident system exists to launch a first-strike nuclear attack and that first-strike weapons violate international law. The navy initially denied that ELF could be used to launch a first strike, but on cross-examination ELF detachment lieutenant commander Wiley Cress admitted that a first-strike message could be sent by ELF. Boyle testified for the defense that it was reasonable for an individual to believe that ELF is part of a first-strike weapons system and thus illegal under international law. Therefore, he argued, individuals are privileged under international law to stop ELF's operation.

Judge Chase refused a defense request for instructions on the affirmative defenses of necessity and coercion. He also turned down the alternative defense request, mistake of international law.[13] However, an alternative defense, mistake of fact, was allowed.[14] The defense also argued that Ostensen believed that his actions to shut down ELF would enhance the national defense by eliminating a destabilizing weapons system.

The jury convicted Ostensen on the first count of sabotage, covering damage to the central transmission site, and it acquitted him on the second count covering damage to the peripheral North Grounds of the ELF facility. Perhaps the jury felt uncomfortable with the severity of sabotage charges for an act of civil resistance and tried to "split the difference" by convicting Ostensen on only one of the two counts. The damage to the central facility represented a small portion of the monetary damage done at the ELF site, suggesting that the jury sought to convict him only on what it perceived as a lesser charge.

On February 12, Judge Chase sentenced Ostensen to thirty-three months in prison. Although an appeal was pending, Ostensen chose to begin serving his sentence.

STATE OF WISCONSIN V. GEORGE OSTENSEN, CASE NO. 87 CR 15116; AND 88 CR 1681; AND 88 CR 2234

. . .

THE COURT: All right, I made my ruling, and my ruling still stands.

MS. HEDMAN: All right. Thank you for allowing us to put it on the record.

MS. HEDMAN: Your Honor, the defense calls Dr. Francis Boyle.

FRANCIS A. BOYLE, DIRECT EXAMINATION

. . .

MS. HEDMAN: At this point, Your Honor, I would like Professor Boyle to be qualified as an expert witness on nuclear-weapons policy and international law, and if the district attorney would like to cross-examine him, he may do so now.

. . .

THE COURT: All right, I'd find that he has specialized knowledge in both of those fields as established by section 907.02 of the statutes. . . . All right, go ahead.

Q (*By Ms. Hedman, continuing*): Dr. Boyle, in your extensive writings about international law, how did you define this concept?

A (*By the Witness*): Well, I think it's important to keep in mind that international law is not an abstract body of rules that's out there floating in the sky but rather has been fully incorporated into and is a part of the United States domestic law. This is the result of two things. First, our own Constitution. Article VI of the United States Constitution says specifically that treaties are the supreme law of the land. And what that means is that treaties and other forms of international agreements to which the United States government is a party are binding on all American citizens, government officials, courts of law, whatever. The second reason for this is a holding by the United States Supreme Court back in 1900 called *The Paquete Habana*, in which our Supreme Court specifically held that international law is a part of United States domestic law, of our common law, that is to be applied by both federal and state courts whenever actions of this nature arise. So in essence this is really our law; it's something that we have either voluntarily subscribed to here in the United States by becoming a party to a treaty; or with respect to international custom, have participated in the formation of that custom by giving our consent to the development of the particular rule you are talking about.

Q: Does this mean that international law is relevant to United States government policies on nuclear weapons?

A: Definitely. As a matter of fact, the United States government itself takes this position. All three branches of our military services take this position. Both the army, navy, and air force issue field manuals to their officers. The navy, *The Law of Naval Warfare* published in 1955; the army, *The Law of Land Warfare* published in 1956; the air force is a bit late in coming out with that manual. . . . I'm most familiar with both the army and navy manuals of '55 and '56, and they make it quite clear that international law binds all members of the United States military forces and all civilian government officials and citizens of the United States as well, to the extent that these rules are involved. So it's the official position of the United States government that these rules apply; and also, with respect to nuclear weapons, the question of nuclear weapons is specifically dealt with in these field manuals. It's made quite clear in these manuals that the threat or the use of nuclear weapons is limited by the rules of international law.

Q: Now, what are the Nuremberg Principles?

A: Well, if you read these manuals, you will see that one of the major sources of law that is applicable with respect to something such as nuclear weapons is the Nuremberg Principles. And again these manuals specifically incorporate and mention the Nuremberg Principles by name and state that they are recognized as a part of the United States law. . . .

These principles go back to the prosecution of the major Nazi war criminals after the Second World War. When the war was coming to a close, Stalin believed that the top 50,000 Nazi leaders should be taken out and shot. Churchill believed that the top 5,000 should be taken out and shot. Our president believed that was not the correct thing to do, that there was something that should make us different from them. And hence these leaders were entitled to a fair trial, due process of law, etc. So the Nuremberg Tribunal was set up by what's known as the London Charter, signed in August 1945, and hearings were held in which the United States government officially participated. We had a judge there, and the court applied what became known as the Nuremberg Principles. I will mention the most relevant portions here. What's known as the crime against peace, namely planning, preparing, or waging a war of aggression or a war in violation of international treaties or agreements. Then war crimes were made a crime prosecutable at Nuremberg; that's violation of the laws and customs of warfare that all troops in all countries are obliged to adhere to. And finally a third category that was new, namely crimes against humanity. This was intended to deal with Hitler's extermination of the Jewish people, the Russian people, the Ukrainian people, Gypsies, and many others. Up until that point in time, civilians had never really been protected in a situation of armed conflict. Nuremberg responded to the fact that literally tens of millions of people, the majority of them civilians, were exterminated in World War II. So a crime against humanity was made a crime.

And if you read the definition of a Nuremberg war crime, you will see one thing made quite clear and said specifically, that the wanton destruction of cities is a Nuremberg war crime. Clearly using a nuclear bomb in a city would be a Nuremberg war crime as defined by the Nuremberg Principles.

In addition to these three crimes, the Nuremberg Charter also recognized what law professors call inchoate crimes; that is, not simply the substantive offense itself but also planning, preparation, conspiracy, incitement, and aiding and abetting, so that you can be found guilty not only of committing the offense but also of preparing and planning an offense. It's the same in a United States domestic court, where you could be found guilty not only, say, of murder but also of attempted murder or conspiracy to commit murder. It was felt at that time—by Mr. Justice Robert Jackson of our own Supreme Court, our own chief prosecutor at Nuremberg—that just making the substantive offense a crime would not be enough to prevent the next war or the next attempt to exterminate large numbers of people. As he put it, the planners, the organizers, the instigators, also had to be held accountable.

Another major point about Nuremberg is that it rejected the defense of superior orders; it is not enough to say that I was just ordered to do this by my commander and therefore I went out and killed a civilian. Those defenses were rejected, as well as the defense known as "act of state," which meant that, "Well, my government was really responsible for this crime, not me. I was just acting as an agent of the government." That defense was rejected, too; again, because the Nazi criminals were saying, "Well, Hitler ordered me to do it," or "Hitler was the one who bore responsibility, I do not."

And the United States government, Russia, France, Great Britain, made it quite clear these types of arguments would not be tolerated at Nuremberg. And eventually several major Nazi criminals were convicted of all three types of crimes, including the inchoate crimes, and some of them were sentenced to death. Similar trials conducted in the Far East in the Tokyo Tribunal drew upon the Nuremberg Principles. After the trials, these principles were enunciated and carried forth in the judgments with the full approval of the United States government. The United Nations General Assembly unanimously approved these Nuremberg Principles as an expression of customary international law, and later formal codification of these principles was drawn up by the International Law Commission, and eventually, as I pointed out, in 1955 the navy incorporated the Nuremberg Principles into their *Law of Naval Warfare*; in 1956, the army incorporated the Nuremberg Principles into their *Law of Land Warfare*, which I should point out are still operative today. They are still issued to soldiers and sailors in the field today, and they are told that they are fully accountable for any violations of the Nuremberg Principles, crimes against peace, crimes against humanity, or war crimes; and the same is true for any civilian government officials who might engage in these activities; and the same is true for any United States civilians. If any of us were to engage in these types of activities, we could be prosecuted for these types of crimes.

Q: Does your research show that the Nuremberg Principles are relevant specifically to nuclear-weapons policy, to the use of nuclear weapons?

A: Well, of course they have a great deal of applicability. Both the army and navy and air force manuals make it quite clear they apply to any time when force is used or when it's planned to be used. Indeed, in the field manuals themselves, they also agree with the proposition of Nuremberg inchoate crimes: planning, preparation, conspiracy, aiding and abetting, and attempt to commit crimes against peace, crimes against humanity, and war crimes. These inchoate crimes are crimes in their own right and can be prosecuted as such. That has been made quite clear by the three services themselves. I know of no international-law professor who is prepared to state that the Nuremberg Principles do not apply to any use or threatened use of any type of force, whether you are talking about an atomic bomb or hydrogen bomb or a new form of tank or anything else. Indeed there's an outstanding DOD [Department of Defense] policy that all such weapons are supposed to be developed in accordance with the requirements of international law.

Q: In your books and writings, have you published information and conclusions that nuclear weapons violate such principles of international law as the Nuremberg Principles?

A: Well, in my—

MR. EATON: At this point I'm going to object to that. That is a legal conclusion. That is not relevant to this case, and perhaps usurped the function of the jury.

THE COURT: What was the question, again?

MS. HEDMAN: I asked whether in his writings and books he has drawn conclusions about whether the Nuremberg Principles are violated by nuclear weapons, and I asked that only to show that the contents of his writings on which Mr. Ostensen has already testified that he reviewed—

THE COURT: Whether or not what the doctor is saying, whether the only reason that the Court is allowing this type of testimony, whether you agree with what he is saying or not, Mr. Ostensen said that he relied on what this doctor said in going to ELF and doing what he did. Of course it becomes, to this Court, I feel it's relevant on the issue of—that was indicated before, the defendant is charged with intentionally damaging property with reasonable grounds to believe that his act would interfere with the preparation for defense by the United States, and that's the only reason I'm allowing this testimony here: has Mr. Ostensen testified that he read Dr. Boyle's books? I so heard him speak, and he was relying on a lot of this information, and either rightfully or wrongfully, that's for you to decide, in going to ELF and doing the things he did. So that's the only reason I'm going to overrule the objection, and I order the question be answered.

MR. EATON: Your Honor, just for the record, I would like to state that its relevancy leads to my objection, but also the connection as far as I know, there has been no showing that there are any type of nuclear devices at the ELF facility.

THE COURT: Okay, the Court will give an instruction that if certain things were testified to by a witness and there are no facts to back up some opinions and conclusions that were made, the jury is to put no weight on that opinion or conclusion. Okay, go ahead.

A (*By the Witness*): Yes. The answer to your question is yes, if we can remember it. It was, have I written on the applicability of the Nuremberg Principles to nuclear-weapons systems? As I said, this went back to the West Point Conference in 1983, where I was speaking to an audience of approximately two hundred high-level generals, colonels, and civilian officials from the Departments of State and Defense, dealing precisely with that question. That's what they asked me to deal with, and somewhat coincidentally, the fellow sitting in front of me was a three-star general in charge of war operations. I pointed out to them that in accordance with the Nuremberg Principles and their own field manuals, that planning, preparation, conspiracy, to commit crimes against peace, crimes against humanity, and war crimes, whether by nuclear weapons or any other form of weapon, is a crime in its own right, and that, based upon my knowledge of the actual plans for the targeting of United States nuclear weapons systems, of which ELF plays a part, it would. It was inconceivable to me that they could plan to use any of the systems they currently had on line without running afoul of the Nuremberg Principles; and I raised this question for them to consider. Later on, then, that presentation that

I was making—and of course I was subjected to some fairly vigorous questioning by service members in the audience—but later on that analysis was written up in great detail with large numbers of footnotes and was published in the *Northwestern Law Review* in 1986;[15] and a Dutch translation of that was published in the Netherlands in 1985. So I have taken that position, yes, that nuclear weapons systems, targeting plans, things of this nature, can create accountability under the Nuremberg Principles.

THE COURT: Yeah, but let me, just for clarification purposes—who is a person or who are the Nuremberg Principles accountable to?

THE WITNESS: Well, Your Honor, they would be accountable in two senses: One, under United States domestic law. In the field manuals, let us suppose that the—you probably saw the movie *Dr. Strangelove* where a United States general actually orders our strategic air command into operation. . . . He would be prosecutable under the United States law or the military law, or he could be prosecuted by some other country that obtains control over him. It's a black-letter rule of international law that's again fully agreed to by the United States government, that there is what's known as universality of jurisdiction for the trial of war crimes. So that if someone were actually to engage in crimes against peace or humanity or a war crime, or planning, preparation, or conspiracy to commit these crimes, any government of the world community that obtained control over these individuals could prosecute that individual. . . .

The third point is that an individual could be held accountable before an international tribunal, which as I said had been set up at the end of the Second World War, held both for the European theater and also the Far East. One would hope that we are not going to need a similar tribunal after a third world war.

. . .

Q (*By Ms. Hedman, continuing*): What's the United States government's position with respect to the Nuremberg Charter?

A (*By the Witness*): Technically, the Nuremberg Charter was annexed to the London Agreement, which was an international agreement entered into by the United States, Great Britain, France, and the Soviet Union that called for the prosecution of the Nazi war criminals. So this agreement is an international agreement similar to a treaty, which as I said before, under Article VI of the United States Constitution, is the supreme law of the land. And then there were two United States Supreme Court decisions interpreting international agreements like Nuremberg saying they are the same thing as a treaty. They are part of the supreme law of the land too. And you can find the Nuremberg Charter in the *Statutes at Large*. It's part of the United States law. Later on this body of law was expressly incorporated into the field manuals of the three services. And it was made quite clear that individuals in the services as well as civilian government officials, and where appropriate, civilians, can also be prosecuted for Nuremberg crimes. And here with respect to the civilians, you dealt with a situation where you had businessmen in Nazi Germany who were using Jewish slave labor or who had been concocting gas for the extermination of Jews; and their response was, "Well, that was just business." But the Nuremberg Tribunals did not accept that argument and found that civilians can be held accountable for this body of law as well.

Q: Now, if we could turn our attention to something called Presidential Directive 59, could you tell us what that is, whether or not you had a chance to examine it in the course of your research?

A: Yes, I have. The plan for the actual targeting of the United States nuclear-weapons systems, the actual use of nuclear weapons is what's known as the single integrated operational plan—

THE COURT: The what?

THE WITNESS: I'm sorry, it's called the single integrated operational plan, or SIOP, S-I-O-P, which is the acronym for it. And these war plans for the actual use of nuclear weapons have gone through several evolutions from the time of the development of nuclear weapons by the United States government. The next to last evolution was in the Carter administration, and that was what was known as Presidential Directive 59. And Presidential Directive 59 called for major revision in the SIOP to include within itself options for the fighting of limited nuclear war, assuming such a thing could actually occur. And also apparently what's known as counterethnic targeting, counterethnic targeting being using nuclear weapons to kill large numbers of civilians simply because of their constituent ethnicity alone; namely we are going to kill these people because they are Russians, not because they are enemies, but because they are Russians. And there apparently were also first-strike options that can be found in Presidential Directive 59. Now, as I said, the actual directive itself is classified. However, there has been more than enough publicity about it, and its terms essentially have been publicized so most people in my area are generally familiar with what it contains.

Q (*By Ms. Hedman, continuing*): What's this first-strike scenario that PD 59 contains?

A (*By the Witness*): Well, there has always been available to the president of the United States, going back to the start of the nuclear age, an option for the president to order the first use of nuclear weapons against an adversary, whether in Europe, using tactical or theater nuclear weapons, or strategic systems, for example, submarine-launched ballistic missiles or ICBMs [intercontinental ballistic missiles]. Here we are talking about submarine-launched ballistic missiles. Now in Europe, of course, the first use of nuclear weapons to repel a conventional invasion is standard doctrine by the United States government; that is, we have officially taken the position that we will be the first to use nuclear weapons if necessary in Europe.

Now, with respect to strategic systems, that is, submarine-launched ballistic missiles, or ICBMs, or bombers, we have never officially stated that we would be the first to use nuclear weapons against an adversary. Nevertheless, to the best of my knowledge that option has always been there. And Presidential Directive 59 contains such an option, and pursuant to that option there has been prepared various forms of nuclear-weapons systems that give the president, or would give the president in the future, the capability to execute that particular variant of the SIOP. For example, the Trident II/Delta V submarine with the missile is generally considered to be by most experts in the field a first-strike system; that is, one whose primary use would be to launch a first strike and, if necessary, to destroy Soviet intercontinental ballistic missiles. You don't need Trident II/Delta Vs to destroy a Soviet city, but it would be very helpful to destroy a fixed silo that is hardened. And you need pinpoint accuracy to destroy that; so there are various systems of that nature. Trident II/Delta V is one of the primary systems to accomplish this objective in the event that the president decides that that's what he wants to do.

Q: Would ELF play a role in the Trident II first-strike scenario?

A: As I understand it from the technical literature on ELF, ELF has been designed primarily to communicate with Trident II submarines. Trident II goes very deep and it goes very fast. And the only way that you can communicate at that depth and speed is through the ELF system. Although a good deal of this is classified, the part that I have read that's not classified indicates that ELF would be useful to transmit messages to Trident II/Delta V submarines to surface or to come close to the surface, where in turn they would receive attack messages from other forms of communication. There are aircraft that fly all the time over the oceans, trailing antenna down to the water or putting out broadcast communications that they would be able to pick up. So ELF, as I understand its primary use, is to communicate with the Trident II/Delta Vs.

Q: Is the first-strike scenario legal under the Nuremberg Principles?

A: No, no. This would clearly constitute a crime against peace, as defined by Nuremberg, namely, waging an aggressive war or a war in violation of international treaties or agreements. It would constitute a war crime. It would also constitute a crime against humanity if you are using nuclear weapons in proximity to cities and killing large numbers of civilians, whatever your objective is. And as I pointed out, wanton devastation of cities is a Nuremberg war crime.

And finally there is one other treaty to which the United States government is a party, going back to 1907, and that's the Hague Convention I on the opening of hostilities, which requires either an ultimatum or a formal declaration of war before you can resort to any type of force against an adversary. And by the way, this is precisely why the United States government was so offended by what happened at Pearl Harbor. The Japanese struck first in a sneak attack without giving any warning, in violation of their commitment under the Hague Convention I of 1907. And once again, you can find that in the *United States Statutes at Large*.[16]

Q: Does that mean ELF, if it's used as part of the first-strike system, is not legal?

A: Certainly if ELF is used as part of a first-strike system, it would be illegal in my opinion, yes.

Q: You have testified that is part of the first-strike system?

A: To the best of my knowledge, from what I have read, yes.

Q: Have you a view as to what if any privilege would exist under the principles of international law, specifically the Nuremberg Principles, with respect to taking action to stop or to oppose ongoing inchoate crimes, planning and preparation for crimes against peace or for war crimes?

MR. EATON: Objection, Your Honor. I think this goes to the mistake-of-law question that we have discussed at length.

THE COURT: Repeat the question, please.

Q (*By Ms. Hedman, continuing*): Have you a view as to what if any privilege would exist under the principles of international law with respect to the taking of action to stop or oppose ongoing inchoate crimes such as planning or preparation for a war of aggression or for ongoing war crimes? I'm simply asking the question to find out if, within his books, he has published information and conclusions about whether someone would have such a belief.

THE COURT: All right, what's the factor or what issue in the case will this evidence tend to prove or disprove?

Ms. HEDMAN: Again, it will go to the reasonableness of my client's belief that when he acted he was somehow interfering with the defense of the United States, because after all, my client did read Dr. Boyle's work. It was just going to show that he either did or did not have a reasonable belief that he was interfering with the defense of the United States.

A (*By the Witness*): If the defense of the United States cannot legally include first-strike weapons systems, he would not believe that he was in any way interfering with the defense of the United States, and that's quite the opposite.

THE COURT: Well, before we get into that, Doctor, you have prefaced your remarks—I think this is quite important—and what you are basing your decisions on, because if we have people relying on some of the things you are saying, you say that you understand it from the technical literature you have read. What kind of stuff have you read?

THE WITNESS: Well, first of all, Your Honor, let me say I have not published anything on the ELF system, per se, or the applicability of the Nuremberg Principles to the ELF system itself, but several articles have been written on the ELF system in the technical literature. For example, Robert Aldridge, who was involved in the design of many U.S. nuclear-weapons systems, particularly for the navy, has written an article on the ELF system. There's a book that was just published by Brookings entitled *Managing Nuclear Weapon Systems.* There is—I get every day from the Pentagon a daily news bulletin that has a compendium of material that is sent out to U.S. military officers in the field. They sometimes have technical material on the characteristics of the ELF system. So that's the type of material that I rely upon. As I said there obviously is better information, but that's all highly classified by the navy, so anyone in my situation who does not have access to classified information relies on this material.

THE COURT: Okay, I'm going to overrule the objection, and the jury can put what weight it chooses on the testimony that is now to be given.

Ms. HEDMAN: Would you like me to redirect the question to you?

A (*By the Witness*): No. As I understand it, have I taken the position in my writings that individuals are privileged to take actions to prevent threatened violations of Nuremberg Principles? And the answer to that question is yes. There is authority both in the Nuremberg Judgments, that is, there's a whole series of judgments, and also in the equivalent in the Far East, the Tokyo Tribunal, that individuals have a privilege to act to the extent that they can take necessary and reasonable steps to prevent international criminal activity. Secondly, it's very similar to United States domestic law, where if you see an individual, say, about to commit a crime, that you have a limited privilege to take necessary and reasonable steps to prevent the commission of that crime. It's a similar principle at work in the international system. Yes.

Q: Dr. Boyle, in your estimation, would it be reasonable for someone to believe that ELF is a first-strike weapon that is illegal under international law and that therefore he could exercise a privilege under international law to stop its operations?

THE COURT: Are you asking if this is reasonable?

Ms. HEDMAN: Yes.

THE COURT: All right, although there was no objection, he is not going to answer that question. That's up to the jury to determine that.

Ms. HEDMAN: All right, Judge, I have no further questions of this witness.

CROSS-EXAMINATION BY MR. EATON

Q: Professor Boyle, is it correct that your analysis of the nuclear-weapons policy of the United States is somewhat incomplete because some of the classified information is simply not available to you?

A: Well, as I said, I would say that the amount of information that's in the public record, if you sit down and read through it all, is pretty enormous. The number of books that were necessary to do my study, I think, occupied maybe four full shelves of materials that have been written. To the extent that you would say it's somewhat incomplete, the actual plans for the targeting of nuclear weapons can be found in Omaha, Nebraska, in the Joint Strategic Target Planning Staff. I have not seen those actual plans. Indeed, I have recommended that Pentagon lawyers be given the opportunity to examine those plans in accordance with the rules of international law. To the best of my knowledge, that has not occurred. But no, I don't have access to the plans themselves, not too many people do.

Q: Well, was your testimony that better information on the subject is held by navy personnel?

A: No, that was not my testimony.

Q: Well, could you explain what degree of knowledge you would hold as opposed to navy personnel?

A: Only a navy person assigned to the Joint Strategic Target Planning Staff [JSTPS] in Omaha, Nebraska, would probably have better knowledge than is generally available in the public record. There are navy personnel, air force personnel, and NATO personnel who are assigned to the JSTPS staff in Omaha, but it's a very small number of individuals, and they do have access, but that information is kept, as I understand it, at highest-level secrecy in the United States government for "eyes only" of the president. I know when President Carter became president, he was the first president ever, as I understand it, to demand to actually see what these plans said; so they are kept very secret; so I wouldn't say that most naval personnel have any better idea at all of what's in there, say, than I do.

Q: You indicated that the United States government has never officially stated that the United States wouldn't use nuclear weapons first; is that accurate?

A: I have stated two things. One, that the official position of the United States government is we will be the first to use nuclear weapons in the event that the Soviet Union invades Europe. Number two, however, we have not said that we would be the first to use nuclear weapons anywhere no matter what happens.

Q: Okay.

A: But we have taken the official position—this is the NATO position—that we will be the first to use nuclear weapons, if necessary, to prevent or impede a Soviet invasion of Europe. That's one circumstance where we have taken this position.

Q: Okay, has the United States ever stated whether it would not be the first to take nuclear action outside the sphere of Europe?

A: Well, certainly President Reagan has stated that he—and recently Gorbachev also stated—that neither of them would be the first to use nuclear weapons. Unfortunately, you know, with all due respect to the president, that statement contradicts our official position on the use of nuclear weapons in Europe; and I should point out that in the event, for example, of a Soviet invasion of Europe, if we are not able to stop it with smaller-scale nuclear weapons, we are fully prepared to go all the way up to the use of larger strategic systems, whether ICBMs or SLBMs [submarine-launched ballistic missiles], whatever it takes. The president has stated this, but unfortunately it's not consistent with the officially announced position with respect to NATO.

Q: And when you say "the officially announced position," are you talking about Presidential Directive 59?

A: No. The officially announced position is found in the NATO planning directive that enunciates the doctrine known as "flexible response." That goes back to the 1960s, and that is official NATO policy. Now, Presidential Directive 59 came at the end of the Carter administration. That has never been officially published. PD 59 is still classified, the text, but the substance of what PD 59 contained was leaked by the Carter administration officials who did this, in my opinion, to combat charges by the Reagan campaign that Carter was somehow soft when it came to the use of nuclear weapons. To counteract that, they leaked the contents of PD 59. We don't have the exact text. We do have the essence of what PD 59 says. There have been several books written by scholars, investigative reporters, and others that deal with the historic evolution of the plans for the targeting of U.S. nuclear weapons, including PD 59. They operate on the basis of fairly reliable sources.

Q: Is ELF usable to send a first-strike launch message?

A: Well, as I understand it, the base—ELF—I mean in theory, it's possible to do that, but as I understand it, ELF would be used primarily to indicate to submarines that they should come closer to the surface to receive a more detailed communication from another source. But on the other hand, it's possible to have a code that ELF could communicate for the first launch of nuclear weapons, yes.

Q: All right, now, the submarines in the United States Navy have conventional weaponry as well as nuclear weaponry, do they not?

A: There are two different types of submarines. There are the submarines that contain the submarine-launched ballistic missiles, and those are the ones that ELF is designed to be communicating with. The other conventional submarines, hunter-killer subs, are designed to go after Soviet submarines containing nuclear missiles. But as I said, from everything I have read in the technical literature, ELF is designed to communicate not with our hunter-killer submarines but with our Trident II/Delta Vs.

Q: Now, the Trident II submarines, what category would that fall under?

A: SLBMs. They carry the strategic ballistic missiles.

Q: Even the Trident submarines carry conventional torpedoes, do they not?

A: I think they might carry some, yes.

Q: And as far as what you have termed killer-hunter submarines, those subs also have ELF communication devices on there, do they not?

A: I don't know if they do or they don't.

Q: Now, the ELF facility, as far as you know, is a communication device, is it not?

A: Yes, to communicate with the SLBM submarines.

Q: And it may well—it may also be used to communicate with the hunter-killer submarines if in fact these submarines do have the ELF communicating device on them, correct?

A: I have no information that conventional submarines have ELF communicators on them, nor do I have any information that ELF is designed for that purpose. All the information I have seen is that ELF is designed to communicate with the Trident IIs.

Q: Now, does the fact that a submarine has nuclear weaponry on it ipso facto make that an offensive weapon?

A: Well, I guess you have to look at what type of weapon you are talking about, and for what purpose the weapon is being used. On the Trident IIs, the SLBMs with the Delta V warheads in my opinion are clearly an illegal system. There is no question at all about it.

Q: Maybe it's a question of terminology or semantics, here, but is "illegal" equivalent to "offensive," are those two terms interchangeable in this discussion?

A: Well, in international law, if we are talking about public international law, yes.

Q: Okay, now, is it your testimony that the ELF facility can be used only in offensive capacity?

A: Well, again I, I don't believe any lawyer, law professor, would go along with a word such as "only" or "never" or anything of that nature. All I can do is testify on the basis of my knowledge of what ELF is to be used for, and that's to be used for the purpose of communicating with the Trident II/Delta V submarines.

Q: Now, the fact that international law outlaws waging war, aggression, does not necessarily protect us nevertheless from attack; is that correct?

A: Well, you are asking me — of course, we can always be attacked, but the key point here, is that — and this is made quite clear at Nuremberg — that even if the United States government is exercising a legitimate right of self-defense, say under the United Nations Charter, the use of force must be consistent with the Nuremberg Principles and the laws of war and the field manuals that I have given to you. So you have a right to defend yourself, but not by any and all means possible. The means that you select must be consistent with the requirements of both international law and United States domestic law.

Q: Let me pose this scenario to you, then. A U.S. aircraft carrier in the Persian Gulf comes under attack by a foreign power using conventional naval vessels. Can the ELF facility be used to send a message to the Trident II system or Trident II submarine to go defend that aircraft carrier using conventional weapons?

A: Again, I would think the Trident II has conventional weapons on there, but I'm not sure. I don't know precisely, but I believe it might have conventional weapons on there. Second of all, I do not believe that the navy will use Trident II submarines to defend an aircraft carrier. Rather, and as I understand it right now in the Persian Gulf, we have nuclear-powered conventional submarines there to do that type of job. So I think that the scenario that you are postulating is pretty improbable. I would not envision that coming about. Aircraft carriers have the task forces, have assigned to them a certain number of submarines with conventional weapons on them, and Trident IIs are simply not used for that purpose.

Q: Okay.

A: The Trident II is, you know, an incredibly valuable, expensive piece of property. To be using that for that purpose, you would also have problems with taking Trident II off its station or its position. So I believe that in the scenario you gave me, the mission would be accomplished by the use of the other subs.

Q: Could the ELF facility not communicate with those other submarines as well?

A: As I said, I don't know if those other subs have ELF communicators on them. From my knowledge, the primary purpose of the ELF is to communicate with the Trident IIs.

Q: You have indicated that it's, in your opinion, legal for an individual to take steps necessary to prevent criminal activity, but those steps must be necessary and reasonable, correct?

A: I have stated that in my opinion under international law, based upon the precedent of the Nuremberg Tribunal and the Tokyo Tribunal, that individuals have a privilege to act to prevent violations of international law and to take steps that are necessary and reasonable under the circumstances.

Q: You have indicated that nations on their own may have jurisdiction over war crimes; also that international tribunals would. Would that include the International Court of Justice?

A: No, not as currently constituted as of today. The International Court of Justice does not have criminal jurisdiction over individuals. On the other hand, there is right now a draft convention for the creation of an international criminal court to deal with war criminals, terrorists, and others. That is under consideration at the United Nations, but as of today that court does not yet exist.[17]

Q: Can only individuals be guilty of war crimes or can governments be guilty of war crimes?

A: Well, again, this goes back to Nuremberg, what the Nazi war criminals argued at Nuremberg: "We weren't guilty of the war crimes, crimes against peace, crimes against humanity, this was our government's responsibility, not ours, and so you cannot hold us accountable." And the Nuremberg Tribunal took the position that what's known as the act-of-state doctrine, namely that these were acts of state, I was acting on behalf of the state as an agent of the state and not in any personal capacity, that defense was rejected by Nuremberg. They had also been rejected by the United States government with respect to its own troops in the Second World War, and they made that quite clear. This defense was not going to be applied, it was not going to be recognized. And so, in the field manuals issued to the army, navy, and air force, it's made quite clear that an act of state is not a defense to the commission of international crimes, that you simply cannot go in there and say, "It's the responsibility of my government, it's not my responsibility," you—

THE COURT: He asked whether it was an individual that could be tried.

THE WITNESS: Certainly, yes.

THE COURT: Okay.

THE WITNESS: In addition to individual responsibility, a government can also be held responsible for international crimes. For example, the Federal Republic of Germany has paid reparations to surviving victims of Jewish slave labor, and war reparations to Israel, which never existed in 1945, on behalf of the crimes committed against the Jewish people by the Nazi regime. So certainly it's possible to have a government be held responsible; but even if that is the case, that would not excuse or condone criminal action by individuals.

Q (*By Mr. Eaton, continuing*): Are you aware of any specific international-law cases dealing with the ELF system?

A (*By the Witness*): No.

Q: So in international law or by an international-law tribunal, the system has never been ruled illegal?

A: Not as of yet. I recently was a chairman of a tribunal that's going to be rendering judgment on various forms of nuclear-weapons systems, but as of yet there has been no authoritative decision on ELF one way or the other that I know of, no.[18]

MR. EATON: No further questions.

REDIRECT EXAMINATION BY MS. HEDMAN

Q: If the United States government were to launch Trident II missiles and were forced to pay reparations for the damage done, if that were found to be illegal, would you estimate that the amount of those reparations would be in excess of $11,000?

A: Well, they would be enormous. The destruction that can be inflicted by one Trident II missile is incredible. A Trident II missile has the capability to accommodate fourteen separate warheads, each of which can destroy a separate target, say a separate city, so one missile alone can destroy fourteen cities in the Soviet Union. And the destruction that would be created by one of these Delta V warheads would be at least perhaps ten to fifteen times the destruction of Hiroshima or Nagasaki, so you could imagine the amount of damage that would be involved by just shooting one missile.

Q: So if we have to pay reparations to victims, how many people would we be talking about?

A: Millions, tens of millions.

Q: Tens of millions?

A: Tens of millions.

Q: For how long has it been the United States' policy to be the first to use nuclear weapons?

A: Well, of course we were the first to use them at Hiroshima and Nagasaki. After the war ended, the plans for use of nuclear weapons were in the hands of the Strategic Air Command [SAC] under General Curtis LeMay. As best as can be reconstructed from the now-declassified documents, the Strategic Air Command's plans to use these nuclear weapons were what was called "Sunday Punch," namely we would use everything we had in our inventory, and we would use it first. General LeMay operated under that scenario, as long as he was at SAC, and indeed apparently kept this plan secret even from the president himself, until finally Eisenhower demanded that he be informed as to what General LeMay was going to do with these nuclear—

Q: You mean the president didn't know?

A: The president did not know, no, did not bother to ask for, for a period of time, and eventually he did. He sent someone out to find out from LeMay. LeMay said, "I'm not going to say," and finally, as I understand it, there was a direct presidential order, and only at that point was the president informed. So we have had first-strike scenarios in our inventory from the very start. Now, the current plan, on the first use of nuclear weapons in Europe, goes back to the Johnson administration, approximately 1965. The program is "Flexible Response," which is that even if the Soviets use conventional weapons, we will respond with the use of nuclear weapons. So that's been official NATO policy now for almost twenty-five years.

Q: What effect has our first-use policy had on the Soviet Union?

A: Well, you look at the policies and the systems that are used to implement the policies. As I said, PD 59 was the policy, but to implement that policy, you needed the system, and the system was Trident II/Delta V together with ELF to help order the thing. And the NAVSTAR communication system to target it. The MX so-called Peacekeeper missile, the Pershing II cruise missiles, and a variety of other things, when you add up the capabilities of these new systems together with the policies, which are matters of public record, certainly if I were a Soviet, I'd be pretty afraid that in the event of a serious crisis, the United States government would either threaten their use or perhaps consider using them. Indeed, I should point out in the Cuban Missile Crisis, John Kennedy initiated the Cuban quarantine, stating that the odds of a nuclear war were probably 50/50 and that was at a time when we had approximately a ten-to-one superiority over the Soviet Union. That's no longer the case today. So when you put on line these very threatening destabilizing systems, Trident

II/Delta V, tied into the NAVSTAR, ELF, or the MX, or the Pershing II, you push the Soviets to move into what's known as a launch on warning.

Q: And what's that?

A: That means in the event their—and by the way, the Soviets have said, "If America goes ahead with the deployment of those systems, that's basically what we probably have to do." In the event that their computer systems, which are far less sophisticated than ours, give an indication of a first strike with nuclear weapons, they will launch immediately rather than wait to find out whether or not there was actually a strike indicated for these weapons, to actually enter space and be identified by other means, or to land.

Q: You mean the machine would make the decision for the Soviets to launch?

A: Well, not a machine. Even in the United States, machines do not make these decisions, but what would happen is that the amount of time involved whereby a human being could make the decision to launch would be reduced. Right now, for example, it's less than eight minutes in the Soviet Union. When we have the Pershing II system, in the Federal Republic of Germany, let's suppose the president decided to use the Pershing II. The Soviets would have less than eight minutes to decide whether they are under attack, number one; and number two, whether or not to respond with nuclear weapons. Well, that would transpire so quickly that probably the instinctual response would be, "Let's use them." So the great danger here is that these systems that we are developing could [leave], if not have left, the Soviets to adopt a strategy that would be almost automatic, but not quite. So that the pressures on the individual in charge of making that decision would be so enormous that he would just say, "Fine, use them." That's the danger of these first-strike systems.

Q: That's not a positive effect for United States' defense and security, is it?

A: I do think it makes it all much more dangerous for all of us. It used to be the case that announced United States policy was that we would wait until nuclear weapons land on our territory and we were sure we were attacked before responding with the nuclear weapons. But now, as I said, with PD 59 and some of these other scenarios, we have abandoned that strategy; and so it makes it much more dangerous, both for us and the Soviets and the whole world.

Q: So Project ELF, if it's used to communicate the launch order or to ring the bell, would not have a very positive effect at all on our national defense, would it?

MR. EATON: Objection, leading.

THE COURT: Sustained. Go ahead.

MS. HEDMAN: I will rephrase.

Q: So do ELF first-strike uses have a positive effect on our national defense?

MR. EATON: Objection, leading.

THE COURT: Sustained. What effect do they have?

THE WITNESS: Well, Your Honor, in my opinion when you tie in ELF to Trident II/Delta V, the effect will be destabilizing and detrimental and make it more likely, not less likely, that the Soviets could panic and decide to attack us first; in my opinion, this would be particularly exacerbated in a crisis situation—for example, another Cuban Missile Crisis or what happened in 1973 in the Middle East War with President Nixon putting our nuclear forces on alert—that in a crisis situation of that nature, the Soviets might conclude that, "Well, the U.S. government has the capability with ELF and Trident II/Delta V to attack us first, so why wait? Let's strike now." I think that's a very dangerous situation.

Q: Now, one final question. If ELF could communicate with nonnuclear submarines, or nuclear submarines with missiles only slated for non-first-use applications, defensive use, would that make it any less in violation of international law?

A: As I said, the navy developed ELF to communicate with Trident II/Delta V submarines. Perhaps there are all sorts of ancillary uses to which ELF could be put. But I don't believe that's why the navy has poured the millions of dollars into that system. It's the primary objective.

THE COURT: There's a question I have to ask, now, about whether his testimony is based upon a reasonable certainty in his profession.

. . .

Q: All right, has all of your testimony been based on a reasonable certainty consistent with the standard in your profession?

A: Yes.

THE COURT: Okay.

RECROSS EXAMINATION BY MR. EATON

Q: Are the Soviets currently in a launch-on-warning scenario, is that their policy at this time?

A: It's hard to say exactly. When the United States government introduced Pershing IIs into the Federal Republic of Germany, the Soviet response was twofold. One, they moved some of their submarine-launched ballistic missiles closer to the United States coast and put them on permanent station there. And two, they moved shorter-range systems into Czechoslovakia and one or two countries in Eastern Europe. And also, they stated that the existence of these Pershing IIs could make it more likely for them to move into a launch on warning and that they might have no alternative. To the best of my knowledge, I don't think that I'd say they have a launch on warning now. But ELF and Trident II/Delta V only make it worse, not better.

Q: And as far as you know, they were not on launch on warning as of August 16, 1987, were they?

A: Well, again, I, I don't believe so, but there's no way we can tell for sure. And the other point that was made very clear in the definitive book published by Paul Bracken called *The Command and Control of Nuclear Forces* is the way nuclear forces are set up on both sides: the United States and the Soviet Union. In the event of the development of a crisis, the interaction of systems on both sides could be such that they will be used anyway, even against the best intentions of leaders on both sides; so although they have not officially adopted launch on warning as their government policy, though they have hinted at it, it could be the case that's where they are today. We just don't know, especially because their computer systems are just not as sophisticated as ours, so there is a danger, there is a risk there, and I think Trident II/Delta V and ELF have made it worse, not better.

Q: You have never read the entirety of the Public [*sic*] Directive 59, have you?

A: No. As I said, the precise language is classified, though the contents were, I think, leaked by the Carter administration to gain an advantage in the 1980 presidential election.

Q: You have no knowledge, firsthand knowledge, of the accuracy of the information leaked in that matter, do you?

A: As I understand it, it was quite hot, and it was leaked at very high levels from the Pentagon on orders, for the purpose of combating charges by the Reagan campaign.

Q: You don't understand my question. I'm asking about your firsthand knowledge here.

A: Could you repeat it?

Q: Do you have any firsthand knowledge about the accuracy of the information leaked?

A: Well, my firsthand knowledge is that that information is pretty accurate based on my reading of a fairly large number of books and articles and newspaper accounts of the contents of PD 59, but I have not myself seen the precise text of PD 59. It's still classified.

Q: Can we understand from your testimony that the leaking of Public [*sic*] Directive 59 was politically motivated?

A: In my opinion, yes, it was. The Reagan campaign was taking the position that the Carter administration was "soft" on détente when it came to the Soviets, and [was] attacking the SALT II Treaty. The Carter administration decided to combat that by leaking the contents of Presidential Directive 59, though not the precise language, in the heat of the presidential campaign. I think all commentators will agree that there is a case of leaking for political advantage.

MR. EATON: No further questions.

THE COURT: Just let me ask a few questions, and if you want to re-recross or whatever, you may.

EXAMINATION BY THE COURT

Q: Let me ask you something. Do you know whether the Soviet Union is bound by the Nuremberg Principles?

A: Yes. As a matter of fact, they participated in the drafting of that document. They voted in favor of the Nuremberg Principles in the United Nations General Assembly. This was a UN General Assembly resolution unanimously approving these principles. A Soviet judge sat on the Nuremberg Tribunal. And as a matter of fact, in 1985 the Soviets sponsored an international conference of lawyers in honor of the fortieth anniversary of the Nuremberg Principles; so the Soviets take those principles quite seriously. As I said, because in the Second World War, of course, they were victims. They lost 20 million of their own people. And so some of that language in there was drafted to deal with what the Nazis had done to the Soviet people. I was there in 1986 lecturing in Moscow, Leningrad, and Kiev on the deterrence policies of both sides. And I pointed out that the same principles apply to U.S. nuclear weapons as applied to their own, and the applicability of the Nuremberg Principles to their own nuclear weapons systems, and they took these facts quite seriously.

Q: Now, the reason I asked that question, now, if you say that ELF is the first-strike system, do you think that the Soviets know that?

A: ELF is part of a first-strike system, and certainly the Soviets have people who read most of the literature that's generated both by the government and by professors like myself, and they read through some of what I read. I haven't particularly discussed ELF with the Soviet Union, but I do know that they view the combination of Trident II/Delta V, of which ELF is a part, as extremely threatening and destabilizing to them, as presenting a potential for first nuclear strike.

Q: Now, to this question—if you don't know it, just say so on the record—do you know whether or not the Soviet Union has a first-strike weapon?

A: In my opinion, they are in the process of trying to develop theirs, yes. The lead in this area was taken by the United States government in the accuracy that we have had with our missiles, going back to the Minuteman III, and then the MX and the Trident II/Delta V, and the Pershing II. These all have pinpoint accuracy that can be used in a first strike. And in response the Soviets, I think, have attempted to develop some capabilities. Whether or not they have that type of pinpoint accuracy at this point, my opinion would probably be no, not yet. But the point is that just because we might be committing violations of the Nuremberg Principles is no justification for their committing violations of the Nuremberg Principles.

Q: That's what I said, that—

A: It's a situation where you have two states engaging in activities that are in violation of basic norms of international law, and one set of violations here could not be used to justify the other; rather I think the appropriate response, which I said, when I was in the Soviet Union lecturing to their people, and I said to our people, is to get rid of these systems that are offensive and in violation of international law. That's the only response. Again this was covered at Nuremberg, where the Nazi war criminals raised a defense known as *tu quoque*, you also: "You also engaged in some of these activities." And Nuremberg didn't accept that either. To be sure, the United States government and some of the allied governments and the Soviet government made violations of laws and customs in World War II, but that did not excuse the fact that others did the same thing. So that defense is not applicable either.

Q: By either country from—

A: By either country. Also the British and the French and Chinese don't have the same capabilities as the United States and Soviet Union, but also possess weapons of mass destruction that raise the same problems.

Q: Thank you. Just one more, just for clarification, now. You said that the United States' official policy over in Europe is that if Western Europe were invaded, that the policy, the policy of the United States would be to use nuclear weapons to counteract that, correct?

A: Yes.

Q: But now I wasn't too clear what you said regarding if the Soviet Union was to attack, attempt to, the United States?

A: Well, again, let us assume that the Soviet Union were to launch its nuclear weapons first on the United States, and we had confirmed evidence that this launch had occurred. Our policy is that we will retaliate by launching our nuclear weapons against the Soviet Union. There is a serious problem with that policy, and the serious problem can be found in our own military manuals, which specifically state that reprisals against civilians are absolutely prohibited for all reasons, so that we cannot kill their civilians even if they kill our own civilians. And this went back again to the Second World War, where the practice—say a German soldier was going through a French town and he was shot at by a member of the resistance and killed—they would march out ten innocent people and just shoot them dead. That was held to be a war crime. It was an illegitimate reprisal, so whether we attack the Soviets first and they respond, or they attack us first and we respond, under no circumstances can we be using these things to blow up cities. Yet to the best of my knowledge, that's what both sides plan to be doing; and again, this raises an accountability problem, Your Honor. The Nuremberg Principles specifically state the wanton destruction of cities is a Nuremberg war crime and that planning, preparation, conspiracy, to wantonly destroy a city is a crime in its own right. So as I pointed out to our military leaders and also to the Soviet government officials, how can you have plans for the wanton destruction of cities without running afoul of the Nuremberg Principles?

REDIRECT EXAMINATION BY MS. HEDMAN

Q: In your opinion, would the Soviets be developing first-strike systems if we hadn't done it first?

A: Well, you can't say what they would or would not have done. You have to look at the historical records, and the historical records go back to the "MIRVing" capability—that's a capability to take one missile and to put on top of that missile several warheads. Each warhead would be capable of hitting a separate target. Now, early on we had the Minuteman III system that had three warheads permissible on each one. They are called "multiple independently targetable reentry vehicles" or MIRV warheads. When the rocket goes up and it enters into space, it separates, and then these warheads are separately targeted to different targets. For the first time this raised the question certainly of a realistic first strike. We were first to develop that technology, and the Soviets followed.

It's the case, if you look at the history of the negotiation of the ABM Treaty, the Antiballistic Missile Treaty, that was negotiated by President Nixon, a conservative Republican president. The Soviets offered a ban on MIRVs, and the Nixon administration decided not to accept the ban at that time but rather to wait until the subsequent negotiations of the SALT II Treaty. In retrospect, President Nixon's secretary of state, Henry Kissinger, and Gerard Smith, who headed up the negotiating team on the ABM Treaty, all have stated that that was probably the worst decision they ever made when it comes to nuclear weapons. That is, not to ban MIRVs, because that decision made first strike in a realistic sense possible on both sides; not at that time, but where we are now or shortly will be in say 1990 or so, with further deployment of Trident II/Delta V, with ELF and NAVSTAR, and with the MX and things of that nature. So all of these officials have now admitted that they should have taken the Soviets up on the offer to ban the MIRVs. But it's a little too late now to do that; we have them.

Q: Will our defense be weakened when the Soviets have finished their first-strike capabilities?

A: Certainly. The Soviets will respond and attempt to mimic precisely what we are doing. Indeed, after we announced the Trident II/Delta V, the Soviets announced what they call a Typhoon system, which is a newer type of submarine. I believe it will have the type of capabilities that ours will. The United States Navy says ours is superior to the Soviets, but it will make the world a lot more dangerous for both of us and undermine our legitimate defense, our ability to survive.

Q: Has the recent INF Treaty made it more or less likely that we will engage in first use?

A: Well, the INF Treaty that was recently signed by President Reagan and General Secretary Gorbachev raises problems with respect to the role of the submarine launch of ballistic missiles. Right now it's under consideration, that as the United States government and Soviet Union remove their theater nuclear weapons from Europe, the targets that had been assigned to these theater nuclear weapons such as the Pershing IIs or the ground-launch cruise missiles that we have would be covered by submarine-launched ballistic missiles. So the ability to order an attack would be put under the command of the supreme allied commander in Europe assigned to NATO to pick up targets that had been picked up by these systems before; from one perspective, that's a drawback to the INF Treaty, that you will see the Trident II/Delta V with the ELF getting drawn to that particular scenario.

Q: Now, going back to something that you mentioned before, is it true that plans for U.S. nuclear targeting are locked away from Department of Defense lawyers?

A: To the best of my knowledge, the plans for the actual targeting of nuclear weapons are maintained in Omaha, Nebraska, with the Joint Strategic Target Planning Staff, and also to the best of my knowledge, I do not believe those plans have been vetted or approved, or run by Pentagon lawyers. They are highly classified, highly secret. Very few people have access to them. As I tried to point out before, when President Eisenhower sent his scientist to look at the Strategic Air Command plans, General LeMay told him to get lost. Now, I have recommended in my writing and also in the presentation I gave at West Point that these plans should be opened up to examination by the Pentagon lawyers, lawyers at the Department of State; that the American people should have a look at this, because some of these plans that have been leaked in the public record raise serious problems under international law, not only the first strike, but also counterethnic targeting. There are several people that pointed out that plan would constitute planning, preparation, conspiracy, to commit a crime against humanity, killing people simply because they are Russians. Now again, as best as I can tell, that has not been done.

Q: Now, do your conclusions with respect to that, or some of these other matters that you have mentioned, carry, as an international-law professor, any special weight?

A: Well, the—

THE COURT: Any special weight for whom, for whom?

MS. HEDMAN: With—

THE COURT: You said "any special weight." Well, with what, whom?

MS. HEDMAN: Well, he indicated that he had made recommendations to the Pentagon to do something, and I'm asking why they—why he would be listened to by the Pentagon.

THE COURT: Oh, how would he know, do you know?

THE WITNESS: Yes, I do.

THE COURT: All right.

A (*By the Witness*): At the West Point conference, as I was pointing out, the problem here is to distinguish the professional military officer from the civilians who give him the orders. As you know, civilians order the military around here, the military take orders, and I said, "Look, some day a civilian such as the secretary of defense might give you a clearly illegal order, say, to use nuclear weapons first, and under the military law, you have been ordered not to obey that order. What are you going to do about it? Are you going to obey a clearly illegal order to destroy cities, to launch nuclear weapons first, or will you refuse to obey a clearly illegal order, which Nuremberg says you must do, and indeed even the United States field manuals, army, navy, air force, all specifically state that military officers must refuse to obey a clearly illegal order." And so I was pointing out that the military has to give serious consideration to this problem.

The professional military officers and the military as a whole take the laws of war quite seriously, and international law, and the Nuremberg Principles, and they have been trained to obey the laws of war; and this created serious problems within the military, especially those branches of the military where people have been assigned to nuclear missions, namely, that some of their officers and enlisted men look at the missions that they have been trained to do and say, "But that mission is inconsistent with what I have been told about the laws of war and international law and Nuremberg accountability." So that's why the military invited me to come and talk about this problem. They didn't know what to do about it.

Q (*By Ms. Hedman, continuing*): One final question, then. Who makes sure that our military isn't making plans in violation of international law?

A: To the best of my knowledge no one. They draw these plans up themselves in Omaha, Nebraska. It gets vetted through their own system. I do not believe it's submitted at all to examination by legal experts. It's approved probably up to the level of the secretary of defense, who might or might not be a lawyer, but probably knows nothing at all about international law. It's kept highly classified. And as I said, as I understand it, we only came to Jimmy Carter, who finally at that point said, "I want to look at the war plans"; and they brought them over and let him have a look at it, for the targeting of nuclear weapons. Carter was unaware of them, and then he looked at them and studied them and sent them back; so I guess the answer is, the military draws these plans up pursuant to presidential directions, but that's it.

REEXAMINATION BY THE COURT

Q: Doctor, in our U.S. Constitution, the military has to take orders from civilians; correct?

A: Well—

Q: The commander in chief?

A: Unless of course it's a clearly illegal order, they—

Q: Okay, illegal order under what?

A: Under international law or United States domestic law.

Q: All right.

A: If the president were to order a soldier to shoot a civilian, the soldier would be under an obligation to disobey that order, and that's made quite clear in the service manuals. No one has the authority to order a soldier or sailor to commit a war crime.

Q: But there's—you are talking about the international law, and the Nuremberg Principles become part of our Constitution and statutes?

A: Part of our laws, yes, and our Constitution by virtue of the supremacy clause, Article VI of the Constitution, with respect to treaties and international agreements such as Nuremberg, and then customary international law by virtue of *The Paquete Habana* of the United States Supreme Court in 1900.

Q: So these things get very complicated, do they not?

A: Well, the army, navy, and air force have attempted to reduce it into these little manuals that I have mentioned to you. That's what is the essence of the laws of war; and every officer that is indoctrinated into the military is ultimately given a copy of this manual. He is supposed to read it and be responsible for what's in it. As far as enlisted personnel, they too, are what they call indoctrinated into the laws of war. They get the basic training as to what they can or cannot do in situations that are in conflict; and to the best of my knowledge, they are told that if you are given something that's a clearly illegal order, you must not obey it. That's also made clear in our Uniform Code of Military Justice, Your Honor.

Q: You could get into a situation where it was a conflict of laws, couldn't you?

A: Well, obviously. The law in this says that the soldier waiting at the bottom of the line has—before he can be held personally responsible, the test—and we found this in the *Calley*[19] case—he has to know—not have reasonable grounds to believe, but must actually know—that the order is illegal. What that means, then, is that soldiers have no license simply to refuse to obey orders, but rather they really have to know that the order that they were given is clearly illegal. As I said, one example of a clearly illegal order would be an officer to tell an enlisted man, "Take that civilian out and shoot him." Any enlisted man now who did that would be responsible for the commission of a war crime and could be prosecuted for it. He could not then plead that he was ordered to do it to exonerate himself, though a judge would consider that order with respect to mitigation of punishment. So with respect to lower-level soldiers, this is not intended as a license for them to disobey orders. But it's made very clear to them and as a basis for the Nuremberg precedent, where this was established, that if an order is given to, say, kill civilians, they cannot carry out that order, and if they do carry out that order, they could be prosecuted.

RECROSS EXAMINATION BY MR. EATON

Q: Could you briefly explain the concept of deterrence?

A: In, in my opinion, the concept of deterrence is a misnomer. All it is, I think, is, is what the judge here was discussing in the little dialogue we had, and that means that the United States threatens to exterminate the Soviet Union and the Soviet Union threatens to exterminate the United States. And in the process both of us are in danger of destroying the entire human race. That's the way I look as a lawyer on the concept of deterrence. I see no validity at all to that notion we have, and the Soviets have. We have no right to threaten to destroy each other or all of humanity for any reason at all, and that again goes back to Nuremberg.

Q: The theory behind deterrence is that we will threaten extermination to avoid extermination; is that not an enigma?

A: Well, you have to distinguish what the theory might be in the academic literature and what the actual plans are for the use of nuclear weapons. Now, with respect to the actual plans of the use of nuclear weapons, there has been an enormous discordance between what some of our elected officials say we might do with nuclear weapons for public consumption and what they (together with the military) are actually planning to do with nuclear weapons. Now, that discrepancy was eliminated by PD 59, where for the first time we began publicly, at least through a leaked version, to say we are no longer relying on deterrence as a theory but rather we are now moving to a nuclear-war-fighting capability, which is different from deterrence as basically defined. Then when PD 59—that came in 1980—was elaborated upon by the Reagan administration and Secretary of Defense Caspar Weinberger's five-year defense guidance statement of 1982, in which they looked at PD 59 and said, "PD 59 is for fighting a limited nuclear war, it's no longer deterring, but we are going to be prepared to fight another nuclear war." And the presidential guidance statement by Weinberger said that's not good enough now, we have to prepare to prevail in a protracted nuclear war. So it moved over from a deterrence strategy, back in the '60s, when that concept was first developed by Secretary of Defense McNamara, to a war-fighting or war-prevailing capability, which is the current operational doctrine of the United States government.

MR. EATON: You brought up another subject matter.

Q (*By Mr. Eaton, continuing*): If the Soviets were presented with a situation where all the Trident submarines had to go to periscope depth because the ELF facility had ceased transmission, would that not present them with an opportunity they might perceive as a chance to win a nuclear war by then destroying those Trident submarines?

A: Well, we can talk about all sorts of scenarios. I think by positing the scenario you have, you have indicated the dangers of the ELF system; that is, we don't know specifically what the Soviets will or will not do once we have the ELF/Trident II/Delta V capability. It makes it extremely dangerous for us because they could conclude—a worst-case scenario. That is, if the ELF transmission goes out for whatever reason and somehow they get word of it, they could very well conclude a first-strike is imminent, and then they might decide to attack first rather than wait to be hit by Trident II/Delta V. I think that ELF raises that problem. If they were to detect an ELF transmission going out, sure, but again it only makes the situation more complex and dangerous, I think.

REDIRECT EXAMINATION BY MS. HEDMAN

Q: My final question, Dr. Boyle, are you aware of any government reports that accept your conclusion that a nuclear war would be tantamount to destruction of all humanity?

A: Well, there's this controversy, as you know, over a nuclear winter, that the use of a certain amount of megatonnage for whatever reason by either side would produce what's known as a nuclear winter, and that the nuclear winter being the type that would create killing conditions all over the globe and make it impossible for food, for flora and fauna, anything, to grow eventually in that part of the world, people being destroyed by heat and blast and then disease, plague, whatever. Eventually they would starve to death. Now, the threshold for that is approximately 100 megatons, which is an infinitesimal fraction of our arsenal or the Soviet arsenal. The Pentagon has, as I understand it, gone along with the nuclear-winter hypothesis. But the argument is precisely where the threshold is. As I said, scientists have drawn it at maybe 100 megatons. The Pentagon is saying it's a lot higher, but as I pointed out, even in the very limited nuclear exchange or first strike or whatever, you are going to be exceeding that quite quickly, quite quickly indeed. So the debate now going on between the scientific community and the Pentagon: where is that threshold where nuclear winter sets in? It's not a debate over, as I understand it, whether or not the theory is correct. It's simply where is that threshold.

THE COURT: Okay, thank you, Doctor, thank you very much.

(Witness dismissed at 4:30 p.m.)

NOTES

1. *Jane's Fighting Ships 2005–2006*, at 857 (2005).

2. Francis A. Boyle, *The Criminality of Nuclear Deterrence* 55–91 (2002); Elliott L. Meyrowitz, *Prohibition of Nuclear Weapons* 24 (1990); Stephen I. Schwartz, *Atomic Audit* 58 n.48 (1998).

3. *Jane's Fighting Ships 2005–2006*, at 812; John Ainslie, *Trident: Britain's Weapon of Mass Destruction*, Scottish CND, March 1999; Natural Resources Defense Council, *British Nuclear Forces, 2005*, Bulletin of Atomic Scientists, Nov./Dec. 2005, at 77.

4. *Jane's Fighting Ships 2005–2006*, at 857.

5. *Jane's Military Communications 2004–2005*, at 341–42 (2004).

6. Mary Thompson, *Wisconsin Protest Case May Signal Redefinition of Sabotage*, Christ. Sci. Mon., Sept. 20, 1996, at 3.

7. George Monbiot, *Our Nuclear Programme Is Illegal*, Guardian (U.K.), Sept. 28, 2000; Stephen C. Neff, *Idealism in Action: International Law and Nuclear Weapons in Greenock Sheriff Court*, 4 Edinburgh L. Rev. 74–86 (2000); Stephen C. Neff, *International Law and Nuclear Weapons in Scottish Courts*, 51 Int'l & Comp. L.Q. 171–76 (2002); *see also* Ronald King Murray, *Nuclear Weapons and the Law*, 15 Med. Conflict & Survival 126–37 (1999) (U.K.).

8. Robert Fox, *Trident: The Done Deal*, New Statesman, June 13, 2005; Patrick Wintour & Martin Kettle, *Britain Faces Long-term Nuclear Threat and Must Plan for It, Says Reid,* Guardian (U.K.), Sept. 13, 2005; Stephen Fidler, *Blair Opts for New Trident Fleet*, Financial Times, Dec. 4, 2006.

9. *Project ELF Closes*, Nuclear Resister, Oct. 15, 2004, at 1; John La Forge, Nukewatch Special Report: *Navy Calls It Quits, Announces Shutdown of Project ELF*, http://www.nukewatch.com/projectelf/navyquits.html; Nukewatch Pathfinder, Winter 2004–2005, http://www.nukewatch.com/pathfinder/#winter0405.

10. Kevin Murphy, *ELF Protestors Found Guilty but Get No Fines from Magistrate*, Daily Press (Ashland, Wis.), Nov. 9, 2004.

11. Natural Resources Defense Council, *U.S. Nuclear Forces, 2006*, Bulletin of Atomic Scientists, Jan./Feb. 2006, at 68, 70 (extended service life for Trident II ends in 2042).

12. In a nutshell, a launch-on-warning policy means that U.S. strategic nuclear-weapons systems would be launched in the event that American nuclear-weapons monitors, sensors, or computers indicated—whether mistakenly or not—that the United States was being subjected to a strategic nuclear-weapons attack before any such weapons had actually struck the United States itself.

13. That is, that Mr. Ostensen was mistaken to believe that ELF/Trident II was criminal under international law.

14. That is, that Mr. Ostensen was mistaken to believe that ELF/Trident II was not necessary for the "defense" of the United States.

15. Francis A. Boyle, *The Relevance of International Law to the "Paradox" of Nuclear Deterrence*, 80 Nw. U. L. Rev. 1407 (1986).

16. Francis A. Boyle, *Foundations of World Order* 77–80 (1999).

17. The Rome Statute establishing the International Criminal Court came into force on July 1, 2002.

18. Francis A. Boyle et al., *In re: More Than 50,000 Nuclear Weapons* (1991).

19. *United States v. Calley*, 48 C.M.R. 19, 22 C.M.A. 534 (1973).

Chapter Four

The Constitutionality of President George H. W. Bush's War against Iraq on Trial

UNITED STATES DISTRICT COURT
FOR THE DISTRICT OF COLUMBIA

Michael Ray Ange,	*Civ. Action No. 90-2792*
Plaintiff,	*(Judge Royce Lamberth)*
v.	*AFFIDAVIT OF*
George Bush, et al.,	*PROFESSOR FRANCIS A.*
Defendants.	*BOYLE*

I, FRANCIS A. BOYLE, depose and declare under penalty of perjury as follows:

I. INTRODUCTION

I am a Professor of International Law at the University of Illinois College of Law in Champaign, Illinois. . . .

This affidavit is submitted as an expert opinion regarding blockade as an act of war under U.S. Constitutional and legal standards as well as pursuant to International Law for purposes of the above captioned case involving the question of blockade and its use in the current Middle East crisis.

II. A BLOCKADE IS AN ACT OF WAR UNDER INTERNATIONAL AND DOMESTIC LAW

A "blockade" is a term used under international law to specifically refer to belligerent measures taken by a nation for the purposes of preventing the passage of vessels or aircraft to and from another country. Customary international law recognizes blockades as an act of war because of the belligerent use of force even against third party nations in enforcing the blockade. Blockades as acts of war have been recognized as such in the Declaration of Paris of 1856 and the Declaration of London of 1909 that delineate the international rules of warfare.

These Declarations were approved by the United States and as such are binding on the United States as part of general international law and customary international law.

As a matter of law in the United States, both the U.S. Supreme Court and former Presidents of the country have recognized blockades as acts of war that trigger the Constitutional requirement of Congressional authorization.

In *Bas v. Tingy*, 4 U.S. (4 Dall.) 37 (1800), the U.S. Supreme Court in addressing the Constitutionality of fighting an undeclared war clearly regarded the seizure of a French vessel as an act of hostility or reprisal requiring Congressional approval. Although the acts of warfare in *Bas* were considered part of an "imperfect" or undeclared war in general terms, the Court held that Congress pursuant to Constitutional war powers had authorized hostilities on the high seas under certain circumstances. The Supreme Court in *Bas* cited *Talbot v. Seaman*, 5 U.S. 331 (1 Cranch) 1801, for the proposition that specific legislative authorization was required in the seizure of a French vessel by an American vessel.

In the case of *Little v. Barreme*, 6 U.S. (2 Cranch) 170 (1804), the United States Supreme Court held that even an order from the President could not justify or excuse an act that violated the laws and customs of warfare. Chief Justice John Marshall wrote that a captain of a United States warship could be held personally liable in trespass for wrongfully seizing a neutral Danish ship, even though the seizure was carried out in accordance with the President's orders. During hostilities with France in the 1790s, Congress attempted to stop Americans from trading with France and authorized the seizure of American vessels bound for that country. On the basis of this Congressional authorization, the President ordered American captains to seize not just ships that were clearly American, but also ships that were effectively American even though covered by foreign papers, and to seize these vessels when they were bound from, as well as bound to, French ports. The genuinely Danish vessel that Captain Little seized on its way from France appeared suspicious, but the Court did not reach the issue of whether probable cause would have relieved the captain's liability. Even if the captain's suspicions had proved correct and the ship had been American, Congress did not authorize seizing any ships bound from France. The fact that the illegal seizure comported with the President's instructions did not help: "[T]he instructions cannot change the nature of the transaction, or legalize an act which, without those instructions, would have been a plain trespass," 6 U.S. (2 Cranch) at 179. The Court did not even discuss whether Captain Little knew that the order exceeded the Congressional authorization or whether Little should have known. The Court's position seems consistent with a typical trespass case, where defendants are liable even when they have a reasonable, good faith (but mistaken) belief in authority to enter on the plaintiff's land.

The clearest enunciation by the U.S. Supreme Court on the matter of blockades as an act of war requiring Congressional authorization came in *The Prize Cases*, 67 U.S. (2 Black) 635 (1862). This case involved President Lincoln's order of a blockade of coastal states that had joined the Confederacy at the outset of the

Civil War. The Court in *The Prize Cases* explicitly set forth that a blockade is an act of war and is legal only if properly authorized under the Constitution.

> The power of declaring war is the highest sovereign power, and is limited to the representative of the full sovereignty of the nation. It is limited in the United States to its Congress exclusively; and the authority of the President to be the Commander-In-Chief, &c., to take care that the law be faithfully executed, is to be taken in connection with the exclusive power given to Congress to declare war, and does not enable the President to declare war or to introduce, without Act of Congress, War or any of its legal disabilities or liabilities, on any citizen of the United States. (*The Prize Cases*, 67 U.S. at 475)

Successive government officials and U.S. Presidents have similarly recognized blockades as acts of war under United States Law.

On May 22, 1948, Ambassador Austin, United States Representative to the United Nations, said in the Security Council:

> It is elementary that a proclamation of a blockade constitutes a claim of belligerent rights. The exercise of belligerent rights depends upon the existence of war, whether it be international war or civil war. The claim to exercise belligerent rights must rest upon a recognition of the belligerency of the opposing party. (Statement by Ambassador Warren R. Austin. May 22, 1948, XVIII Bulletin, Department of State. No. 465, May 30, 1948, pp. 695, 697. See also U.N. Security Council Off. Rec. 3d year, No. 72, 302d meeting, May 22, 1948, p. 43)

In a speech on November 29, 1954, Secretary of State Dulles stated:

> We have agreed, by the United Nations Charter, to try to settle international disputes by peaceful means in such a manner that international peace is not endangered. Therefore, our first duty is to exhaust peaceful means of sustaining our international rights and those of our citizens, rather than now resorting to war action such as a naval and air blockade of Red China. ("The Goal of Our Foreign Policy," Speech by Secretary of State Dulles, Nov. 29, 1954, XXXI Bulletin, Department of State No. 807, Dec. 13, 1954, p. 890. See also Secretary Dulles' Remarks at a News Conference, Dec. 1, 1954, ibid., p. 888)

On December 1, 1954, President Eisenhower commented during the course of a White House news conference:

> A blockade is an act in war intended to bring your adversary to your way of thinking or to his knees. In fact, in the rules of war that were studied in my former life, were clearly established the conditions that must prevail before you could legally proclaim a blockade. You couldn't, even if you were a belligerent, merely say, "We blockade Antarctica," or any other country. You had to make the blockade effective, and you were not justified in stopping anyone's ship unless you had the means present at the spot to make the blockade effective, indicating that the word "blockade" is, so far as I know, an act of war, a part of war. (Public Papers of the Presidents of

the United States: Dwight D. Eisenhower, 1954 [1960] 1073, 1076. See also XXXI
Bulletin Department of State, No. 807, Dec. 13, 1954, pp. 887, 889)

At a press conference on March 6, 1963, President Kennedy in response to a
request for comment regarding Cuba's reliance on Soviet oil, stated:

To deny the oil would require, of course, a blockade, and a blockade is an act of war
. . . you should not be under any impression that a blockade is not an act of war, because when a ship refuses to stop, and you then sink the ship, there is usually a military response by the country involved. (Public Papers of the Presidents of the
United States: John F. Kennedy, 1963 [1964] 236, 242)

At a hearing before the Senate Committee on Foreign Relations and the Senate Committee on Armed Services, September 17, 1962, Chairman Russell '
asked, "Is a military blockade still recognized as an act of war under international law?" Secretary of State Rusk replied:

I would say this about blockades; that war normally involves the application of a
blockade, so we can say that to start with.

Secondly, blockade is an act of force which, if not accepted by the other side,
would be interpreted and approached as an act of war.

All that a pacific blockade is is an announcement by the blockading party that
these steps you are taking are all that you have in mind. If the other side refuses to
accept that measure, it is an act of force which would be interpreted or could be interpreted as an act of war.

In the same Committee session, Chairman Russell said: "I thought it was very
clearly defined internationally where one country had the power to impose a
blockade, that they had the right to do it."
Secretary of State Rusk replied:

Senator, I think the situation would be quite different if, in fact, there was a state of
war between the two countries. I had supposed we were talking about a blockade
short of the existence of a state of war when I commented on it earlier. ("Situations
in Cuba," Hearing Before the Committee on Foreign Relations and the Committee
on Armed Services, United States Senate, 87th Cong., 2d sess., Sept. 17, 1962, pp.
35, 60–61)

These official statements by U.S. government officials in recent history re-
flect the long-standing position that under U.S. law, blockades are acts of war.
As interpreted by the U.S. Supreme Court such acts of war require Congressional approval under the Constitution.

In accordance with the universally accepted principle that blockades are acts
of war, Iraq has stated its position that the United States and its allies have "em-
barked on the implementation of an economic blockade by force of arms against
Iraq, including food and medicines, and this is an act of war under world norms
and international law." *New York Times*, Aug. 19, 1990 at 2 (late edition).

III. CONCLUSION

International law and U.S. Constitutional law dictate compliance with the universally recognized norm that blockades represent acts of war. Most specifically, case law and precedent in the United States demonstrate that blockades trigger requirements under the Constitution of Congressional statutory authorization for acts of war. Therefore, this is the standard by which the instant case before this Court must be measured.

Respectfully Submitted,
Francis A. Boyle
Professor of Law
Dated: November 28, 1990

On August 2, 1990, Iraq invaded Kuwait. At the time, Jeff Paterson was a corporal serving in the U.S. Marine Corps at Kaneohe Bay, Hawaii. The next day President George H. W. Bush imposed an economic embargo on Iraq and moved the U.S. aircraft carrier *Eisenhower* to the eastern Mediterranean Sea so that its attack planes would be able to hit Iraq. Five days after the Iraqi invasion, President Bush ordered U.S. armed forces to deploy to the Persian Gulf. And on August 10, President Bush unilaterally imposed a blockade against Iraq, including a ban on shipments of food.

Corporal Paterson joined the Marine Corps in 1986 at the age of eighteen. But over time he became troubled about a conflict between his developing moral beliefs and his activities as an active-duty member of the U.S. armed forces. This situation crystallized on August 11, 1990, when Corporal Paterson was informed that he might be deployed for military duties in the Persian Gulf. After consultations with counsel, members of his family, and some friends, Corporal Paterson filed an application to be discharged from the Marine Corps on grounds of conscientious objection, pursuant to Marine Corps Order 1306.16E. Despite popular misconceptions, members of the U.S. all-volunteer armed forces have the constitutional right to apply for a conscientious-objector discharge at any time: "To qualify for discharge from military service as a conscientious objector, an applicant must establish that (1) he or she is opposed to war in any form, *Gillette v. United States* (S.Ct. 1971); (2) his or her objection is grounded in deeply held moral, ethical, or religious beliefs, *Welsh v. United States* (S.Ct. 1970); and (3) his or her convictions are sincere, *Witmer v. United States* (S.Ct. 1955)."[1]

During the processing of an application for discharge as a conscientious objector, Marine Corps Order 1306.16E required that reasonable efforts be made to assign the applicant to duties that conflicted minimally with his or her beliefs. Nevertheless, on the morning of August 29, 1990, Corporal Paterson was ordered to prepare his gear and get ready to board an airplane that evening for deployment to Saudi Arabia. Corporal Paterson appeared for the deployment as ordered, but then nonviolently refused to board the airplane. He was arrested, and then incarcerated, though later set free pending a court-martial. Corporal Paterson thus bore the great distinction and honor to become the first military resister, indeed the very first civil resister, to President George H. W. Bush's unconstitutional and criminal war against Iraq.[2]

Corporal Paterson was later charged with (1) violation of the Uniform Code of Military Justice (UCMJ) article 86, alleging that he refused to appear at a personnel muster preliminary to deployment to the Persian Gulf; (2) violation of UCMJ article 87, alleging that Corporal Paterson "did . . . through design miss the movement by military aircraft" by which his unit was transported to the Persian Gulf; and (3) violation of UCMJ article 90, alleging that Corporal Paterson refused orders to "muster with all equipment" and to board a military aircraft as part of his deployment to the Persian Gulf.

The Center for Constitutional Rights (CCR) in New York City together with Eric A. Seitz of Honolulu, Hawaii, who was Corporal Paterson's civilian attorney of record, filed a motion to dismiss these three charges on November 1, 1990, on the grounds that the orders concerning deployment to the Persian Gulf that Corporal Paterson disobeyed were illegal and thus that he could not be prosecuted for refusing to obey them. A special hearing on this motion was held before a Marine Corps judge on November 19, 1990, at Kaneohe Bay Marine Corps base.

The proceedings started with Mr. Seitz arguing to the military judge that the government must prove beyond a reasonable doubt that the orders given to Corporal Paterson to ship out to the Persian Gulf were "lawful," as required by the ruling of the U.S. Supreme Court in *In re Winship*, 397 U.S. 358 (1970). After hearing the oral argument against this proposition by the Judge Advocate General (JAG) Corps lawyer, the military judge ruled in favor of Mr. Seitz's argument, concluding that the government bore the burden of proof and that the standard of proof was proof beyond a reasonable doubt. That is, the government had to prove beyond a reasonable doubt that the order given by President Bush to Corporal Paterson to ship out to the Persian Gulf was "lawful."

At that point I took the stand and for about three and one-half hours, testified on behalf of Corporal Paterson as an expert on whether President Bush's order to Corporal Paterson was "lawful." The direct examination of me was conducted by José Luis Morin, an attorney with the Center for Constitutional Rights (CCR). Working in conjunction with CCR, I also submitted an affidavit in the contemporaneous case of *Ange v. Bush*, 752 F. Supp. 509 (D.D.C. 1990), that raised similar constitutional war-powers issues and is reprinted at the beginning of this chapter. This *Ange* affidavit sets forth a succinct written constitutional-law analysis that I had previously just argued orally in the *Paterson* court-martial proceedings.

We won a great victory for peace, justice, international law, the U.S. Constitution, and civil resistance in the general court-martial of Corporal Paterson. On December 5, 1990, the Marine Corps commanding general at Kaneohe Bay granted Corporal Paterson an administrative separation from the Marine Corps with an "other than honorable discharge," including reduction in rank. In other words, Corporal Paterson was fired by the Marine Corps. Nevertheless, he walked out of the Marine Corps as a free man. Because of his conscience and principles, Jeff Paterson triumphed over both the Bush administration's and the Pentagon's heedless, senseless, and criminal rush to war against Iraq. His courageous and principled example inspired numerous other members of the U.S. armed forces to refuse to participate in this unconstitutional and criminal war.

For that reason, this case is of great historical significance. It stands as an important precedent to be used by all current members of the U.S. armed forces and their lawyers and their supporters who today refuse to participate, on grounds of conscience and principle, in the unconstitutional and criminal war being waged against Iraq by President George W. Bush as this book goes to press. The *Paterson* precedent also can be used by nonmilitary civil resisters against this war. Finally, the *Paterson* precedent applies directly to the second Bush administration's outstanding threats to attack Iran, Syria, and North Korea in gross violation of the war powers clause of the U.S. Constitution, Congress's 1973 War Powers Resolution, and the UN Charter, as well as the Nuremberg Charter, Judgment, and Principles.

Despite the best efforts by the American peace movement, on January 14, 1991, pursuant to the terms of the 1973 War Powers Resolution, Congress finally authorized President George H. W. Bush to use military force against Iraq to expel Iraq from Kuwait in accordance with UN Security Council Resolution 678 of November 29, 1990. On January 15, 1991, Congressman Henry B. González of Texas, former U.S. attorney general Ramsey Clark, and I launched a national campaign to impeach President Bush if he went to war against Iraq, initially for the purpose of deterring him from doing so.

Nevertheless the war started, and the very next day Congressman González appeared on the floor of the U.S. House of Representatives to introduce his impeachment resolution against President Bush.[3] It was my great honor and privilege to serve as counsel to Congressman González as he tenaciously investigated President Bush's actions and pursued impeachment. I wrote a bill of particulars against President Bush, which served as the basis for the articles of impeachment submitted by Congressman González. In response to

González's resolution, President Bush initiated a CIA investigation against this beloved congressman known affectionately to his friends as "Henry B."

I will not review here the complete contents or the constitutional bases for the impeachment resolution against President Bush. But in a nutshell, there were five articles of impeachment in Congressman González's resolution, the gist of which were as follows:

Article I, that President Bush violated the equal protection clause of the U.S. Constitution by forcing poor white, black, and Mexican-American soldiers "to fight a war for oil to preserve the lifestyles of the wealthy";

Article II, that President Bush bribed, threatened, and intimidated others, including the members of the UN Security Council, to support belligerent acts against Iraq;

Article III, that President Bush prepared, planned, and conspired to engage in a massive war against Iraq employing methods of mass destruction that would result in the killing of tens of thousands of civilians, many of whom would be children;

Article IV, that President Bush committed the United States to acts of war without proper congressional consent and contrary to the UN Charter and international law; and

Article V, that President Bush planned, prepared, and conspired to commit crimes against the peace by leading the United States into aggressive war against Iraq in violation of article 2(4) of the UN Charter, the Nuremberg Charter, other international instruments and treaties, and the Constitution of the United States.

Of course, Congressman González proved prophetic in his prognostication of the subsequent course of President Bush's war against Iraq and genocidal slaughter of the Iraqi people. Yet even more prophetically, Congressman González's five articles of impeachment against President George H. W. Bush apply equally to President George W. Bush and his criminal war of aggression against Iraq launched in March 2003.[4] Sometimes history repeats itself—most sadly and tragically for all concerned. As George Santayana perspicaciously stated: "Those who cannot remember the past are condemned to repeat it."[5]

On Tuesday, March 11, 2003, Congressman John Conyers Jr. of Michigan, the ranking member of the House Judiciary Committee (which has jurisdiction over bills of impeachment), convened an emergency meeting of forty to fifty of his top advisors, most of whom were lawyers. The purpose of the meeting was to discuss and debate immediately submitting impeachment resolutions against President George W. Bush, Vice President Dick Cheney, then–secretary of defense Donald Rumsfeld, and then–attorney general John

Ashcroft, to head off the impending war. Congressman Conyers invited former U.S. attorney general Ramsey Clark and me to come to the meeting to argue the case for impeachment.

This impeachment debate lasted two hours. It was led by Congressman Conyers, who quite correctly did not tip his hand one way or the other on the merits of impeachment. He simply moderated the debate between Clark and me on the one side, favoring immediately filing bills of impeachment to prevent the threatened war, and almost everyone else there who was against impeachment for partisan political reasons. Obviously no point would be served here by attempting to digest a two-hour-long vigorous debate among a group of well-trained lawyers on such a controversial matter at this critical moment in American history. But at the time, I was struck by the fact that this momentous debate was conducted in a private office right down the street from the White House on the very eve of war.

Suffice it to say that most of the "experts" there opposed impeachment not on the basis of not wanting to enforce the U.S. Constitution and the rule of law, whether international or domestic, but on the partisan political grounds that it might hurt the Democratic Party's effort to get their presidential candidate elected in the 2004 campaign. As a political independent, I did not argue that point. Rather, I argued the merits of impeaching Bush, Cheney, Rumsfeld, and Ashcroft under the U.S. Constitution, U.S. federal laws, and U.S. treaties and other international agreements to which the United States is a party.

Congressman Conyers allowed me to make the closing argument in the debate. The concluding point I chose to make was historical: "The Athenians lost their democracy. The Romans lost their republic. And if we Americans do not act now we could lose our republic! The United States of America is not immune to the laws of history!" After two hours of most vigorous debate among those in attendance, the meeting adjourned with revised draft bills of impeachment sitting on the table.[6]

Certainly, if the U.S. House of Representatives can impeach President Clinton for oral sex and lying about oral sex, then a fortiori the House can, should, and must impeach President Bush for commencing this war, lying about this war, and threatening more wars. All that is needed is for one member of the House of Representatives with courage, integrity, principles, and a safe seat to file these revised draft bills of impeachment against President Bush, Vice President Cheney, and Attorney General Alberto Gonzales, who bears personal criminal responsibility for orchestrating the Bush administration's systematic torture campaign.[7] Failing this, the alternative is likely to be their further expansion of an American empire abroad, continued construction of a U.S. police state at home, and recurrent wars of aggression to sustain them both.

The longer we delay this necessary and principled impeachment process against President Bush and his neoconservative apparatchiks, the greater will be the disaster for all the peoples of the world and even here in the United States. Witness the racist and class-based criminal mistreatment inflicted by the Bush administration on the victims of Hurricane Katrina.[8] President Bush, Vice President Cheney, and Secretary of Homeland Security Michael Chertoff must all be impeached for denying equal protection of the laws, in violation of the Fifth and Fourteenth Amendments to the U.S. Constitution, to the Katrina victims because they were African Americans and because they were poor. Their criminal negligence and its resulting mass homicides constitute "other high Crimes and Misdemeanors" within the meaning of Article II, Section 4 of the U.S. Constitution: "The President, Vice President and all civil Officers of the United States, shall be removed from Office on Impeachment for, and Conviction of, Treason, Bribery, or other high Crimes and Misdemeanors."

There is one recent precedent for introducing an article of impeachment against an incumbent American president for such equal protection violations amounting to massive discrimination on the grounds of race and class that cost the lives of numerous American citizens—article I of the 1991 González impeachment resolution against President George H. W. Bush:

> In the conduct of the office of President of the United States, George Herbert Walker Bush, in violation of his constitutional oath faithfully to execute the office of President of the United States and, to the best of his ability, preserve, protect, and defend the Constitution of the United States, and in violation of his constitutional duty to take care that the laws be faithfully executed, has violated the equal protection clause of the Constitution. U.S. soldiers in the Middle East are overwhelmingly poor white, black, and Mexican-American, and their military service is based on the coercion of a system that has denied viable economic opportunities to these classes of citizens. Under the Constitution, all classes of citizens are guaranteed equal protection, and calling on the poor and minorities to fight a war for oil to preserve the lifestyles of the wealthy is a denial of the rights of these soldiers. In all of this George Herbert Walker Bush has acted in a manner contrary to his trust as President and subversive of constitutional government, to the great prejudice of the cause of law and justice and to the manifest injury of the people of the United States.
>
> Wherefore George Herbert Walker Bush, by such conduct, warrants impeachment and trial, and removal from office.

As Congressman González so eloquently and presciently stated when he introduced his impeachment resolution against President Bush on the floor of the U.S. House of Representatives on January 16, 1991:

My resolution has five articles of impeachment. First, the President has violated the equal protection clause of the Constitution. Our soldiers in the Middle East are overwhelmingly poor white, black, and Mexican-American or Hispanic-American. They may be volunteers technically, but their voluntarism is based on the coercion of a system that has denied viable opportunities to these classes of our citizens. Under the Constitution, all classes of citizens are guaranteed equal protection, and calling on the poor and the minorities to fight a war for oil to pre-serve the lifestyles of the wealthy is a denial of the rights of these soldiers.

Let me add that since 1981 we have suffered the Reagan-Bush and now the Bush war against the poor,[9] and to add insult to injury, we now are asking the poor to fight while here, as a result of this fight, even the meager programs that the Congress had seen fit to preserve as a national policy will suffer be-cause the money for those programs will be diverted to the cause of this un-necessary war.[10]

Of course the same constitutional arguments apply today to justify the im-peachment of President George W. Bush for his unconstitutional and criminal war against Iraq to steal oil, a war that is being coercively waged by poor whites, blacks, and Latinos in the U.S. armed forces for the purpose of sup-porting the extravagant lifestyles of the racist power elite who effectively govern America and criminally abandoned the black and poor Katrina victims to their cruel and grisly fate. We must impeach them all immediately for the good of the people of the United States as well as the people of the world.

On the evening of January 10, 2007, in a nationally televised address to the American people from the White House, President George W. Bush an-nounced that he was implementing a "surge," sending an additional 21,500 U.S. troops into Iraq. Both President Bush and Vice President Cheney also made it perfectly clear that they would initiate this "surge" against the mani-fest will of the American people expressed in the elections of November 2006 and without obtaining authorization from Congress. Both President Bush and Vice President Cheney invoked the president's alleged powers as com-mander in chief of the U.S. armed forces under Article II, Section 2, Clause 1 of the U.S. Constitution as authority for their unilaterally determined "surge." But that provision was included in the Constitution for the express purpose of guaranteeing the supremacy of civilian control over the U.S. mil-itary establishment.[11] Article I, Section 8, Clause 11 makes it clear that only both houses of Congress acting together have the power "[t]o declare War, grant Letters of Marque and Reprisal, and make rules concerning Captures on Land and Water." This is popularly known as the war powers clause of the U.S. Constitution.

Pursuant to its constitutional power under this war powers clause, and act-ing to prevent another Vietnam War, Congress enacted the 1973 War Powers

Resolution over President Richard Nixon's veto, which means that the resolution was adopted by at least a two-thirds majority in both the House and the Senate.[12] My testimony set forth below in the *Paterson* court-martial proceedings provides extensive commentary about the origin, purpose, meaning, and application of the War Powers Resolution. In the case of the troop "surge" announced in January 2007, the War Powers Resolution explicitly required that President Bush obtain additional authorization from Congress before proceeding, which he failed to do, unilaterally sending additional troops to Iraq without specific congressional authorization. Section 4(a)(3) makes it quite clear that the requirements of the War Powers Resolution are triggered "[i]n the absence of a declaration of war [which we do not have for Iraq], in any case in which United States Armed Forces are introduced . . . (3) in numbers which substantially enlarge United States Armed Forces equipped for combat already located in a foreign nation." The Bush administration simply ignored section 4(a)(3) of the War Powers Resolution.

At the time, we had about 132,000 troops in Iraq. Sending in an additional 21,500 troops would "substantially enlarge" those armed forces. Therefore, the Bush administration required further authorization from Congress for this euphemistic "surge," which was really a substantial escalation. The Bush-Cheney refusal to obtain additional authorization from Congress for this substantial enlargement of U.S. armed forces in Iraq constitutes an impeachable offense as a violation of both the war powers clause of Article II, Section 4 of the U.S. Constitution and the War Powers Resolution.

The same constitutional arguments apply to the Bush administration's proposed substantial enlargement of U.S. armed forces in Afghanistan by one combat brigade of about 3,500 U.S. troops in addition to the 21,000 U.S. soldiers already there.[13] Of course, President Bush requires authorizations both from the U.S. Congress under the War Powers Resolution and from the UN Security Council before he can attack Iran, which he is currently threatening and preparing to do. If President Bush and Vice President Cheney are not stopped immediately by means of impeachment, they could readily set off World War III in the volatile Persian Gulf, Middle East, and Central Asia, where two-thirds of the world's hydrocarbon resources are up for grabs among the United States, Russia, China, and India. *The Guns of August*, indeed.

What follows is the transcript of the testimony I gave under oath and subject to cross-examination by JAG lawyers and the military judge during the *Paterson* court-martial proceedings. The transcript excerpts have been corrected and edited for style, length, and typographical errors, but should provide a good account of what actually happened in the Marine Corps courtroom when we put President George H. W. Bush's war against Iraq on trial as an unconstitutional violation of the war powers clause of the U.S. Constitution and an illegal violation of Congress's War Powers Resolution of 1973.

COURT MARTIAL PROCEEDINGS OF LANCE CORPORAL JEFFREY PATERSON, HEARING ON NOVEMBER 19, 1990, UNITED STATES MARINE CORPS, KANEOHE BAY, HAWAII

MR. MORIN: Professor Boyle, are you familiar with the issues that are being raised in this case, the papers that are concerned with this motion, and the case of Corporal Paterson?

A: Yes, I've read all the pleadings in this case and have reviewed them all and have also personally met with Corporal Paterson to speak with him about it, too.

Q: The motion in this case and the pleadings have a rather extensive discussion on the issue of blockade. Can you describe for the court what you think is a blockade?

A: Well, a blockade technically is an act of war. And that is made very clear in international law and also in United States constitutional law; for example, *The Prize Cases* decided by the Supreme Court. When a government proclaims a blockade as President Bush did in the Persian Gulf—a blockade of Kuwait and Iraq in August—this is indeed an act of war.

Q: In the beginning the president called it a boycott, any difference?

A: Well, Your Honor, what has happened is this—there has been a historical evolution since back in the nineteenth century when some European countries tried to blockade Venezuela. They called it a pacific blockade to avoid the implication of its being an act of war. They did not want to call it a blockade so they called it a pacific blockade. At that time the United States government officially took the position that there is no such thing as a pacific blockade. A blockade is a blockade—it's an act of war.

. . .

A: That's right. And the U.S. government at that time officially took the position that there is no such thing as a pacific blockade. A blockade is an act of war that triggers the laws of war, the laws of neutrality. And indeed I was interviewed as an expert on this subject by the *Washington Post*—I think Mr. Morin has a reference to that interview on the subject of the blockade being an act of war.[14] Now, what has happened is this was always the position of the United States government up through and including the Eisenhower administration. And indeed there is a statement that I think Mr. Morin would have available to the effect that President Eisenhower stated that a blockade is an act of war—there is no other way around it. Starting with the Cuban Missile Crisis, there was an attempt to apply euphemisms . . . in an effort to deflate the pressures and tensions surrounding the crisis. The Kennedy administration decided not to call the blockade of Cuba a blockade, even though everyone recognized full well it was a blockade and an act of war. To avoid or try to avoid the various implications behind that, they called it a quarantine. But I think it is the general consensus of all international-law professors that whether you agreed with it or you didn't, it clearly was a blockade. Eventually, with respect to the Persian Gulf, although President Bush did start out calling it a boycott and at one point I think it was called an interdiction, they finally did openly and publicly admit this was a blockade. So to make a long story short, as far as law professors are concerned, you can call it what you want to avoid the implications, but a blockade is an act of war and that's how the Supreme Court defined it in *The Prize Cases*. And once a blockade is proclaimed, it then triggers the laws of neutrality and the laws of war, the Geneva Conventions. For example, one of the points I pointed out in the *Washington Post* interview was that of course this has to be a blockade that triggers the laws of war because if any of our servicemen are captured by Iraq or Kuwait, we would certainly insist that they be treated in accordance with the Geneva Conventions. And so you know you have to recognize the legal consequences of what you are doing simply for the safety of your own people.

. . .

Q: Professor Boyle, you mentioned the boycott and the situation in the Persian Gulf at this point. Can you describe to the Court when this was instituted and how.

A: Well, as you know, President Bush unilaterally, on his own authority, as he said, as commander in chief of the armed forces, decided to deploy U.S. military forces to Saudi Arabia. At the time, his presidential spokesperson, Marlin Fitzwater, stated that as far as the president was concerned, he had the authority to do this under his powers as commander in chief of the armed forces and that the War Powers Resolution was unconstitutional, so in theory he just wasn't going to pay any attention to it. Shortly after U.S. forces arrived—I believe it was around August 10, you can correct me on the date, but I believe on August 10—President Bush unilaterally proclaimed a naval blockade of Iraq and Kuwait. He did this without any approval by Congress and he also did this without any approval by the United Nations Security Council. So the president unilaterally undertook an act of war as we law professors and the Supreme Court and everyone else looks at acts of war without authorization by anyone to do this. In response, the Iraqi government stated that they considered this blockade of Iraq and Kuwait to be an act of war. And technically they were within their rights under the laws of war and international law to treat the blockade as an act of war. Iraq also stated that as far as they were concerned, henceforth they were in a state of "holy war" with the United States. Now I'm not exactly sure what that meant. It did seem to me that that statement was ambiguous. It did not seem to me that that necessarily meant that they considered themselves to be in a state of war with the United States. There is a distinction between acts of war and a formal state of war. But clearly we committed an act of war and Iraq treated it as an act of war, and then two days later, in an effort to enforce this blockade, U.S. naval forces did fire upon Iraqi tankers. So there was shooting. These were armed hostilities within the meaning of—

MAJ. QUIGLEY: I want to object here at some of the conclusory language of the witness regarding whether or not there is a state of war or whether or not the blockade is an act of war or whether or not these are hostilities. These are basically issues for the court to decide.

MR. MORIN: Your Honor, if I may please present some critical issues in this case. There are standards of law and the fact that Professor Boyle is corroborating here that is essential to an understanding of this situation given that the situation in the Middle East is of such a complex nature, and given that there are so many elements to this situation including blockades, including hostile acts, all of which are important to this case and—

THE COURT: Your objection is overruled. I can use whatever help I can get with this.

MR. MORIN: Professor Boyle, in your expert opinion, what kind of authorization is required under the Constitution?

A: Well of course we must always start—if we're talking about the president engaging in an act of war, which in my opinion he has by proclaiming this blockade, and I also note in this *Washington Post* article Professor Thomas Mallison of George Washington Law School also agrees with me separately and independently. We were independently interviewed as experts on this area and we both agreed that this blockade was an act of war that triggered the laws of war and the Geneva Conventions. The question is, what is his authority under either the United States Constitution or international law to engage in acts of warfare? The Constitution made this quite clear. It set up a tripartite system of power. The model that they wanted to avoid was that of George III as described in the Declaration of Independence. They did not want a president who would be a monarch waging foreign wars without approval by Parliament and taxing the people to pay for these wars and oftentimes without their representation. No taxation without representation. So to deal with this situation, they divided the powers—the power to declare war or to go to war, make war; the power to wage war once the formalities had been made to go to war; and then the power of the purse, that is, to pay for the war. . . . It was the George III model that they were trying to avoid. So then the question was with respect to popular participation, which house of Congress. There was a proposal that the Senate and the president could do it together. That was defeated. And ultimately the decision was made that because of the awesome consequences of our society going to war, the only authorities that should have the right to declare war or make a war would be both houses of Congress. The president would have nothing at all to do with it. And so both houses of Congress would have to declare war together. And then once that war was declared by Congress, it would be up to the president to conduct a formally legally constitutionally proclaimed war as commander in chief. So at that point the commander-in-chief clause would kick in. And indeed the model they feared there—that they wanted to deal with there—was George Washington having to deal with the Continental Congress. George Washington did not want to have to conduct the Revolutionary War and constantly report back to the Continental Congress on how to do it. So what they wanted was, Congress would declare the war and then the president would conduct the war, subject of course always to the power of Congress to pay for that war. And even if the president is conducting a validly proclaimed war, nevertheless if Congress decides to cut off the funding for that war, that decision is definitive. The president would have no authority to continue waging a war once Congress has cut off the funding. And indeed that is precisely how the Vietnam War ended. Congress simply cut off the funding. And President Nixon, despite his opposition to this decision, took no effort whatsoever to contest that Congress had the ultimate authority with respect to powers of the purse.

Q: Professor Boyle, are there any differences in types of war, and if so which require authorization?

A: Yes. As I said before, under the Constitution and U.S. Supreme Court decisions, it has been recognized that there are what the Supreme Court has called perfect and imperfect wars. A perfect war is when Congress has gone out and formally adopted a declaration of war—for example, in the Spanish-American War, the First World War, and the Second World War, where you had joint resolutions of Congress that were then signed into law by the president. And this is what the Supreme Court has called a perfect war. However, the Supreme Court also recognizes such things known as imperfect wars— that is, the ability of the United States government to engage in acts of war short of formally proclaiming an all-out war or the existence of a formal state of war. As I said before, there is a well-recognized distinction between acts of war and a state of war. It is possible to engage in acts of war without necessarily being in a state of war. It is also possible to have a formally existing state of war without there being acts of war. For example, after Hitler invaded Poland, war was proclaimed by the various European states, but there were no hostilities for nine months. This was called the so-called Phony War, but under international law, a state of war did exist. Now, with respect to imperfect wars, that is, acts of war short of a formally proclaimed state of war, Congress reserved that power too. That power was reserved to Congress in the Constitution in what is called the marque-and-reprisal clause. It says quite clearly that only Congress has the power to issue letters of marque and reprisal. And what that meant was that it would be possible for Congress to authorize . . . hostilities short of warfare. But of course the power pursuant to the war powers clause would always lodge in Congress, not in the president.

Q: Given that constitutional framework, how would you describe the situation in early August?

. . .

A: With respect to the deployment to the Persian Gulf, as I stated, President Bush through his spokesperson Marlin Fitzwater stated that as far as he was concerned, the War Powers Resolution was unconstitutional and he was simply going to deploy these forces to the Persian Gulf under his powers as commander in chief of the armed forces. And then the next step of course was to proclaim a blockade. The problem is, Congress had never authorized this at all. It did not authorize the deployment, it had not authorized the blockade.

Indeed, in those cases where we do have troops deployed abroad, in situations where hostilities are either indicated or clearly indicated by the circumstances taking place, we have had treaties of alliance with other states that have authorized the deployment of troops abroad—for example, NATO. The NATO Alliance is a treaty that received the advice and consent of two-thirds of the Senate, and it has also been executed by the United States Congress voting to implement the terms of the NATO Pact. Pursuant to that treaty, we have had troops deployed abroad in Europe for quite some time. The same applies to Japan. We have a treaty of defense with Japan. We had no treaty whatsoever with respect to either Saudi Arabia or Kuwait. And as a matter of fact, that was admitted by Assistant Secretary of State John Kelly in his open congressional hearings. We had no treaty, no treaty obligation, no treaty commitment, that had been approved by the Senate and Congress to deploy troops to Saudi Arabia or to institute the blockade, this act of war in the Persian Gulf.

MR. MORIN: Your Honor, at this point I'd like to mark this document for evidence. . . . Professor Boyle, you have before you exhibit 11. Can you please identify what that document is?

A: This is a letter sent by President Bush to the Speaker of the House dated August 9, dealing with his rationale for deploying U.S. military forces to the Persian Gulf region.

Q: Unlike those discussions regarding the Constitution and the war powers clause of the Constitution, there is a specific requirement under the War Powers Resolution. Is that correct?

A: Yes there is.

Q: And perhaps you can describe what those requirements are and whether this letter falls in line with those requirements.

A: Sure. Well, the important point about this letter, of course, is that the president states that "I have taken these actions pursuant to my constitutional authority to conduct our foreign relations and as Commander in Chief." As I tried to point out, the commander-in-chief clause does not justify the deployment of U.S. military forces to the Persian Gulf or proclaiming the blockade or an act of war concerning Iraq and Kuwait. So clearly, what we are seeing here is the president saying that he alone has the authority to do this when the Constitution clearly allocates both types of decisions to Congress and not to the president. With respect to the War Powers Resolution, the War Powers

Resolution required the president as a matter of law to submit a report to Congress in the event that he introduced U.S. military forces into a situation of hostilities or into a situation where hostilities are clearly indicated by the circumstances. I believe the report has to be submitted within forty-eight hours. This one was not. Ah, the —

MAJ. QUIGLEY: Objection, Sir — conclusion. . . . Your Honor, we will be willing to proceed, but I don't recall anywhere where one could say it was submitted or not submitted. My recollection of the facts is very different from the professor's as to the type of —

A: Well I have stated my opinion, Your Honor, on the basis of the letter itself. Now maybe the Xerox is no good here, but it said U.S. forces began arriving on August 6, 1990, and this letter is dated August 9, so perhaps I am incorrect, but I was trying to operate in accordance with the letter.

. . .

A: In any event, the War Powers Resolution requires a formal report. The president makes it clear that this is not a report under the War Powers Resolution. And indeed his spokesperson made that fully clear. He was not reporting under the War Powers Resolution. He put the language in here saying that he was only informing Congress, that Congress be fully informed consistent with the War Powers Resolution. But he made it very clear this was not a report under section (4)(a)(1) of the War Powers Resolution.

THE COURT: I apologize, but I'm going to ask a question. Ah, I've read the War Powers Resolution. It states a report is required, but I didn't notice anything that stated format and what the report must be. Is there something from which you're deriving an opinion that this does not comport with the formal report required under the War Powers Resolution?

A: Well, Your Honor, as I said . . . the president stated that as far as he was concerned, the whole War Powers Resolution was unconstitutional. And so this language "consistent with" as a matter of public record was also drafted so that he could continue to assert that the War Powers Resolution was unconstitutional. I think it's an important issue here and that if the president deployed all these forces to the Persian Gulf on the assumption that the War Powers Resolution was unconstitutional, I would submit that he did not have the authority to do that under the Constitution. If you are the president, first, you have taken an oath to uphold the Constitution and laws of the United

States. Second, you also have a separate constitutional obligation to take care that the laws be faithfully executed. Now if the president did not believe the War Powers Resolution was constitutional, it was up to him to go to court and get a ruling from the Supreme Court that indeed the War Powers Resolution was unconstitutional and he was free to ignore it. And in this regard I'll point out that in the Senate Foreign Relations hearings on this matter, Senator Kassebaum from Kansas, a Republican, made the exact same point with Secretary of State Baker, saying, well I don't really support the War Powers Resolution either, but it is the law of the land and the president has to take care that the laws be faithfully executed and if he didn't like it that's too bad, he has no separate constitutional authority to ignore the supreme law of the land which is the War Powers Resolution.

THE COURT: Well maybe I wasn't clear with my question. The War Powers Resolution required a report, right?

A: Yes sir.

THE COURT: Is there anything that says what format or form that report must take?

A: The War Powers Resolution does—I believe Mr. Morin hopefully will have a copy of it there—it does state what the elements of the report must contain. It did not specifically say, here is a form that you have to use.

THE COURT: All right, thank you.

MR. MORIN: Professor Boyle, isn't it correct that the War Powers Resolution speaks about the necessity in terms of format of this report by being the scope and duration of the deployment of troops?

A: Yes. And here the president specifically stated that he really had no idea what the scope or duration is and that, as he said, although it is not possible to predict the precise scope and duration of this deployment, our armed forces will remain so long as their presence is required. Again, that does not fulfill the reporting requirements of the War Powers Resolution.

Q: I'd like to draw your attention as well to the fourth paragraph on the first page, the first sentence where the letter reads: "I do not believe involvement in hostilities is imminent."

A: Yes.

Q: Professor Boyle, does this in any way contravene the War Powers Resolution?

A: Well, I think the facts are that the very next day the president proclaimed the blockade on August 10. Now this letter is dated August 9. On August 10 he proclaimed the blockade, which clearly [represents] hostilities. A blockade, as I've said before, is an act of war. And in the legislative history of the War Powers Resolution, they originally were going to have the language that would trigger the War Powers Resolution as armed conflict. Now to a law professor, armed conflict has a definite threshold test. What is an armed conflict, when the Geneva Conventions and the laws of war and things of that nature kick in? Hostilities obviously could be something less than an armed conflict and they changed the language precisely for the purpose of setting the threshold for reporting lower than simply an armed conflict. And as I said here, the War Powers Resolution requires the report not only if troops are introduced into combat but also where hostilities are indicated by the circumstances. And as I said, on the ninth the president sent this letter over. On the tenth he proclaimed the blockade, which clearly was an act of war.

Q: Is it correct, then, to say that at the beginning of the blockade on the tenth, under the War Powers Resolution, the president should have reported that to Congress?

A: Clearly he should have, yes. However you want to look at the letter of August 9, and in any event, as of the tenth with the proclamation of the blockade, this was an act of war, and it definitely should have triggered a formal report under [section] 4(a)(1), however you want to characterize this August 9 letter. And as I said, two days later, then, we actually began firing on Iraqi tankers. So between the ninth, the tenth, the twelfth, there should have been a letter reporting that formally under the terms of the War Powers Resolution. And this is the only letter that the president has sent, to the best of my knowledge. The formal, open, official letter stating what he's doing in the Persian Gulf.

. . .

Q: Professor Boyle, in response to this letter and the president's actions, what has Congress done?

A: So far? Congress has not authorized in any way, shape, or form anything President Bush has done in the Persian Gulf. The War Powers Resolution specifically requires authorization by Congress in the event that the president decides to keep U.S. military forces in this type of situation after sixty days. The president can request a thirty-day waiver. If he desires he has to formally request it and explain why he needs it. President Bush has not done that. So the withdrawal requirement of the War Powers Resolution started sixty days after the resolution kicked in. And as I said, depending on how you want to count it, whether it was the ninth with this letter, which I believe was constitutionally deficient, but if you don't want to accept that, clearly the tenth with the imposition of the blockade, which was an act of war, and certainly no later than the twelfth, when we actually began firing on Iraqi tankers. These were armed conflicts, hostilities, acts of war, clearly a report should have been sent in by the president within forty-eight hours, it was not, but the clock started ticking — the sixty-day clock — certainly no later than August 12. When October 12 rolled around, there was no request by the president for further authorization from Congress to continue to deploy U.S. military forces in the Persian Gulf. And here I think it is very instructive to look at the Lebanon intervention by the Reagan administration, and here I have personal experience with that because I served as an adviser to Senator Moynihan's office on the drafting of the Lebanon War Powers Resolution. Shortly after the marines were introduced into Lebanon in the summer of 1982, Senator Moynihan was very concerned that those marines would get killed if they were not pulled out very quickly. And I shared the same concerns myself. And I dealt with his office, they called me and asked, what can you recommend we do here? And I said, well, the president is going to have to ask for permission under the War Powers Resolution to keep the marines there after sixty days. Right now, you have a United Nations peacekeeping force down on the border with Lebanon. There are 5,000 men sitting around with nothing to do. It seems to me what you need to do is to bring some of those UN peacekeeping forces up from the border of Lebanon and bring them up to Beirut and then pull those marines out. And what you have to do then is demand in the Lebanon war powers authorization that the president remove the marines and put UN peacekeeping forces in there. What happened was that the Congress did adopt a War Powers Resolution authorization for the continued deployment of marines in Lebanon. However, Congress only requested, they did not demand, that the president replace the marines with United Nations forces, and the president paid no attention to the request by Congress. Now as a matter of law, he was not obliged to pay any attention to a request by Congress even though, in my opinion, it was a wise request. Unfortunately, then, as both Senator Moynihan and I feared and others who worked on that, those marines were killed by the suicide bombing at the barracks, and I believe 260 men lost their lives. And then eventually President Reagan withdrew the marines from Lebanon. But the significant point here was that in a situation where far fewer marines were deployed to Lebanon than troops we have seen deployed to the Persian Gulf, the Reagan administration did request and receive formal authorization from Congress for their continued deployment, and Congress did give them that. In this case, the Bush administration has not requested and it has not received formal authorization from Congress for anything—the stationing of troops, the blockade, firing shots across the bow, these military maneuvers that are going on right now in Saudi Arabia of Operation Imminent Thunder, things of that nature. The president has no authority, no authorization from Congress to do any of this.

Q: Professor Boyle, I'm not sure if I misheard you or misunderstood concerning the deployment after the forty-eight-hour mark. Let's assume that that is not done in the time we have. Let's assume it is not done at all. The president still has a sixty-day period to get his authorization from Congress, right?

A: Well, assuming that the troops were lawfully sent there in the first place, which we've already dealt with in the first portion of my testimony—that is, the War Powers Resolution made it very clear that the passage of the resolution itself did not get into the question of whether or not the president had lawful authority to send troops in the first place. And they made it very clear that nothing could be inferred from the compliance with the resolution that somehow the president was given a blank check just to introduce U.S. forces whenever he wanted to so long as he got authorization sixty days later.

. . .

Q: Does the fact that there wasn't a report within the forty-eight hours or even at all affect the legality of the troops being there?

A: The War Powers Resolution made it quite clear that the sixty days gets triggered the moment the president either submits the report or should have submitted the report, so that it is not subject to the will of the president here. If the president fails or refuses to file a report, the statute makes it quite clear that the sixty-day clock starts running immediately on the factual basis, that is, at the deployment of the troops.

THE COURT: What were the consequences though? . . . There doesn't seem to be any difference. The president ignored the report; same thing happened if he filed the report?

A: That's exactly correct. The reason why Congress wanted the report was they were demanding an explanation from the president why he did this. Congress felt that under the war powers clause, if troops are used, there had better be a good accounting for them. So they are separate and independent requirements in the resolution. That's correct. There had been, Your Honor, instances in the nineteenth and early twentieth centuries where United States presidents had deployed U.S. military forces for the protection of U.S. lives or property abroad. And Congress wanted to make sure that if something of that nature was asserted by the president as the basis for what he was doing, that he had better explain it to them, that he better tell them precisely what he was doing and why he was doing it and what if any authority he had to do it.

THE COURT: Thank you.

MR. MORIN: Your Honor, I have another document I'd like to submit into evidence. . . . Is that your order attached to the reply brief that is exhibit B where it's going into Congressional Record October 5, 1990? . . . Professor Boyle, can you identify the document that you have before you?

. . .

A: Yes, this is Senate Resolution 376. It was drafted as a joint resolution. It would have [satisfied] or it did attempt to satisfy the requirements of the War Powers Resolution, and you note also Senator Moynihan was involved in this one just as he was involved in the one on Lebanon.

Q: Are you saying that exhibit 10 authorized—

A: It attempted to but it never succeeded. The resolution was introduced, but it only passed as a concurrent resolution without any binding legal significance at all.

Q: Weren't these required under the War Powers Resolution?

A: You need, well of course here the distinction [is] between concurrent resolutions which are purely hortatory and nonbinding on the president, and resolutions that are binding.

Q: I want to be sure—hortatory—I'm not sure I understand. Can you give me a simpler word or a translation?

A: Sure, well, it was like the request to the president in the Lebanon resolution—it's a request. It is asking the president to do something. It is not ordering that he do it. It is not specifically ordering him to do anything.

Q: Well, are you saying that the concurrent resolution was this request you were talking about?

A: Yes. It was passed by the Senate. The House adopted a completely different version. The two were never reconciled, and they were never signed into law by the president. The War Powers Resolution requires that for there to be authorization for the continued deployment of U.S. military forces beyond the sixty- or ninety-day period, there must be a statute that is enacted into law by the president that specifically refers to the War Powers Resolution by name. And this did happen with respect to Lebanon, and the sending of U.S. Marines to Lebanon. It has never happened yet with respect to the U.S. expedition in the Persian Gulf.

THE COURT: Excuse me, Professor—then what is required then, in other words, is a joint resolution?

A: Yes, well, a joint resolution or you could have—it must be passed by both houses formally, and then signed into law by the president. You simply cannot have concurrent resolutions where the House passes one thing and the Senate passes another and that's it. It was originally labeled a joint resolution, as Senate Joint Resolution 376, but there was no equivalent in the House and the versions that were passed in the House and the Senate were different, they were never reconciled, and they were never signed into law by the president. And as I said, this is precisely what did happen in Lebanon.

Q: Are you familiar with any other attempts to authorize this?

A: A resolution was introduced into the House. It too was purely hortatory; indeed, it was not even labeled a joint resolution; it was labeled a concurrent resolution, which meant that it was simply asking the president—it was not authorizing him. The resolution was passed but that was it—that's as far as it got. It was never reconciled with the Senate version, nor was it signed into law by the president. So, so far, Congress has not authorized anything here.

. . .

MR. MORIN: Professor Boyle, I will present you with another document. If we can identify that document for the record.

A: Yes, these are the hearings before the Committee on Foreign Relations of the United States Senate on October 17, 1990, on the U.S. policy in the Persian Gulf, and I have read through these hearings beforehand.

Q: Ah, Professor Boyle, in the interest of time due to the fact that you have a plane to catch, can you briefly describe the nature of these hearings and what occurred on October 17?

A: Well basically, the senators were very concerned with the legal authorization for the Bush administration to send U.S. military forces to the Persian Gulf. And they asked Secretary Baker to appear and explain the administration's position—what authorization if any they thought they had.

Q: Professor Boyle, can you please turn to page 57 of the document. There is a discussion there with Secretary Baker and if you can, can you please summarize for the court what is occurring on page 57?

A: Well the senators involved want in these hearings to get a commitment from Secretary Baker that if the United States goes to war with Iraq, either in Iraq itself or Kuwait, that he will ask for formal approval from Congress. And at this point in the hearings, Secretary Baker was referring to these two preceding congressional resolutions that I mentioned to you before that simply have the status of concurrent resolutions. They are not binding as matters of law on the president or anyone else. And in it, Baker says, "I think in both bodies—and here he's referring to both the House and the Senate resolutions I discussed—there should be nothing in there that could even suggest authority to move in the future and there is not." Now what the secretary, then, is saying is that there is nothing in these resolutions giving authority to the Bush administration to launch an attack upon Iraq or Kuwait, at least according to my reading of what he was saying.

Q: Professor Boyle, can you please turn to page 86 and describe to us what is happening at this point in the hearing?

A: I'll have to look at it here again. [Pause.] That's where again Secretary Baker is referring back to these two resolutions—one from each body as he said, a path the people could look at. And that's certainly a lot more than we had when we began to engage on the subject. So in other words, Secretary Baker is admitting that they started out with no authorization from Congress at all and now they at least have two resolutions saying something. The key point on all these hearings that struck me certainly as a constitutional lawyer, as an international lawyer, is that all the senators involved expressly asked Secretary Baker, would the Bush administration ask Congress for authorization to launch a military attack on Iraq and Kuwait? And Secretary Baker expressly refused to say yes. But all he said was that he would consult with Congress. He did not say at any point in time as I remember it that he was going to ask for any authorization from Congress to engage in military operations against Iraq. And as I said, to me it sounds as if Secretary Baker is simply saying that he doesn't care all that much about the war powers clause. The president is going to go ahead and if he sees fit, launch military operations without seeking approval by Congress for these operations.

Q: Professor Boyle, in the interest of time I will proceed to the other copy. We've noted your expertise with regards to the U.S. Army field manual as well as the Nuremberg Principles. What is the general rule involving soldiers participating in illegal orders?

A: Well generally, the principles go back even further than that to *Little v. Barreme*, decided by the United States Supreme Court in the nineteenth century; *Mitchell v. Harmony*, a whole series of cases; and even in Winthrop on *Military Law and Precedents*, which you can indeed read—it says quite clearly that a soldier is under an obligation to disobey an illegal order. And an illegal order as defined by Winthrop is either one of two types of orders—an order that is not authorized by law or an order to commit an act that is clearly illegal, for example, as a war crime. So in this case we're dealing with the first variant of what is an illegal order. Did the order that Corporal Paterson receive to deploy to the Persian Gulf—was that authorized by law?

Q: Given your familiarity with the Paterson case, what is your determination so far as the ability for Corporal Paterson to disobey orders?

A: As I said, it's made very—

MAJ. QUIGLEY: Objection, sir, that asks for a legal conclusion.

. . .

MR. MORIN: Right. The professor has stated that he is familiar with the case at hand of Corporal Paterson. I am only requesting to see whether the orders as disobeyed in this matter, whether they are in compliance with the principles that he just finished elaborating to the court.

. . .

THE COURT: Major Quigley, it sounds as though your objection is based on the witness giving an opinion of the ultimate issue in the case, is that right?

MAJ. QUIGLEY: Yes, sir.

THE COURT: Well, Federal Rules of Evidence Rule 704 states that testimony in the form of an opinion otherwise admissible is not objectionable because it embraces an ultimate issue decided by the trier of fact. . . . Objection's overruled.

. . .

Q (*By Mr. Morin*): Professor Boyle, given that standard that you have elaborated in court with regard to rules involving disobeying illegal orders and given your familiarity with Corporal Paterson's case, what in your expert opinion can you conclude in terms of Corporal Paterson disobeying the orders?

A: If you take a look at the letter by the president that he did send to the Speaker of the House, he said I have taken these actions—that is, the whole deployment that Corporal Paterson was ordered to participate in—pursuant to my constitutional authority to conduct our foreign relations and as commander in chief. Well, the authority to conduct our foreign relations has nothing at all to do with dispatching military forces abroad. As for commander in chief, as I have explained before, the powers of commander in chief do not give the president the authority to deploy U.S. military forces into these types of situations here in violation of the War Powers Resolution and to engage in acts of warfare, which he has done. . . . Those powers are not the powers of the president as commander in chief. They are not the powers of the president. So under the two-prong test that you can find in Winthrop [Winthrop's *Military Law and Precedents*] that an illegal order is an order that is either to do an illegal act or an order that is not authorized by law, it seems to me that this order here was not authorized by law. And since it was not authorized by law, I do not believe that Corporal Paterson had an obligation to obey it.

Q: Thank you professor, I have no further questions at this time.

. . .

THE COURT: Gentlemen, are we ready to go? The court will come to order, all parties are present. Now Counsel, you may cross.

MAJ. QUIGLEY: Thank you. Sir, have you read the government's response to the motion?

A: I did.

Q: Do you agree that the president did address the United States from the White House on the eighth of August 1990?

A: Well I do remember, I can't remember the exact date, I do remember listening to his address and reading it, yes.

Q: On the ninth of August, he did submit his letter to Congress?

A: Yes, the letter that we discussed, yes. I have the letter right here in front of me.

Q: On the twenty-eighth of August, were you aware that he conducted a briefing of members of Congress at the White House on the status of the efforts?

A: Yes sir. Those are matters of simple consultation.

Q: Just consultation?

A: Consultation at best.

Q: On September 4, were you aware whether or not the members of the House and Senate met with the president to discuss the Persian Gulf current crisis?

A: Well, again, I cannot recall the exact dates but I certainly will admit that members of the House and the Senate have discussed the issue with the president, yes. These are questions of consultation, not authorization.

Q: On September 4 Secretary of State Baker testified before the Foreign Affairs Committee?

A: I seem to recall that. I have not reviewed that testimony of September 4. I have reviewed his testimony of October 19.

Q: On September 18 the Subcommittee on Europe and the Middle East held a hearing to receive testimony from the State Department witnesses regarding the current crisis?

A: Again, I do have a recollection of those hearings being held.

. . .

Q: Sir, I'd like to hand to you what is marked as exhibit 14. Is that a copy of the House resolution?

A: Yes it is. It's the one I had previously discussed.

Q: In section 4 of that resolution, will you refer to that?

A: The international implementation, or—oh, okay, the war powers finding, I'm sorry, yes.

Q: Paragraph 1 indicates that the president did report to Congress that he had ordered the deployment of forces. Is that correct?

A: Well, the House said that, but the president didn't. You see, that's the point, that the House is in this point saying that they believe the president reported. The president made it clear in his letter that he was not reporting under the War Powers Resolution. So what you have here is a resolution by the House that's trying to put the best face on what the president did. And you'll note they point that out in paragraph 2, that the report was only consistent with the War Powers Resolution and that language was put in there expressly by the president to indicate that he was not reporting as required by the War Powers Resolution.

Q: Yes sir, now section 6 under that, can you read that?

A: The president has consulted with the Congress and has kept Congress informed. I would agree with that—he has certainly consulted with them. Although he's done a lot better job consulting with various countries in Europe and in the Middle East and Arabian countries than he has with our own Congress. And trying to—

Q: The fact is the House passed a resolution indicating to Congress that the president has consulted with Congress in the course of the War Powers Resolution. Is that correct?

A: Well, the president has consulted with the Congress. But the War Powers Resolution requires authorization. And he has received no authority at all from the House or the Senate for anything he has done. But we have consulted.

Q: That's your interpretation?

A: Yes. And as I said, this resolution here is simply a concurrent resolution. That was its final status. It is not binding as a matter of law. It was never presented to the president as a matter of law. So it's of purely hortatory significance.

Q: That is your interpretation?

A: Yes.

Q: Congress has subsequently appropriated a billion dollars for support of Operation Desert Shield. Is that correct?

A: Yes, I have examined the legislative history of the supplemental appropriation, and again, it is defective under the War Powers Resolution. What happened here was quite simple.

Q: Excuse me, sir—

A: Defective under the War Powers Resolution.

Q: Is that your opinion?

A: As an expert on the subject, yes, it is my opinion, and I'm happy to explain why.

. . .

Q: Also, has Congress also amended title 10, section 673(b) of United States Code, authorizing the president to extend on active duty the army reserve in combat units for up to 180 days?

A: There is a serious question whether or not that is correct, counsel. I know you state that here in your section E. The problem is this, and I have researched the legislative history of that. When the bill was originally introduced into the House, it had that provision in it. During the course of the debates and before the vote, that provision was removed from the legislation as approved by the House. Also, the legislation as approved by the Senate did not contain any authority for the president to call selective reserve combatants up for 180 rather than 90 days. What happened, according to the *New York Times*, which is a matter of public record that experts in my field rely on, is that Congressman Murtha of his own accord added that into the conference version of the report, but it had never been approved by either house of Congress, to the best of my knowledge and relying on the research that I was able to do before I came here. So what happened was that particular provision was snuck in by Congressman Murtha without having been approved by either the House or the Senate, and I have severe doubts as to whether or not this provision here, section 673(b), which has never been approved by either the House or the Senate, is constitutional. And I would think that any serviceman or woman who is called up under this provision would have a very good constitutional challenge to the extension from 90 to 180 days.

Q: You understand that was not approved?

A: Well, it appeared in the final legislation, but it was not approved by either house of Congress.

Q: All right.

A: . . . it was snuck in by Congressman Murtha.

Q: All right, we need not belabor this point. . . . Sir, you are familiar with the case of—excuse me, sir. Under the president's authority to conduct foreign affairs, he has deployed troops on numerous occasions throughout U.S. history, is that correct?

A: They have not been cited under the president's authority to conduct foreign affairs, no. The president has stated and—all these cases arose before the War Powers Resolution. But the president has stated that he was acting to defend either the lives or property of American citizens in foreign countries from attack, but he never stated powers under foreign affairs.

Q: But he has deployed troops under this?

A: No, he has sent troops in to defend the lives and properties of U.S. citizens that were under attack or in jeopardy or in danger. That is not precisely what's going on now in the Persian Gulf.

Q: Are you ever aware of the time in United States history when the president's acts in a foreign country have been questioned by Congress?

A: They have been questioned, yes, indeed, and many times in these circumstances the president—

Q: My question was, was it censured by Congress?

. . .

A: Yes. The one instance I do know and I believe there are others, although I cannot recall them off the top of my head, is of course when Nixon bombed and invaded Cambodia without any congressional authorization at all. There was an article of impeachment introduced. Although, as you know, the president resigned before impeachment proceedings were brought. When Woodrow Wilson sent troops into Mexico, General Pershing, there was a serious dispute with Congress as to the propriety of his doing that. Ah, I don't believe that he ultimately was censured for it. Eventually he did report to Congress on what he did after the fact, and he did get authorization from Congress after the fact as to what he did.

Q: The government's aware of four cases involving the War Powers Resolution. Are you aware of those at all?

A: Which cases are you referring to?

. . .

Q: Regarding the War Powers Resolution, *Crockett v. Reagan*,[15] *Sanchez-Espinoza v. Reagan*,[16] *Conyers v. Reagan*,[17] and *Lowry v. Reagan*.[18] Are you aware of those cases?

A: Yes, I have, I've read all of them.

Q: In each of those cases are the requests for an order of relief of the court dismissed?

A: None of those cases are relevant to the proceedings here. This is a criminal case. These were all civil actions in which various plaintiffs were trying to use the War Powers Resolution as a sword in order to prevent various types of governmental action. In this case, the government is going after Corporal Paterson. This is a criminal proceeding. So all these cases are totally irrelevant to these proceedings. The same applies to the so-called amicus curiae brief submitted by the Washington Legal Foundation. All the cases mentioned in that brief are civil cases in which various plaintiffs tried to impede governmental conduct in one fashion or another, and for a variety of reasons, those cases were dismissed. That is not the type of proceeding we have here, where the government is seeking to prosecute Corporal Paterson. So I don't believe that any of these cases have any bearing or relevance at all to a criminal proceeding.

Q: That's your opinion?

A: Yes.

Q: Also, you are familiar with the military case of *United States v. Johnson*?

A: I'm sorry, no, I am not familiar with that case. And I have not read it, and I do apologize.

Q: Also in regard to—are you familiar with *Berk v. Laird*[19] and *Orlando v. Laird*?[20]

A: Yes.

Q: In both of those cases, didn't the court ultimately decide that the issue of whether or not the orders given to an individual was legal action of the president or nonaction of the president were basically nonjusticiable issues?

A: Not exactly, no. Again, Mr. Morin I think will be discussing those in his oral argument. But basically what was found in those Vietnam War cases, and again these were civil actions, not criminal actions, counsel, was that Congress in one fashion or another had authorized the Vietnam War. Whether it was a combination of the Gulf of Tonkin Resolution, together with appropriation of funds and together with the continuation of conscription. And so for that reason again, one combination or another of those three actions, the courts had found that Congress gave the constitutional decree of authorization for the Vietnam War. I should point out that here in this case we do have the War Powers Resolution that did not apply then. But, in any event, those were all civil proceedings—this is a criminal case, and here you have the burden of proof to establish that this was a lawful order. That was not an issue in these cases. The issue in these cases was, had Congress given authorization for the Vietnam War?

Q: The cases rose out of criminal prosecution, is that correct?

A: Well, some of them did and at some point, yes.

. . .

Q: Sir, in regard to Corporal Paterson, there are two orders in issue. One is an order to muster on the twenty-ninth. Do you believe that that is also unauthorized?

A: I have not seen the order to muster, so I really could not comment. It has not been provided to me.

Q: Which order are your referring to, then?

A: The order to deploy to the Persian Gulf.

Q: The order to get on the aircraft?

A: Well again, I have not been precisely told what orders were issued to Corporal Paterson.

MAJ. QUIGLEY: I have no additional questions.

THE COURT: Redirect.

MR. MORIN: Professor Boyle, have you been paid for your services in testifying today?

A: No, I have not. I simply requested reimbursement for my out-of-pocket expenses, but I have received no fee at all for coming here to testify today.

Mr. Morin: Thank you.

The Court: Anything on that Major Quigley?

Maj. Quigley: No sir.

[Examination by the military judge.]

The Court: Professor Boyle, two points I'd like to clear up for my own un-, derstanding.

A: Sure.

Q: Going back to an earlier statement you made on direct, you said the president had no authority to send troops to the Persian Gulf, and I took that to mean that regardless of the War Powers Resolution. Did I get that right?

A: Well, my argument—

Q: His authority as stated in his letter, whichever exhibit that is—exhibit 11—the president stated he was sending troops under his office or his authority as commander in chief, and in conducting foreign affairs you said both of those are bogus reasons . . . was of no consequence, therefore his act in sending the troops in the first place was unlawful. Did I get that right?

. . .

A: Let me repeat. There had been, as I pointed out in the redirect, examples in the nineteenth century, where the president of the United States has dispatched troops abroad under his own authority as he sees it, and this has always been a gray area in dealing with Congress, for the very limited purpose of protecting the lives and property of United States citizens. Now originally when the war powers clause of the Constitution was drafted, it was recognized by the framers that the requirement for the president to seek a formal declaration of war would not apply in two instances: (1) if there was an attack upon the United States of America itself or (2) if Congress was not in session, could not meet because of the exigencies of an attack, or something of that nature. Now over the nineteenth century, there had been developed a practice by the president to dispatch U.S. military forces in situations where the lives and properties of U.S. citizens abroad were subject to threat of death and destruction. And these I take it are some of the instances that were referred to here at the cross-examination. At best it seems Congress might have acquiesced in those instances throughout the nineteenth century. Although, as I tried to explain, in the War Powers Resolution, they intended to plug the gap to try to resolve that one way or the other. But, clearly, whatever you think of that precedent and what constitutional significance that has, limited military actions for the purpose of protecting U.S. lives and property is not what the president was doing in the Persian Gulf. And it clearly was not what was at stake. There was no assertion here by the president in this letter that he was sending U.S. military forces to the Persian Gulf for the purpose of protecting the lives and property of United States citizens.

. . .

Q: The president's actions, in your opinion, in sending troops to Saudi Arabia and other places there were not lawful?

A: Well, I don't believe it was authorized by the Constitution.

Q: Well, does that not make it unlawful?

. . .

A: That would be correct, yes. If it's not authorized by the Constitution, and as I said the president here says, "I have taken these actions pursuant to my constitutional authority to conduct our foreign relations and as Commander in Chief." Now this is the authority he has cited. Again, conducting foreign relations does not include military force. Commander in chief kicks in when Congress has authorized him to use force. In theory, if we had a treaty obligation, for example, Your Honor, to defend Saudi Arabia or Kuwait, as we do with NATO, and that treaty had received the advice and consent of the United States Senate and authorizations by Congress, under those circumstances, for example, if there was an emergency in Europe or Japan, where we also have a treaty of alliance to come to their defense, I believe the president probably would have had authority to dispatch U.S. military forces to defend states that we do indeed have treaty commitments to defend. But in the case of Saudi Arabia, Iraq, Kuwait, we have no treaty commitments to do anything to them. So I'm not exactly sure where the president got the authority to dispatch all these troops.

Q: What I'm driving at is that I detect in here an unstated basis for defense for an illegal act, although this is all traveling under the banner of the War

Powers Resolution. If there was no War Powers Resolution, your opinion would still be the same?

A: Yes, I don't believe the president here has cited any constitutional authority for what he has done.

Q: Now, moving over to the War Powers Resolution, assume that the president had sent troops in . . . protecting lives and property of citizens who were being rounded up by the Iraqi government. That was day one. On day two he made the report. . . . By day three he should have made the report. By day sixty-three he'd have to have the resolution by Congress or get out. Get the troops out. Would an order given on day ten be lawful even if the president had not reported as required? . . .

A: Well, Your Honor, let me back up just a bit here. The nineteenth-century precedent that I cited for the deployment of troops abroad was limited deployments. That is, the troops would go in, they would protect U.S. lives and property, and they would go out, they would go home. None of those precedents at all dealt with sending large-scale forces in, occupying countries, and things of that nature. So it's an open question whether Congress acquiesced in that, felt that it violated the war powers clause as opposed to the resolution, or whatever. Now what the War Powers Resolution did is try to impose limits on that particular type of deployment of forces—that is, if the president was saying, well, I believe it's necessary for me to send marines in here to protect the lives and property of U.S. citizens, the War Powers Resolution would kick in for that purpose. But here, the president is not saying that he is sending U.S. military forces to the Persian Gulf, including acts of war such as a blockade, simply for the purpose of protecting the lives and property of U.S. citizens. He is asserting a far broader power, and that's basically to send now up to half a million men and women to this region of the world without any authorization from Congress. That's been his position right from the start. And all the authority he is citing for it is this power to conduct foreign relations, which does not apply to military forces, and the commander-in-chief clause. I do not believe our founders had in mind under the commander-in-chief clause that the president could just commit a half million men and women anywhere in the world for extended periods of time. But to specifically answer your question, again, what was in mind in these earlier nineteenth-century precedents was going in, grabbing our citizens and our property, and getting out.

Q: Back under this War Powers Resolution, now what I'm getting at is, can an order be retroactively illegal, but legal at the time it's given? For comparison's sake let's say on day ten he's given an order to deploy. Now the president has till day sixty-three to get authorization to lead. Up to that point, his actions are lawful. Let's say on day sixty-three he hasn't got the power yet. Does that make the orders given up to that point, all of them unlawful? It seems to me that the crucial point is the time at which the order is given. Is it lawful at that point?

A: Well, let's look at the —

Q: Is it in violation of the war powers clause until another, say, sixty-three days down the road?

A: Well, Your Honor, in this case of course the president took the position that the War Powers Resolution was unconstitutional and he wasn't going to pay any attention to it right from the outset of the operation.

Q: Well I understand that —

A: So it seems to me the answer to your question, sir, that he's saying I don't care about the war powers clause, I'm just going to go ahead and do this.

Q: Well I realize what the president is saying, looking at the letter, but in spite of the fact that he might be saying I don't care about it, he obviously does or he wouldn't have written this letter. Ah, why don't we go on to another point.

A: Well, could I return, then, to you with a question that you asked. The second thing that the president did here, and I take it this was before Corporal Paterson was asked to muster, or ordered to muster, was the imposition of the blockade. Now, however you want to look at the — also the order to send the troops over there. The blockade was a second independent constitutionally deficient act here by the president. So he sent the troops over, and then shortly thereafter he imposed the blockade, which was an act of war. So that when Corporal Paterson was ordered to muster, our government technically was committing acts of war. The president was committing acts of war in the Persian Gulf region. And he had no authorization to engage in any types of acts of war from Congress. Congress never authorized an act of war on the part of the president. And these events did occur, as I understand it, before Corporal Paterson was ordered to muster. And then you have the president, well, even assuming if you want to for your purposes that the original deployment might have been lawful, certainly after the point he began to engage in acts of warfare without congressional authorization, which occurred before the time Corporal Paterson was ordered to muster, it seems to me that that created the serious constitutional problems that I have been discussing here.

Q: Let me try for a yes or no. If the president's actions were not in violation of the War Powers Resolution, at this point the order was given on day ten, but they do run afoul of it and become not in compliance on day sixty-three, does that relate back and make the original order lawful or unlawful?

A: Well, here, I believe that however you want to interpret the letter, the moment he began to use military force, he imposed the blockade and used military force at that point, he was out there on his own without authorization from Congress to do it. So one could say there is a gray area at best between the time he sent the forces and the time he imposed the blockade and started using military force to enforce it. But thereafter, I don't believe there was any legality in the further steps he had taken from that point in time. So I'm assuming arguendo what you're saying.

Q: Well, it appears that it would work completely off the war powers problem and just are now going on the problem if orders are illegal ab initio.

A: Well, certainly, I believe they are. But I'm assuming your premise that they are not. You've given me a hypothetical that they were not illegal ab initio, and so on the basis of that assumption, I'm saying, okay, let's explore your hypothetical and let's take your hypothetical from the day the deployment was ordered and say, maybe on the basis of your hypothetical, the president might have had an argument between that day and the day he imposed the blockade and began firing, which I believe was August 12. At that point in time, clearly he had no authority to engage in acts of war under the war powers clause or the War Powers Resolution—he had no authorization to do this. And that was prior to the time that Corporal Paterson was ordered to go.

Q: When trial counsel referred to court cases where a court declined to take up the matter, that it was not justiciable, you said that they were civil cases.

A: Yes.

Q: But the criminal cases are different. Is that merely your opinion, or do you have some other authority you can point to?

A: Well, the political-question doctrine happens or gets applied in circumstances where plaintiffs, whether private individuals or congressmen, try to use the war powers clause and the War Powers Resolution as a sword.

Q: What doctrine?

A: The political-question doctrine or nonjusticiability—they're basically the same thing. In those cases that counsel is referring to, the plaintiffs were using the war powers clause and the War Powers Resolution as a sword to go after some type of military action that the president was taking. In those types of cases, it has happened that courts for one reason or another have determined that this is a political question; we're not going to be getting involved in a struggle between Congress and the president, or it's nonjusticiable, or we're going to stay out of it and they come up with one reason or another. That isn't this case, Your Honor. In this case, the government is prosecuting Corporal Paterson. My testimony here, expert-witness testimony that I have given you, is directly relevant to the issue here in dispute, an element of the crime that you have stated yourself, namely, that the government has the burden of proof beyond a reasonable doubt, to establish that this order was lawful. My testimony goes to the question that this order was not lawful, and I believe today I have certainly created a reasonable doubt on that issue. Now of course that's for you to decide, Your Honor, but if you agree with me [that] I have created a reasonable doubt, then it seems to me that Corporal Paterson is entitled to acquittal. And those are the rules of evidence applied by the United States Supreme Court in *In re Winship* and *Mullaney v. Wilbur*, and the rules in *Winship* and *Wilbur* of course come after Winthrop [Winthrop's *Military Law and Precedents*]—I don't know what version or edition they were citing to, Winthrop—but *In re Winship* and *Mullaney v. Wilbur* are the law of the land when it comes to the government having the burden of proof beyond a reasonable doubt on all elements of an offense. That has nothing at all to do with political question. This is simply a question of the relevance of my testimony to that element of the offense. So the political-question doctrine comes up in civil proceedings when plaintiffs, usually, typically, congressmen, have tried to use the War Powers Resolution to stop something that the president is doing. The political-question doctrine does not come up in criminal cases, where you are governed by the rules of evidence, burdens of proof, burdens of persuasion, and things of that nature. Those are independent requirements imposed by the Supreme Court.

Q: That's strange why I've never heard it before in court in all my criminal work. Okay, thank you. Gentlemen.

. . .

A: Thank you very much, Your Honor, for your patience.

NOTES

1. Charles A. Shanor & L. Lynn Hogue, *National Security and Military Law* 443 (2003).
2. Francis A. Boyle, *Destroying World Order* 53–91 (2004).
3. H.R. Res. 34, 102d Cong. 1st Sess. (1991), later reintroduced as H.R. Res. 86, Feb. 21, 1991.
4. Boyle, *supra* note 2, at 140–57.
5. George Santayana, *The Life of Reason*, vol. I, 284 (1905).
6. Francis A. Boyle, *A Guide to Impeaching President George W. Bush*, in *Destroying World Order* 158–72.
7. Francis A. Boyle, *War Criminal as Attorney General?*, Counterpunch, Nov. 18, 2004, http://www.counterpunch.org/boyle11182004.html.
8. Associated Press, *Video Shows Bush Was Warned before Katrina*, Mar. 1, 2006.
9. *See, e.g.*, Herbert J. Gans, *The War against the Poor* (1995); David Macarov, *What the Market Does to People* (2003) (footnote not in the original).
10. 137 Cong. Rec. H521 (daily ed. Jan. 16, 1991).
11. Louis Fisher, *American Constitutional Law* 296 (5th ed. 2003).
12. *Id.* at 298–303.
13. David S. Cloud, *Gates Sympathetic to Pleas for More Troops in Afghanistan*, N.Y. Times, Jan. 18, 2007.
14. Spencer Rich, *Rules on Detainees' Treatment Depend on Whether War Exists*, Washington Post, Aug. 20, 1990, at A16.
15. *Crockett v. Reagan*, 720 F.2d 1355 (D.C. Cir. 1983), *cert. denied,* 467 U.S. 1251 (1984).
16. *Sanchez-Espinoza v. Reagan*, 770 F.2d 202 (D.C. Cir. 1985).
17. *Conyers v. Reagan*, 765 F.2d 1124 (D.C. Cir. 1985).
18. *Lowry v. Reagan*, 676 F. Supp. 333 (D.D.C. 1987).
19. *Berk v. Laird*, 429 F.2d 302 (2d Cir. 1970), *on remand to* 317 F. Supp. 715 (E.D.N.Y. 1970), *aff'd, Orlando v. Laird*, 443 F.2d 1039 (2d Cir. 1971), *cert. denied*, 404 U.S. 869 (1971).
20. *Orlando v. Laird*, 443 F.2d 1039 (2d Cir. 1971), *cert. denied*, 404 U.S. 869 (1971).

Chapter Five

President Clinton's Invasion of Haiti on Trial and the Laws of War

United States

v.

Rockwood, Lawrence P.

CPT, 261-29-6597

HHC, 10th Mountain Division (LI)

Fort Drum, New York 13602

U.S. Army

Request for Production of Witnesses

18 April 1995

1. The accused, CPT Rockwood, through counsel, hereby requests that the Government produce the following witnesses to testify at trial. This request is intended to comply with the requirements of RCM 703, 1001, and the Rules of Court.

. . .

COL Michael L. Sullivan, Commander, 16th Military Police Brigade (Abn). He is expected to testify about his 1 October 1994 visit to the Haitian National Penitentiary.

. . .

Prof. Francis Boyle, Illinois Law School, Champaign, IL. He is expected to testify as an expert in International Law, Humanitarian Law, and laws protective of human rights. He will testify on different aspects of those fields of law, the duties they impose on military commanders, officers, and personnel, and how these laws relate to the charges against CPT Rockwood and to establish the legal basis for a reasonable belief that the conduct charged was required, justified, or protected.

. . .

CPT (Ret) Hugh Thompson, Jr. . . . He is expected to testify, on the basis of actual military precedent, about military discipline in situations of operational necessity concerning human rights violations.

. . .

2. The defense assumes by this request that the witnesses listed above will be produced unless otherwise notified.

Judith Camarella
CPT, JA
Associate Defense Counsel

On September 19, 1994, President Bill Clinton illegally invaded Haiti without authorization by Congress and thus in violation of the war powers clause of the U.S. Constitution and the 1973 War Powers Resolution. The 10th Mountain Division of the U.S. Army, from Fort Drum, New York, was part of that invading force. Its counterintelligence officer was Captain Lawrence P. Rockwood II, a career military officer who had already spent fifteen years in the U.S. Army. Captain Rockwood was a fourth-generation soldier in the U.S. military.

When Captain Rockwood was a young boy, his father took him to visit the Nazi concentration camp near Dachau, Germany, on his last military assignment and lectured him about how "the world's cynicism and blind obedience to authority played in" its construction.[1] That visit to Dachau and lecture by his father would have a decisive impact on Captain Rockwood's courageous and heroic decision to act to prevent human rights abuses in Haiti a generation later.

During the summer of 1982, I likewise had the opportunity to visit that same Nazi concentration camp just outside of Dachau, Germany. Given the proximity of the town to the camp, my immediate reaction was, "This town is so close to the camp that the citizens of Dachau must have known what was going on out there. Why did they not do anything about it?" Unlike Dachau's inhabitants, Captain Rockwood acted in Haiti at personal risk to his life, his liberty, and his cherished military career in the U.S. Army.

Before entering Haiti, Captain Rockwood had begun to receive intelligence information about the horrific human rights conditions in Haitian prisons, and in particular at the National Penitentiary in Port-au-Prince, which even after the U.S. invasion remained under the control of the "officials" appointed by the regime of General Raul Cedras. Captain Rockwood did everything humanly possible to convince the superior officers in his chain of command that they must immediately secure the Haitian prisons to terminate and prevent ongoing human rights violations there. Instead of so acting, Captain Rockwood's superiors informed him that their main objective was "force protection" for U.S. soldiers and that so-called Haitian-on-Haitian violence was not a priority. Therefore, nothing was done to secure the National Penitentiary, despite the fact that it was completely surrounded by thousands of U.S. armed forces—that is, until Captain Rockwood acted of his own accord as required by the Geneva Conventions of 1949, the Hague Regulations of 1907, and the U.S. Army's *Field Manual 27-10* (1956), all of which he had studied.

On the evening of September 30, Captain Rockwood secretly left his base in Port-au-Prince to travel to the National Penitentiary, alone and at risk to his own life, to inspect the human rights conditions there. The conditions were atrocious and every bit as horrendous as had been reported in the prior intelligence he had received. Nothing had changed at the National Penitentiary, despite the public promise given by President Bill Clinton that the primary purpose for the U.S. invasion of Haiti was to secure human rights and democracy for its people. Given the hellacious human rights conditions in the prison, Captain Rockwood proceeded to draw up a list of the names of the prisoners to prevent and deter their death or "disappearance."

Captain Rockwood's humanitarian efforts at the National Penitentiary were terminated upon the arrival of a U.S. Army major from the U.S. embassy's military attaché's office, who ordered Captain Rockwood to leave the National Penitentiary, which he did. The U.S. Army major had been summoned by the Cedras "official" in charge of the prison. Notice that the U.S. Army major, the U.S. military attaché's office, and the Cedras warden worked in tandem with each other to stop Captain Rockwood's humanitarian mission at the National Penitentiary.

Captain Rockwood was later subjected to a general court-martial from May 8 to May 14, 1995, at Fort Drum, New York, facing a potential sentence of about ten years of incarceration in a military prison if convicted on several charges. The military court convicted Captain Rockwood of five specifications on three charges under the Uniform Code of Military Justice (UCMJ)—charge 1: article 86, specification 1 (failure to report for duty), specification 2 (unauthorized leave); charge 2: article 89 (disrespect toward a superior officer); charge 3: article 90 (willful disobedience to superior orders); and charge 5: article 133 (conduct unbecoming an officer). The military court acquitted Captain Rockwood of both specifications in charge 4 under UCMJ article 92, specification 1 (failure to obey an order) and specification 2 (dereliction of duties).

Although Captain Rockwood faced a substantial term of incarceration for the charges upon which he had been convicted, the military court did not sentence him to prison, but did dismiss him from the army with forfeiture of pay. In other words, a military jury of his own peers of professional military officers basically agreed with the defense's contention that Captain Rockwood did what he had to do under international law to terminate and prevent grievous human rights abuses and war crimes at the National Penitentiary. Captain Rockwood walked out of the U.S. Army as a free man. He was deeply disappointed to have his treasured career as a military officer so unjustifiably terminated. But he left the U.S. Army as an acknowledged and eternal hero to the worldwide human rights movement.

I have included, toward the end of this chapter, excerpts from the testimony I gave during the course of the general court-martial proceedings against Captain Rockwood. The direct examination of me was conducted by my friend and colleague Ramsey Clark, who served as U.S. attorney general during the presidency of Lyndon Johnson and who was Captain Rockwood's civilian attorney of record. Note the monumental statement made by the military judge to Ramsey Clark in front of the military jury toward the end of my testimony (highlighted in bold): "You covered the priority of the law, and I think it's clear that international law would supersede the UCMJ under appropriate circumstances."

Appearing as the defense's expert witness on the charges of "dereliction of duty" and "conduct unbecoming an officer" was the storied but now deceased Hugh Thompson, another human rights hero. As a warrant officer during the Vietnam War commanding a scout helicopter armed with machine guns, Hugh Thompson almost single-handedly ended the My Lai massacre by threatening to kill Lieutenant Calley and his soldiers if they did not immediately cease and desist from their murderous rampage against old men, women, and children. Without Hugh Thompson's courageous intervention, the death toll at My Lai would have been greater than the reported 504 victims. Hugh Thompson's riveting but low-key testimony in Captain Rockwood's court-martial stood for the proposition that a soldier could threaten to kill his superior officer to prevent serious human rights abuses and that the U.S. Army should award him a medal for it, as the Pentagon belatedly did for Hugh Thompson some three decades later—instead of a court-martial. Perhaps some day the U.S. Army will realize the error of its ways and award a medal to, and reinstate, Lawrence Rockwood for his similarly heroic and principled actions in Haiti.

Captain Rockwood fought a ferocious and lonely battle of courage, integrity, and principle against the Pentagon to uphold human rights, international law, and the laws of war in Haiti—and won! For that reason alone, his case is of monumental importance, not just for the past but also for the future and most importantly for the present. The principles of international law, human rights, and the laws of war applicable to U.S. armed forces in Haiti in 1994 apply with full force and vigor to U.S. armed forces in Iraq today as a result of the Bush administration's illegal invasion in March 2003. It is not my purpose here to provide a detailed critique of the numerous illegalities surrounding the Bush administration's criminal invasion of Iraq. But for the purposes of this particular analysis, I intend to relate my testimony in the

Rockwood case to the laws of war and human rights violations of the Bush administration's war against Iraq.

On March 19, 2003, President Bush commenced his criminal war against Iraq by ordering a so-called decapitation strike against the president of Iraq, in violation of a forty-eight-hour ultimatum he had given publicly to the Iraqi president and his sons to leave the country.[2] This duplicitous behavior violated the customary international laws of war set forth in the 1907 Hague Convention on the Opening of Hostilities, to which the United States is still a contracting party,[3] as evidenced by paragraphs 20, 21, 22, and 23 of the U.S. Army's *Field Manual 27-10* (1956). Furthermore, President Bush's attempt to assassinate the president of Iraq was an international crime in its own right. Of course, the Bush administration's war of aggression against Iraq constituted a crime against peace as defined by the Nuremberg Charter, the Nuremberg Judgment, and the Nuremberg Principles, as well as by paragraph 498 of *Field Manual 27-10* (1956).

Next came the Pentagon's military strategy of inflicting "shock and awe" upon the city of Baghdad. Article 6(b) of the 1945 Nuremberg Charter defines the term "war crimes" to include "wanton destruction of cities, towns or villages, or devastation not justified by military necessity." The Bush administration's infliction of "shock and awe" on Baghdad and its inhabitants constituted the wanton destruction of that city, and it was certainly not justified by "military necessity," which is always defined by and includes the laws of war. Such terror bombings of cities have constituted criminal behavior under international law since before the Second World War:[4] Guernica, London, Dresden, Tokyo, Hiroshima, Nagasaki—Fallujah.[5]

On May 1, 2003, President Bush theatrically landed on a U.S. aircraft carrier sailing off the coast of San Diego to declare, "Major combat operations in Iraq have ended." He spoke before a large banner proclaiming "MISSION ACCOMPLISHED." As of that date, the U.S. government became the belligerent occupant of Iraq under international law and practice.

This legal status was formally recognized by UN Security Council Resolution 1483 of May 22, 2003, the relevant portions of which are excerpted below:

Noting the letter of 8 May 2003 from the Permanent Representatives of the United States of America and the United Kingdom of Great Britain and Northern Ireland to the President of the Security Council (S/2003/538) and recognizing the specific authorities, responsibilities, and obligations under applicable international law of these states as occupying powers under unified command (the "Authority"), . . .

5. Calls upon all concerned to comply fully with their obligations under international law including in particular the Geneva Conventions of 1949 and the Hague Regulations of 1907.

In that May 8, 2003, letter from the United States and the United Kingdom to the president of the Security Council, both countries pledged to the Security Council that "[t]he States participating in the Coalition will strictly abide by their obligations under international law, including those relating to the essential humanitarian needs of the people of Iraq." No point would be served here by attempting to document the gross and repeated violations of that solemn and legally binding pledge by the United States and the United Kingdom, since it would require a separate book to catalog all of the war crimes, crimes against humanity, and grave human rights violations inflicted by the United States and the United Kingdom in Iraq and against its people.[6] Suffice it to say that both the United States and the United Kingdom have been the belligerent occupants of Iraq, subject to the Four Geneva Conventions of 1949, the 1907 Hague Regulations on land warfare, the U.S. Army's field manual and its British equivalent, the humanitarian provisions of Additional Protocol I of 1977 to the Four Geneva Conventions of 1949, and the customary international laws of war. I discussed and analyzed all of these basic sources of international law with respect to the U.S. military occupation of Haiti, on behalf of Captain Rockwood during his general court-martial proceedings. My comments and analyses in connection with that court-martial apply with respect to the belligerent occupation of Iraq by the United States and the United Kingdom that tragically still continues apace as this book goes to press.

For example, my *Rockwood* testimony applies with full force and vigor to the torture scandal at the Abu Ghraib prison in Iraq that was then under the direct control of the U.S. government. The same legal analysis applies to other locations of detention and torture controlled by U.S. armed forces throughout Iraq and Afghanistan, such as at the Bagram and Kandahar bases. I do not take the position that the United States is the belligerent occupant of the entire state of Afghanistan. But certainly the laws of war and international humanitarian law apply to the United States in its conduct of hostilities in Afghanistan as well as to its presence there.

It is not generally believed that the United States is the belligerent occupant of Guantánamo Bay, Cuba. But those detainees held there by U.S. armed forces who were apprehended in or near the theaters of hostilities in Afghanistan and Iraq are protected by either the Third Geneva Convention protecting prisoners of war or the Fourth Geneva Convention protecting civilians. In any event, every detainee held by the U.S. government in Guantánamo Bay is protected by the International Covenant on Civil and Political Rights, to which the United States is a party. My *Rockwood* testimony reprinted at the end of this chapter should provide a good guide to the gross and repeated violations of international law, human rights, and the laws of war inflicted by U.S. military forces at these detention and torture facilities. A similar analysis likewise applies to those numerous but unknown detention and torture facilities operated around the world by the Central Intelligence Agency.[7] America's own *Gulag Archipelago*. No wonder the Bush administration has done everything humanly possible to sabotage the International Criminal Court!

The U.S. government's installation of the so-called interim government of Iraq during the summer of 2004 did not materially alter this legal situation. Under the laws of war, this interim government is nothing more than a "puppet government." As the belligerent occupant of Iraq, the U.S. government is free to establish a puppet government if it so desires. But under the laws of war, the U.S. government remains fully accountable for the behavior of its puppet government.

These conclusions are made quite clear by paragraph 366 of the army's *Field Manual 27-10* (1956):

366. Local Governments Under Duress and Puppet Governments

The restrictions placed upon the authority of a belligerent government cannot be avoided by a system of using a puppet government, central or local, to carry out acts which would be unlawful if performed directly by the occupant. Acts induced or compelled by the occupant are nonetheless its acts.

As the belligerent occupant of Iraq, the U.S. government is obligated to ensure that its puppet interim government obeys the Four Geneva Conventions of 1949, the 1907 Hague Regulations on land warfare, the U.S. Army's *Field Manual 27-10* (1956), the humanitarian provisions of Additional Protocol I of 1977 to the Four Geneva Conventions of 1949, and the customary international laws of war. Any violation of the laws of war, international humanitarian law, and human rights by its puppet interim government are legally imputable to the U.S. government. Because the United States is a belligerent occupant of Iraq, both the U.S. government itself and its civilian officials and military officers are fully and personally responsible under international criminal law for all violations of the laws of war, international humanitarian law, and human rights committed by its puppet Iraqi government—for example, reported death squads operating under the latter's auspices.[8]

Furthermore, it was total myth, fraud, and outright propaganda for the Bush administration to maintain that it somehow magically transferred "sovereignty" to its puppet Iraqi government during the summer of 2004. Under the laws of war, sovereignty is never transferred in the first place from the defeated sovereign such as Iraq to a belligerent occupant such as the United States. This is made quite clear in paragraph 353 of the U.S. Army *Field*

Manual 27-10 (1956): "Belligerent occupation in a foreign war, being based upon the possession of enemy territory, necessarily implies that the sovereignty of the occupied territory is not vested in the occupying power. Occupation is essentially provisional."

If there were any doubt about this matter, paragraph 358 of that field manual makes this legal fact crystal clear:

358. Occupation Does Not Transfer Sovereignty

Being an incident of war, military occupation confers upon the invading force the means of exercising control for the period of occupation. It does not transfer the sovereignty to the occupant, but simply the authority or power to exercise some of the rights of sovereignty. The exercise of these rights results from the established power of the occupant and from the necessity of maintaining law and order, indispensable both to the inhabitants and the occupying force.

Therefore, the U.S. government never had any "sovereignty" to transfer to its puppet interim government of Iraq. In Iraq, the sovereignty still resides in the hands of the people of Iraq and in the state known as the Republic of Iraq, where it has always been. The legal regime described above will continue so long as the United States remains the belligerent occupant of Iraq. Only when that U.S. belligerent occupation of Iraq is factually terminated can the people of Iraq have the opportunity to exercise their international legal right of sovereignty by means of free, fair, democratic, and uncoerced elections. As of this writing, the United States and the United Kingdom remain the belligerent occupants of Iraq despite their bogus "transfer" of their nonexistent "sovereignty" to their puppet interim government of Iraq.

Even UN Security Council Resolution 1546 of June 8, 2004, "welcoming" the installation of the puppet interim government of Iraq recognized this undeniable fact of international law. The preamble to the resolution referred to "the letter of 5 June 2004 from the United States Secretary of State to the President of the Council, which is annexed to this resolution." In other words, that annexed letter is a legally binding part of the resolution. In that letter, U.S. Secretary of State Colin Powell pledged to the UN Security Council, with respect to the so-called multinational force (MNF) in Iraq, "In addition, the forces that make up the MNF are and will remain committed at all times to act consistently with their obligations under the law of armed conflict, including the Geneva Conventions."

This brings the analysis to the so-called constitution of Iraq that was allegedly drafted by the puppet interim government of Iraq under the impetus of the U.S. government. Article 43 of the 1907 Hague Regulations on land warfare flatly prohibits the change in a basic law such as a state's constitution during the course of a belligerent occupation: "The authority of the legitimate power having in fact passed into the hands of the occupant, the latter shall take all the measures in his power to restore, and ensure as far as possible, public order and safety, while respecting, unless absolutely prevented, the laws in force in the country." This prohibition was expressly incorporated in *haec verba* in paragraph 363 of the U.S. Army's *Field Manual 27-10* (1956). Nonetheless, the United States has demonstrated gross disrespect toward every law in Iraq that has stood in the way of its imperial designs and petroleum ambitions, including and especially the preinvasion 1990 interim constitution of Iraq.

UN Security Council Resolution 1637 of November 9, 2005, extended the foreign military occupation of Iraq until December 31, 2006, but expressly subject to the October 29, 2005, letter by U.S. Secretary of State Condoleezza Rice to the president of the Security Council guaranteeing that "[t]he forces that make up the MNF will remain committed to acting consistently with their obligations under international law, including the law of armed conflict."

More recently, UN Security Council Resolution 1723 of November 28, 2006, extended the mandate for the 160,000-strong multinational force in Iraq—which included 132,000 troops from the United States—for one year, but once again, only after Secretary of State Rice promised on behalf of the United States—this time in a letter dated November 17, 2006, and annexed as an integral part of the UN resolution—that "[t]he forces that make up MNF will remain committed to acting consistently with their obligations and rights under international law, including the law of armed conflict." In connection with this letter by Secretary of State Rice, France's foreign affairs minister, Philippe Douste-Blazy, publicly labeled the United States and the United Kingdom as the belligerent occupants of Iraq: "The French foreign minister pointed out that there is an occupant, referring to US and Great Britain, and an occupied in that Arab country, thus admitting the real nature of those two countries presence in Iraq."[9]

As for any subsequent Security Council resolutions, the UN Security Council has no power or authority to alter the laws of war, since they are peremptory norms of general international law. For the Security Council even to purport to authorize U.S. violations of the laws of war in Iraq would render its member states aiders and abettors to U.S. war crimes and thus guilty of committing war crimes in their own right. Any Security Council attempt to condone, authorize, or approve violations of the international laws of war by the United States and the United Kingdom in Iraq would be ultra vires, a legal nullity, and void ab initio.

In fact, the United Nations itself has become complicit in U.S. and U.K. international crimes in Iraq in violation of the customary international laws of war set forth in paragraph 500 of the U.S. Army's *Field Manual 27-10* (1956): "[C]omplicity in the commission of, crimes against peace, crimes against humanity, and war crimes [is] punishable." The United Nations is walking down the path previously trod by the League of Nations toward Leon Trotsky's "ashcan" of history. And George Bush and Tony Blair are heading toward their own judgment at Nuremberg, whose sixtieth anniversary the rest of the world gratefully but wistfully commemorated in 2006. Never again!

Set forth below is a transcript of the testimony I gave under oath and subject to cross-examination by JAG lawyers and the military judge during the course of the general court-martial proceedings against Captain Rockwood. The transcript has been corrected and edited for style, length, and typographical errors, but it should provide a good account of what actually happened in the U.S. Army courtroom when we put on trial President Clinton's hypocritical and unconstitutional invasion of Haiti.

THE COURT: Okay. Are we ready for the court members? Apparently so. Okay. Go ahead and bring them in.

. . .

Francis A. Boyle, civilian, was called as a witness for the defense, was sworn and testified as follows:

DIRECT EXAMINATION

. . .

MR. CLARK: Good morning, Professor Boyle.

A: Good morning, Mr. Clark.

Q: Have you been in the courtroom during the testimony of Captain Rockwood?

A: Yes. I've heard the testimony of Colonel Sullivan, Captain Rockwood, Mr. Messing, and Captain Thompson.

Q: So you were here all day yesterday?

A: Yes.

Q: And today?

A: Yes.

Q: And there's a reason that you were, contrary to the usual rule, able to stay in the courtroom because you're an expert witness?

A: That's correct.

Q: And did you listen carefully to the testimony?

A: I listened very carefully because I figured I'd be called upon to express some opinion.

. . .

Q: I guess first I should ask you, how is it that international law has anything to do with the United States? We make our laws. Or with the United States citizens?

A: Well, as you heard yesterday in some of the testimony, international law is part of the United States law. The United States Constitution says in Article VI that treaties are the supreme law of the land, and the same applies to executive agreements. That is, international agreements that don't have the approval of the Senate. Say, for example, the Nuremberg Charter is an executive agreement concluded by the president under his constitutional authority as commander in chief. And then customary international law, the United States Supreme Court has held in *The Paquete Habana* case and other cases that this is part of our law. That customary international law is federal common law, so it applies to all of us. And this law that I'm discussing here has also been explicitly recognized and incorporated into the *Field Manual 27-10, The Law of Land Warfare* by Judge Richard Baxter, my teacher. He says the same thing that I'm saying to you here, so it's also been incorporated into military law that applies to all of us. The field manual says correctly that the laws of war apply not only to members of the armed forces but also to civilians to the extent that any of us do get involved in these types of situations.

Q: Now, identify the major treaties—the really important ones—that would have applications to this matter, this case here.

A: Well again, to go back to the field manual, the field manual is based first on the Hague Conventions of 1899, 1907. And particularly here, Hague Convention number 4, on the law of land warfare, regulating the conduct of land warfare, the Hague Regulations, which are a treaty. Again, the supreme law of the land. It's still on the books. We're still bound by it. Other countries are bound by it. The Nuremberg Judgment and the Tribunal held that the Hague Regulations were also customary international law. So everyone's bound by the Hague Regulations, and that's a pretty high authority of the Nuremberg Tribunal. The second major source, of course, would be the four Geneva Conventions of 1949. Particularly, in this case you would be dealing with the Fourth Geneva Convention with respect to the treatment of civilians. Then there are principles of international law that have been derived from the World War II prosecution of war criminals at Nuremberg and Tokyo, principles of command responsibility, the *Yamashita* case—that an officer has an obligation to act on information that troops or others subject to his control have committed or are about to commit a war crime. Other cases left over from Nuremberg dealing with inchoate responsibility for war crimes, that is, not the substantive offense itself, but conspiracy, incitement, attempt, and complicity. A lot of this goes back to the Nuremberg Charter, Judgment, and Principles. So those would be the basic principles—so obviously the field manual is quite extensive. A good deal of it would not necessarily apply to this situation, but some of it clearly does.

Q: Those treaties that you identified, let me ask you, what happened to General Yamashita?

A: Well, as you probably know, he was the commander in the Philippines, and troops subject to his control committed atrocities on U.S. forces—prisoners of war—and there was no knowledge that he had knowledge of this, but he was tried and the matter went to the U.S. Supreme Court, and the test was articulated that those commanders who knew or should have known that troops or other individuals subject to their control were about to commit a war crime or had committed a war crime and had either failed to prevent that war crime or to prosecute the perpetrator, were themselves vicariously responsible for those war crimes, and so General Yamashita was executed.[10] There was a request for a writ of habeas corpus from the Supreme Court, it was denied, and he was executed, upholding that principle. The *Yamashita* principle has been expressly incorporated; Judge Baxter did not reference it by a citation to the case itself, but he put that principle—I believe it's in paragraph 501 of the field manual itself.

. . .

Q: Do those treaties that you talked about—Nuremberg, Hague, the four Genevas—apply to Haiti?

A: Yes. If you read the field manual, particularly in the outset, paragraphs 8 and 9, they make it very clear that this body of law applies in the case of any type of occupation. As you know, war can start or occupation can start in a number of ways as a matter of law. The 1907 Hague Convention on the Opening of Hostilities allows a war to start even without a declaration of war, but an ultimatum. And of course, in this case you had an ultimatum that was given to the de facto authorities there. The field manual tries to deal with all these contingencies whether you're actually having a hostility or a declaration of war without hostilities, or even an occupation that is not resisted. And the field manual expressly states that in the event of an occupation that's not resisted, nevertheless, the laws of war come into play. So certainly, it's my opinion that given the circumstances here where the United States had surrounded Haiti, there was massive overwhelming force there ready to be used, an ultimatum had been given and indeed General Cedras, according to President Carter, capitulated only when he was told that U.S. paratroopers had already been sent on their way and were into their mission, and at that point he capitulated to the ultimatum, and went along with the occupation, and I think that if you read the field manual, it's clear that under those circumstances the laws of war and the other treaties applicable would apply.

MR. CLARK: Now, let me advise the court that we offer Professor Boyle as an expert witness on international public law or public international law, and the laws of land warfare and peacekeeping activities.

CAPT. O'BRIEN: No objection, Your Honor.

THE COURT: Okay.

MR. CLARK: Did you hear that long hypothetical I asked Captain Thompson this morning?

A: Yes, and I also heard all the testimony yesterday upon which it was based, by Captain Rockwood.

Q: And are you able to base your testimony, obviously giving primary weight to all the evidence that you heard, but also to the hypotheticals only as hypotheticals given to Hugh Thompson?

A: Yes. I can respond to those issues. Sure.

Q: 'Cause that will save us a lot of time. I won't have to go back through all that.

A: I'm certainly prepared to express an opinion on what I heard Captain Rockwood testify to yesterday.

. . .

Q: First, I'd like to you to state your opinion on this matter. Does international law—and U.S. law, including any positive U.S. military law that's applicable—impose an affirmative duty to act, a legal duty, on an individual soldier to prevent imminent death or serious bodily injuries where he reasonably believes that death or injury will occur unless he acts to prevent it? And he has made every reasonable effort, taken every opportunity, to avoid the violation of any regulation, military policy, or order in the commission of his effort to save those lives or prevent harm?

. . .

A: Yes. I formulated an opinion listening to all the testimony yesterday; both Colonel Sullivan, who I think gave very compelling testimony as to the human rights situation, and also Captain Rockwood, explaining his attempts to stop the human rights violations as he saw it going on at the prison. The field manual makes it clear in the outset that one of the purposes of the laws of war is to protect the rights of civilians under these circumstances. They are very clear about that: the human rights of civilians. And here, we're talking about civilians at this prison. Under the Hague Regulations, the United States government, as the occupant, would have the obligation to preserve law and order and take care of the well-being of these people. Under the Geneva Conventions, the Fourth Geneva Convention has far more extensive protections for civilians, even in prison. As long as there are civilians in this type of situation, in my opinion they are entitled to the protections of the Fourth Geneva Convention. Indeed, the convention makes it clear that it would apply in the case of an occupation—not just armed conflict, but an occupation under these circumstances—and that is also referenced in the field manual itself. The field manual also makes this clear. Professor Baxter made that very clear. It is a factual test: "Is there an occupation?" That is, it's a matter of fact. Is there an occupation in Haiti? I think that we can all agree that there was an occupation. Certainly, in Port-au-Prince you had close to 10 to 15,000 troops just there. I don't know how much out in the countryside, and under these circumstances then, the civilians in the prisons had to be protected by the occupying power. There was an obligation by the United States government, and particularly the army, to protect these people, their lives, their well-being, their health, their safety. There are quite extensive protections in the Fourth [Geneva] Convention. There are several articles that would directly apply here. If someone wants to give them to me, I would be happy to go through them, but there are 147 articles in there that apply to protect all civilians. And in my opinion it would apply to protect the civilians in that prison. It did not appear to me that in the time frame we're talking about here—two weeks— that anything had been done to protect the civilians in that prison, despite the existence of the obligation to protect. Now, certainly perhaps in the first twenty-four to forty-eight hours when the troops are deploying and getting organized, one can understand that they had other things to do, and, you know, the laws of war do recognize the problem with ongoing military operations, but as the operations terminate, more obligations come into effect. But clearly, at some point in time here within the two-week framework we're talking about, someone was obliged to go to that prison and to secure the welfare of the prisoners in that prison. And as I understand it, that even was the position taken by Colonel Sullivan on the same day that Captain Rockwood acted in the recommendation he made. And I would fully concur. You know, this should have been done probably before then. I can't say exactly when because I wasn't there, but there was a clear-cut obligation to take care of these civilians. They were protected persons within the meaning of the Geneva Convention, and the truth of the matter is that protected persons within the meaning of the Geneva Convention are entitled to even more protection than either you or me under the laws of war. They have absolute protected rights that must be secured by the occupying power, and the Geneva Conventions are quite clear that the United States government must respect and ensure respect for that Fourth [Geneva] Convention in all circumstances. So, to get back to your question, Mr. Clark, I would base my opinion on the field manual, the Hague Regulations, on the Geneva Conventions, that there was an obligation on U.S. forces there in Haiti to go into that prison, and to guarantee the human rights for the prisoners who were there, and it did not appear to me that this had been done within the two-week time in which Captain Rockwood acted, and he had made every effort as he was not only privileged to do but obliged to do. Captain Rockwood was obliged to take those steps, whatever steps that he could and certainly to bring this to his commanding authorities—to his commanders, to his superior authorities. He had an obligation to do this, and I noticed in the testimony of Captain Thompson, he stated his opinion that based on his experience, Captain Rockwood's superior officers were derelict in their duties to not act on the reports that they received from Captain Rockwood. I would agree with that conclusion. When the information that Captain Rockwood had about the situation was brought to the attention of the superior officers, they had—his superior officers—they had an obligation to act and to do something at that prison to secure the lives and well-being of those prisoners, and it does not appear that this happened.

Q: Now, you followed—professionally, you followed all these operations: Panama, the Gulf, and in history earlier ones, Grenada—

A: I've written and lectured on them all. Yes.

Q: Do you know that in Panama, the U.S. forces went to the prisons within a matter of several hours? The U.S. Army in Grenada was in the prisons within forty-eight hours.

. . .

A: Mr. Clark, I had heard Mr. Messing's testimony yesterday, and I am in full agreement, although he was not qualified as an expert on international law and I know this created some problem as to his testimony yesterday. But I am in full agreement with the testimony he gave as to the urgency of the need to enter the prisons and to secure and guarantee the human rights of the prisoners. The testimony that Mr. Messing was giving on the basis of his own personal experience in the armed forces, on the basis of the field manuals that he had studied and helped draft, is fully consistent with the requirements of the laws of war and international law as recognized in the field manual. As I said, I'd be prepared to recognize that it might take a day or two given the confusion necessary with the vast deployment of troops for everyone to get there and get into a location, but I would agree with what Mr. Messing said that at that point they had to get into those prisons and secure those prisoners and guarantee their safety, especially in a life-threatening situation as in Haiti, where everyone knows, at least myself as a human rights expert, that the lives of those people were in imminent threat of harm.

Q: On that last point, as a part of your studies and teachings and writings on the law of human rights so to speak, is it fair to say that it was—and had you been in that activity, for instance, a member of the Board of Directors of Amnesty International and worked with other—

A: Yes, I was elected to the Board of Directors of Amnesty International here in the United States for four years, and I served in that capacity dealing with—actually, we dealt with human rights at a board level—problems in Haiti—

Q: There's a big flow of international human rights information going all over the world that you had access to?

A: That's correct. And I stay on top of that. Sure.

Q: And from that access, do you know that Haitian prisons were considered among the most dangerous in the world for anybody who is in there?

A: That—that's correct. That was on the reports I had seen.

. . .

Q: (*Pause*) You heard the defendant's testimony?

A: I did. Yes.

Q: And you heard what he testified to about human rights conditions here, including what he believed human rights conditions were in the prison?

A: Yes I did, and the reports that he received from the State Department—the delayed report on the conditions in the prison. Yes.

Q: And Colonel Sullivan, what he saw?

A: I heard—yes. I heard his very compelling testimony as to the conditions in that prison and the report he made and the recommendation that he made, which I believe was fully warranted as a matter of international law. Yes.

. . .

Q: From what you have heard here and in light of your qualifications as an expert witness on the law of international human rights, do you believe that the testimony supports an urgent need for immediate protection of protected people, prisoners in the National Penitentiary and elsewhere in Haiti?

A: Of course. Certainly. The prisoners there—the testimony I heard, and certainly from Colonel Sullivan, was that these people were being subjected to cruel, inhuman, degrading treatment, perhaps torture, and that clearly is prohibited under the Fourth Geneva Convention, and we had an obligation once we became the occupant. An occupant, under the laws of war, has both rights and responsibilities, and we have rights as an occupant in Haiti to preserve law and order—if necessary, at gun point—and you heard some of that testimony yesterday that Captain Rockwood gave, that we were prepared to use military force under certain circumstances against Haitian civilians. The law of war recognizes that within limitations. On the other hand, there are also obligations that we must assume as an occupant, and since the government of Haiti effectively collapsed as a legal matter upon our presence, whatever authority that was there was superseded by our own. The law of war cannot tolerate a vacuum of that nature. The occupant must step in and secure the rights of the people in the areas that it's occupying, and secure the basic human rights of these people. So again, it's my opinion that we had an obligation to secure that prison with our own troops and to provide for the basic human rights and human needs of the people living in that prison, and probably I would say within, say, sometime about forty-eight hours.

Q: Now, is *27-10* just a book that describes some international law, or does it impose duties directly on superior officers and junior officers for which they will be accountable?

A: Yesterday you heard, I think, some objection to some of the field manuals that Mr. Messing was relying on saying, "Well, that's just army policy." This field manual is different. There is a requirement in the Hague Conventions and the Geneva Conventions that we must, the U.S. government, as a contracting power, issue instructions to all of our troops as to the law that applies in this type of situation. So, this field manual here is effectively required by a treaty and it states what are the obligations that are incumbent primarily upon military personnel, but also upon civilians. The field manual recognizes that—again, going back to Nuremberg and the experiences in the Second World War—civilians can commit violations of laws and customs of war and can be held accountable for that, as we saw at Nuremberg. But primarily, the thrust of this field manual is the obligation incumbent upon military personnel. However, the obligation comes from international law, from the Hague Regulations, the customary international law, the Geneva Conventions, things of that nature. The field manual is an attempt to distill all of these rules in a manner in which certainly commanders can read and can understand.

Q: And as it comes from international law directly, does it also come by incorporation through Article VI of the U.S. Constitution?

A: That is correct. The supreme law of the land. Again, these, for the most part, are treaties that are the supreme law of the land under Article VI of the Constitution, and the field manual points that out in those words, that even the military personnel are bound by these treaties, on pain of prosecution themselves if they fail to discharge their obligations. And then other provisions in the field manual that are not directly tied in to a treaty are based upon customary international law, and you can see that in the commentary. Where there is a treaty provision they put it in bold—Professor Baxter put it in bold—with a citation to the relevant treaty. Those provisions that are based on customary international law are in there without a reference to a treaty.

Q: So there's no question in your mind that international law, through the Constitution and otherwise, imposes direct obligations, and imposed direct obligations, on the multinational force and U.S. troops in Haiti, of the types that you described?

A: That's correct. And the field manual again deals directly with the problem of a military operation authorized by the Security Council, and it says quite clearly in there that in the event U.S. armed forces participate in a military operation authorized by the Security Council, the laws of war still apply—I mean, they apply all the time. They apply even to United Nations troops themselves that are not part of the U.S. command but subject to the command of the United Nations in peacekeeping operations. So, yes. And again, that contingency was expressly dealt with in the field manual.

Q: And are you familiar with Security Council Resolution 940?

A: Yes, I have read it.

Q: And is that such a Security Council resolution that you were talking about?

A: It too is the supreme law of the land under Article VI. The United Nations Charter is a treaty, received the advice and consent of the Senate; it's the supreme law of the land. And the charter delegates decision-making authority to the United Nations Security Council to adopt enforcement resolutions of this nature. And so that Security Council decision is entitled to the same degree of respect under the supremacy clause, Article VI, as would be a treaty.

Q: And the United States is a member of the Security Council?

A: Yes.

Q: It participated and voted for the resolution?

A: Yes.

Q: And approved the resolution?

A: Yes.

Q: And has agreed to the applicability of the Geneva Conventions to this operation?

A: Well, the United States government takes the position in many of these military operations, and I believe it's taken the position in Haiti, that it does not want to get into a legal quibble one way or the other. It is simply going to apply the Geneva Conventions in any event. And there's been a history of the U.S. government applying the Geneva Conventions to these types of operations, while preserving its position on the formal applicability. But certainly, you heard the testimony yesterday that the ICRC, the International Committee of the Red Cross, was in there inspecting our detainees—that is, not the prison but the detainees—and the reason they were in there inspecting the detainees is very simple, because the Red Cross was taking the position that indeed the Fourth Geneva Convention applied to protect these detainees. And also, if they were members of the Haitian armed forces, they would be protected by the Third Geneva Convention—and prior to the operation, the U.S. government did, as I understand it, issue a statement to the Red Cross to the effect that they would adhere to these conventions as a matter of policy.

Q: Now, you've talked about all that law and the duty to act positively to protect the civilian rights of the Haitian people under these circumstances, but what's that got to do with an individual captain?

A: Well, the captain—all members of the armed forces, and especially officers—the higher the rank, the more responsibility they bear under international law—and again, the field manual makes this very clear, that they are all bound personally on pain of criminal prosecution to adhere to the laws and customs of war and the Geneva Conventions. And again, the more responsibility you have, the higher your rank, the more responsibility you have to carry out the laws of war and the Geneva Conventions. So he was perfectly correct in his statement yesterday that he felt he had an obligation under international law to do something about the situation at that prison—and, you know, maybe he hadn't made as extensive a study of international law as I might have, but his conclusions were correct.

Q: Did you hear his testimony about his assignment as a counterintelligence officer?

A: I did.

Q: And how they gathered information and wrote up their reports and all that?

A: I—yes.

Q: Did the fact that he was perhaps the focal point—the first real officer with direct-line responsibility for basic information, intelligence gathering about human rights violations, prison conditions, and all the rest, so that he had to see it all, uniquely really, perhaps, among the officer corps—impose any special responsibilities on him to act?

A: I believe so. He was in a unique situation to have access to all the information. He was aware of it. He had more information, from what I understood, than just about anyone else as to the conditions at that prison, and the extent of your obligation depends on your knowledge. Obviously, if you don't know anything, you know, even—you have a lesser obligation, although you still have an obligation to find out, if you are an officer. But in his case, under the *Yamashita* test, he knew that there were serious problems with the conditions at that prison. It's not just that he should have known, all right, but he knew. He went out, he got this information, and he knew. And he acted on the information that he had. To give you a comparison, you probably remember the case of UN secretary-general Kurt Waldheim. He was an intelligence officer in the Nazi army in the Balkans, and his unit is alleged to have committed war crimes. Now, I haven't seen any evidence that Waldheim himself personally committed war crimes, but he was an intelligence officer in that unit, and when this information came out, the United States government accused him of being a war criminal and put him on the watch list that bars him from entry to the United States of America on the grounds that he is a suspected war criminal because of his role as an intelligence officer attached to this unit in the Balkans. So here you have, I think, an analogy that's kind of close to Captain Rockwood. He's an intelligence officer, he had this information, unlike Waldheim he acted on the information to try to secure the lives and well-being of civilians, these protected persons within that prison.

Q: Did the United States place Kurt Waldheim on that list with all the implications it has for their international relations at the very time that he was president of Austria?

A: Yes. It shows you how important this principle is that Waldheim had been secretary-general of the United Nations. He was then elected president of the Republic of Austria, which we have very good relations with, we even have treaty relations guaranteeing its neutrality, and despite that, on the basis of the evidence that they had, they put him on the watch list for the role he played as an intelligence officer attached to a unit that did commit atrocities in the Balkans. So again, intelligence officers, a recognition that they have information, perhaps more information than many others, and they're obliged to act on this information they had—and as I understand the testimony yesterday from Captain Rockwood, he acted on the information he had, he was correct in his conclusion that he had an obligation under international law to act. It is unfortunate that his commanding officers did not act—his superior officers. I personally believe, as Captain Thompson said, they should have acted once they got that information. They were obliged to act, they did not act, and—again, I don't know any of these gentlemen personally, one way or the other, but from the testimony I heard yesterday and the facts that have been introduced in the evidence, and also my examination in the news media of this case, I believe they were derelict in their duties in not going and securing that prison and guaranteeing the basic human rights of these protected persons under the Fourth Geneva Convention. Yes.

Q: Now, did you hear the testimony yesterday about what I'll call "facially"—that's a lawyer's phrase, unfortunately—that facially, the facial violation of orders or a policy or something not to climb over a fence, not to travel downtown, and to be at your duty station, and not to argue with your superiors or show disrespect when they don't seem to be willing to listen to you when you're trying to tell them that there are human rights violations that have to be acted on, and you feel that if you're sent home it's the end of any hope for those people, in the face of—and you leave a hospital to come to your lieutenant colonel to try again [chuckled]—please don't send me home, I want a full accounting of these human rights violations—there's got to be a full accounting of these human rights violations—and you've read the charges here, of course, is there anything in those provisions of the Uniform Code of Military Justice and all that would excuse in any way Captain Rockwood for failing to try to do something about the National Penitentiary, knowing what he knew?

A: Yes. The field manual is very clear on this point. It says, every violation of the laws of war is a war crime. So what you had going on in the prison, a failure to stop the abuse of protected persons as confronted Captain Rockwood—as he saw it, these were war crimes over here in the prison. On the other hand, you had military regulations and orders that he had received, and of course those normally should be obeyed. But when you have threatened war crimes over here and war crimes accountability, not only for Captain Rockwood himself but also for his superior officers who knew or should have known what was going on in that prison and they refused to do anything about it, and perhaps culpability on the part of the army for failing to do anything about that prison, I think Captain Rockwood made the right choice in terms of trying to stop the war crimes, which are, from an international-law perspective, and I think even a military-law perspective, are far more serious than the military regulations. And I think that certainly at common law is known as the defense of justification or necessity or choice of evils. It's called by different names in different jurisdictions, but military law does recognize that type of a defense. And I believe the basic defense is the choice of the lesser evil, and between allowing war crimes, potential war crimes to continue at that prison, and violating the military regulations, I believe that Captain Rockwood chose to stop the greater evil. A war crime is always the greater evil.

. . .

Q: And the question is, did Captain Rockwood have an affirmative duty—legal duty—as an individual soldier to act to prevent imminent death or serious bodily injury where he reasonably believes death or injury will occur unless he acts to prevent it, and has no reasonable further opportunity to avoid doing the act without risking the lives and health of the people in the prison?

A: Yes, he had that obligation, and also the field manual makes it very clear that "superior orders" is never a defense to the commission of any type of war crime. So in that area it is recognized that you can't plead superior orders. So the fact that there were other orders given by superiors to Captain Rockwood, in my opinion, just is not relevant here to his attempt to prevent what he believed were violations of the laws and customs of war, which would be war crimes.

Q: And what's the preeminent international authority for the proposition that obedience to the order of a superior is not a defense to a war crime?

A: That goes back to Nuremberg. If you have a look at the Nuremberg Charter, superior orders was rejected as a defense to any type of war crime, though it was recognized as mitigation of punishment. Indeed, that principle in the Nuremberg Charter even goes back further to the old War Department *Field Manual 27-10* of 1940, which was the predecessor to the 1956 manual, and

I've also studied that and written about that. And in the fall of 1944, probably in anticipation of the war-crimes prosecutions, the Department of War put out a revision of this War Department field manual of 1940, enunciating this principle that superior orders is not a defense. So in other words, if the captain here did feel there were these orders but there are war crimes over there, again in my opinion, he was justified in trying to prevent the violations of the laws and customs of warfare.

Q: Did I hear you say that the principle that obedience to the orders of a superior is not a defense where war crimes are serious—

A: Any war crime.

Q: —abuses are going on, in the U.S. military law before Nuremberg?

A: That's correct. I did a study of this with respect to some other matters arising out of the Second World War, and we were the ones that adopted this rule first in the fall of '44, and then later this same principle appeared in the Nuremberg Charter. Yes.

Q: Well, you've made my day. Are there provisions in all of these laws that you talked about, and if not, which don't have them, that impose the individual obligation to act to prevent the type of activity that was alleged or that was reasonably believed by Captain Rockwood to be occurring down at the penitentiary?

A: Well, again, as I said, in my opinion he was obliged certainly under the Geneva Conventions to protect these people. Yes, they were protected persons. And also under the Hague Regulations to protect them, yes.

Q: He had a personal duty?

A: He had a personal duty as a member of the armed forces, and you'll note in the soldiers' code—the oath—the first obligation is to the Constitution of the United States, the president comes second. And that Constitution includes the treaties as the supreme law of the land. So in my opinion, he was carrying out the soldiers' oath and trying to deal with the conditions at the prison in violation of the Hague Regulations and the Geneva Conventions.

Q: Now, can you tell us how the—let's go from—quickly from the Security Council Resolution 940 down through Governors Island Agreement and

President Clinton's speeches and directions to the public—you've studied all this—

A: Yes, I've looked into it.

Q: —and till we hit the beaches, do you find that within the language of those documents and persons there was an expression of an intent to protect the very rights that we're talking about?

A: Yes, the 940 resolution—940 talks about a stable, secure, safe environment in Haiti for the people of Haiti. It refers to the Governors Island Agreement, and if you read the Governors Island Agreement, it also talks about securing human rights in Haiti. But I should point out, even if Resolution 940 said nothing at all about human rights in Haiti, the human rights in Haiti still had to be protected under the laws and customs of warfare, and the Hague Regulations, the Fourth Geneva Convention. And the field manual says this very clearly. But that resolution, I think, provided even more reinforcement to the conclusions reached by Captain Rockwood that even the Security Council, the president of the United States, were aware of the importance of securing, guaranteeing, the human rights in Haiti.

Q: But if it came down through his commander's intent, he would have that individual independent duty?

A: Certainly Nuremberg makes clear that a soldier is a moral agent. You are always a moral agent, and in a situation like this, you must make a moral choice.[11] That's very clear from Nuremberg. And this Security Council resolution, the statement by President Clinton, all had, I think, a very important bearing on the moral choice as Captain Rockwood saw it. And I believe all of this is relevant in your evaluation of his motivations and the moral situation as he saw it.

Q: Did you hear that little short statement on television that the prosecution—

A: I did hear that, yes, that the second speech, the primary purpose was the protection of troops.

Q: The nineteenth?

A: Yes.

Q: Yeah. And then of course the television stopped there, and then did you hear Captain Rockwood read the rest—the next paragraph?

A: I did.

. . .

Q: Was anything said there that either did or legally could have altered the testimony you've given about an individual duty of a captain to act under these circumstances to prevent the continuance of these prison conditions?

A: No. Indeed, of course it's critically important to protect the lives of U.S. military personnel in a situation like this, but by the same token, there is still the obligation under the Fourth Geneva Convention to protect the civilians in Haiti, and failure to do that could lead to personal accountability on the part of individuals involved. So you just can't say, well we're going to do everything to protect our troops and the hell with the Haitian people. That's certainly not what President Clinton said from the testimony I heard yesterday from Captain Rockwood, that appeared to be the attitude of some of the—

CAPT. O'BRIEN: Objection, Your Honor, we're getting into irrelevant territory here.

THE COURT: Well, it's not irrelevant, but we need to make it clear that you're assuming what he said was true.

. . .

A (*By the Witness*): But for a commander to take an attitude that the civilian population in this situation is worthless, I believe is a gross dereliction of duty under the Geneva Conventions and Hague Regulations. Those people have to be protected, and you can't take that attitude under the Geneva Conventions. And even if your first priority is always the protection of U.S. forces, you can't just treat people in a situation of occupation under the Geneva Conventions as throw-away lives. The laws of war make that very clear. And again, if what Captain Rockwood said is true, I believe, again, it would support also the opinion stated by Captain Thompson that these superior officers were derelict in their duties if that is true.

Q: Did the President Carter negotiations with the de facto government—this triumvirate or whatever it was—alter anything that you said regarding the duty of Captain Rockwood under the circumstances?

A: Well, I believe it made it even more emphatic in the following sense, in that we agreed to cooperate with the de facto authorities that we had already stated were a bunch of thugs, goons, and murderers, so we knew that they had committed enormous violations of human rights. Even in our own government, State Department officials were saying that these were crimes against humanity, which go back to Nuremberg. So here we enter an agreement between President Carter and President Jonassaint, the de facto president, as authorized by President Clinton, cooperating with these people. So under those circumstances, we had a very strong obligation under the accomplice liability as recognized by the field manual, to make sure that whatever cooperation we had with these people, that the laws and customs of warfare were not being violated. And again, the field manual is very clear in its section on inchoate responsibility that aiding and abetting, attempt, incitement, and complicity in war crimes are crimes in their own right. So this cooperation elevated—in my opinion, this agreement basically made the Haitian authorities our agent, that we were responsible for what they were doing. And by allowing them to continue to exercise certain authority, we became responsible for what they were doing under these circumstances.

Q: This certainly wasn't incorporated in the prior question, so I don't think you had any need to address it, but it's fair—is it fair to say that the cooperation you were talking about was a very limited cooperation for a very limited purpose—

A: Yes.

Q: —and a very limited period of time?

A: Well, it said until Aristide was restored to power, and obviously until he was able to exercise some degree of effective control; although I haven't been down to Haiti, I've been kind of busy, but my reading of the situation is that President Aristide is still, to a great extent, dependent on the United Nations force and with a substantial component of U.S. military forces still down there. But certainly at the time Captain Rockwood acted, that agreement was in effect. And if we're going to be cooperating with people we've called criminals, then we have an obligation to make sure that they are no longer going to be carrying on their criminal acts.

Q: There was nothing in the agreement to that degree of cooperation that we would agree to cooperate in their criminal conduct, certainly?

A: No.

Q: We were just trying to get things settled down so we could get them out and—

A: That was the philosophy of the mission, as I understand it, yeah.

Q: But none of that affects the international law you described—

A: No.

Q: —and the duties of Captain Rockwood?

A: No. These—

Q: Or affects the Security Council Resolution 940, which I believe you testified imposes a direct duty on him to do this?

A: Well, as I said, I think it entered into, properly so, his assessment of the situation as an officer and as a moral agent as recognized by Nuremberg.

Q: Let me go into it a little bit more. It's hard for me to specify in questions, so try not to repeat what you've already said, but did you pick up that—you heard about his IG complaint, his inspector general, complaint in his testimony?

A: Yes.

Q: And you heard about his—the early document that he gave to the staff judge advocate, the SJA, that listed laws and it said the Universal Declaration of Human Rights or the Commission on Human Rights?

A: Yeah.

Q: What does the Universal Declaration of Human Rights have to do with this situation?

A: The Universal Declaration of Human Rights is a General Assembly resolution adopted in 1948. Basically, the United States government drafted it; it was adopted by a consensus by the UN General Assembly. The United States government takes the position that this is customary international law, that it binds the United States government, and we've taken that position also with respect to other governments—for example, the former Soviet Union, or other states that are violating human rights. So, clearly, that had relevance as to what human rights were at stake in this prison, and I think he was correct to ask for a statement since this is customary international law, and again, we're bound to protect the rights set forth in this declaration.

Q: You heard Captain Thompson talk about the *Calley*[12] case?

A: I did.

Q: Had you ever seen him before?

A: No, I never have.

Q: Had you read the *Calley* case before?

A: Yes.

CAPT. O'BRIEN: Objection, Your Honor. Any opinions on the *Calley* case are irrelevant to this case.

THE COURT: Where are you going?

MR. CLARK: I'd like to ask him what relevance he thinks the decision in the *Calley* case has to the situation here.

THE COURT: Okay. I guess that's the question. Do you have an answer?

A (*By the Witness*): Yes, well again, I think it shows, as Captain Thompson pointed out—again, in *Calley*, in some of the instructions that the judge, the military judge, gave to the members of the jury, he pointed out patterning that language from Nuremberg, that soldiers are always moral agents and they must always make moral choices, and they must not simply blindly carry out whatever orders they might be given. And certainly, the *Calley* case and the whole precedent of My Lai stands for that proposition. You know, it's fair to say that there you had people being murdered right there on the spot, but again, as Captain Rockwood thought, he feared that people might be getting murdered in that prison, and other violations of human rights. So it's simply, I think, a question of degree here, that he felt that there were human rights violations, perhaps murder, torture, who knows what, going on in that prison and he acted to the extent that he could to try to stop it.

Q: Now, if you were testifying in a case in which Captain Rockwood was being prosecuted for failing to act to protect lives at the National Penitentiary, knowing what he knew, and he raises a defense that he was under orders, multiple orders, not to climb the fence, to be at his post at 8 p.m., to shut up, calm down, to stay in the hospital, and behave in a manner becoming to an officer and a gentleman—there may be another one that I forgot about—what would your opinion be as to the effectiveness of those orders as a defense to the charges against him?

A: I'd give the same testimony I'm giving here today.

CAPT. O'BRIEN: Your Honor, this is a matter that's left to the panel in this case.

THE COURT: Yeah, that's a matter for my instructions, and I'm not going to allow him to give an opinion on that particular issue. You've covered the basic groundwork fine.

MR. CLARK: It's really just a way of having him testify as to whether the superior orders here would have protected him if he were charged with the offense of not doing his duty—his international-law duty.

THE COURT: I think you've already covered that. You covered the priority of the law and I think it's clear that international law would supersede the UCMJ under appropriate circumstances.

. . .

THE COURT: Captain O'Brien?

CAPT. O'BRIEN: Thank you, Your Honor.

CAPT. O'BRIEN: Good morning, Professor Boyle.

A: Good morning.

CROSS-EXAMINATION

. . .

Q: Sir, I believe in your direct testimony you testified that you were not in the courtroom for the government evidence?

A: That's correct, I—due to problems in plane reservations and things, I could not get here any sooner than yesterday.

Q: Okay. But whatever the reason, you were not here for the government's evidence?

A: That's correct, I was not.

Q: So isn't it true, Professor Boyle, that your opinion is based solely on the defense evidence, the testimony of the accused, and what you've read about this case in the media?

A: That is—well—that is correct. Everything I heard yesterday, and I did ask my research assistant to pull whatever he could off the Internet, and I have read that, yes.

. . .

REDIRECT EXAMINATION

. . .

MR. CLARK: As a matter of law, would there be an obligation to inspect the prison when you come in if it's just average third world conditions—and I'll add one other element to the hypothetical—and if the State Department report of, that had as to 1994, there had been an increase in routine beatings in the prison, would that impose an obligation—an urgent obligation—to go in and inspect the prisons?

A: Well again, I think this goes back to the point I think that Captain Rockwood made yesterday when he was asked by the other officer why should he care about—this is just another third world prison—and the answer he gave was not given in legal terms, but he was correct that this prison is—once the United States government became the occupant in Port-au-Prince, under the Geneva Conventions and the Hague Regulations, we were responsible for this prison, unlike all the other prisons out there in the third world, which are deplorable. There's no question about it. But this one was different because we had thousands of troops right there, and we were responsible for it. And under those circumstances then, we had to at least bring that prison up to the minimal levels of protection required by that Fourth Geneva Convention, and clearly those standards were severely deficient.

Q: And you have to go there to do it, you have to inspect the prison to do it and see?

A: Of course. And the notion of taking the names down is critically important in the laws of war in human rights practices. One of the first things, you know, that the Red Cross will tell you, if they can get a name of a POW or a detained person, that increases, incredibly, the likelihood that that soldier or that civilian is going to live, because there's a name on a list held by an outside authority. So it's very important to get names of people on lists so you can ensure that they're not just going to disappear.

Q: And in a condition of political turmoil in which a de facto government of thugs is still in power and political prisoners and other political people are being assaulted and killed, does that enhance the responsibility—increase the responsibility—to move quickly to the prisons?

A: Certainly on the basis of the situation in Haiti—you know, I wasn't there, but from everything I read it seemed to be pretty critical to get into those prisons and protect people from being executed. Sure.

Q: Urgent?

A: Urgent.

MR. CLARK: Thank you.

. . .

EXAMINATION BY THE COURT-MARTIAL

. . .

THE COURT: If there were no reports of executions in the prison, yet there were daily reports for the ten days prior to the accused going into the prison of people being murdered on the street by what you might call a "terrorist," is there some sort of priority that an occupying force should use in deciding what problem to work on first?

A: Well, generally, Your Honor, we're under an obligation to both stop the Haitian-on-Haitian violence as well as dealing with that prison—

Q: I understand that.

A: —and that's our obligation.

Q: I understand that. But assuming you only have a limited resource, is there some way that you have to prioritize your responsibilities?

A: Well, as I understand it, in Haiti we had almost 20,000 troops in Port-au-Prince.

Q: No, I'm not interested in what you think. I'm asking you, do we have to prioritize what we do based upon our resources? Just yes or no.

A: Well, the obligations are absolute to protect civilians—yes.

Q: I asked you a yes or no question. Is your answer yes or is it no?

A: Your Honor, with respect, I think as an expert I'm entitled to respond as an expert.

Q: No, as an expert you're going to answer the question that I asked you. Is— do—does the command have to use, knowing how many resources they have, do they have to prioritize in some fashion?

A: They must respect civilians. That's the only answer I can give you in good faith, Your Honor.

Q: Well, if people are being killed in one location and not being killed in another, do they have an obligation to protect the people that would be killed first? Yes or no?

A: Yes, you must prevent the worst violations first if you can, but you have to prevent all violations and protect the civilians.

THE COURT: Yes, I understand. Okay. Does the court have any questions?

MEMBER (*Col. Dubik*): No, Your Honor.

NOTES

1. Lawrence P. Rockwood, *In the Oath I Took, the Constitution Comes First*, Army Times, March 27, 1995.
2. Bob Woodward, *Plan of Attack* 385–86 (2004).

3. Francis A. Boyle, *Foundations of World Order* 77–80 (1999).

4. Francis A. Boyle, *The Criminality of Nuclear Deterrence* 55–91 (2002).

5. Francis A. Boyle, *Obliterating Fallujah: A War Crime in Real Time*, Counterpunch, Nov. 15, 2004, http://www.counterpunch.org/boyle11152004.html.

6. *In the Name of Democracy* (Jeremy Brecher, Jill Cutler & Brendan Smith eds., 2005).

7. Dana Priest, *CIA Holds Terror Suspects in Secret Prisons*, Washington Post, Nov. 2, 2005, at A1.

8. Sinan Salahedden, *AP: Bodies Found in Iraq Since April*, Associated Press Dispatch, Oct. 7, 2005; BBC, *Iraq Death Squad Caught in Act*, Feb. 16, 2006.

9. Prensa Latina, *France Advises U.S. Retreat from Iraq*, Nov. 15, 2006.

10. *In re Yamashita*, 327 U.S. 1 (1946).

11. *See* Francis A. Boyle, *Foreword* to Rick Anderson, *Home Front: The Government's War on Soldiers* (2004).

12. *Calley v. Callaway*, 519 F.2d 184 (5th Cir. 1975), *cert. denied*, 425 U.S. 911 (1975).

Chapter Six

President George W. Bush's War against Iraq on Trial

The first Iraq War veteran to refuse further involvement in the war was Staff Sergeant Camilo Mejia of the U.S. Army Reserve. After serving in combat in Iraq from April to October 2003, he returned on leave to the United States to take care of personal matters. When his two-week furlough ended, Staff Sergeant Mejia failed to rejoin his Florida National Guard unit. After a great deal of moral reflection and anguish, he concluded as a matter of conscience and principle that he could not continue fighting in Iraq. So he filed for discharge from the army as a conscientious objector, in part on the grounds that the invasion and occupation of Iraq were illegal and immoral.[1]

Instead of respecting his constitutional right to a conscientious-objector discharge, the U.S. Army decided to charge Staff Sergeant Mejia with desertion under the Uniform Code of Military Justice (UCMJ). Staff Sergeant Mejia might have gone AWOL (absent without leave), but he certainly did not desert, a far more serious offense. This "overcharging" and persecution of Staff Sergeant Mejia by the Pentagon was an attempt to send a strong message to all other U.S. military personnel around the world that they would pay a high price for exercising their constitutional right of conscientious objection to the Bush administration's war of aggression against Iraq.

Consequently, Staff Sergeant Mejia's special court-martial hearing at Fort Stewart, Georgia, in May 2004 was deliberately designed by the Pentagon to be a combination of kangaroo-court proceedings and show trial that was broadcast and reported quite extensively to all U.S. military personnel worldwide through its internal television, radio, and newspaper outlets. The military judge improperly rejected and prevented the valid defense that we had prepared under the UCMJ, the U.S. Army's *Field Manual 27-10* (1956), the U.S. Constitution, and international law. After the preordained finding of "guilty" by the military jury, I was permitted to testify during the sentencing stage of the court-martial proceedings, though under severe limitations arbitrarily imposed by the military judge. The following excerpts from an interview with Professor Mark Levine—part of a roundtable discussion on war crimes— represent the gist of my testimony in the Mejia court-martial proceedings:

LEVINE: In my own research on war crimes committed by U.S. forces in Iraq, I counted at least two-dozen classes of offenses systematically committed by the Occupation administration and U.S. or U.S.-allied military forces in the invasion and subsequent period of CPA (Coalition Provisional Authority) rule. This includes violations of articles 17, 18, 33, and 147 of the Geneva Convention covering the killing, hostage-taking and torturing of civilians.

BOYLE: As I just argued at Fort Stewart, Georgia, in the court martial proceedings for Sgt. Camilo Mejia for desertion, the accountability here goes directly up the chain of command under the terms of the U.S. Army *Field Manual 27-10*. Specifically, paragraph 501 makes clear that commanders who have ordered or knew or should have known about war crimes and failed to stop it are themselves guilty of war crimes. If you look then at the public record, it is clear that Gens. Sanchez and Miller ordered war crimes and both should be relieved of command immediately: abuse of prisoners in violation of the Geneva Conventions. As for General Abizaid, the overall commander of U.S. forces in Southwest Asia, he admitted in his Senate hearings that he should have known about the war crimes at Abu Ghraib, so basically he's already incriminated himself under the rules of the U.S. Army *Field Manual 27-10*. In addition, above Abizaid you have Rumsfeld and Wolfowitz. Again my reading of the public record, including the Taguba and Red Cross reports, is that they either knew or should have known about all these war crimes. Indeed, if you read the ICRC [International Committee of the Red Cross] report—and as I testified under oath and under cross-examination (and was not contradicted) at the Mejia court-martial proceedings—the widespread and systematic nature of these abuses rise to the level of crimes against humanity, going all the way up through the chain of command. Culpability also extends to Undersecretary of Defense for Intelligence General William G. Boykin and Defense Undersecretary Stephen Cambone, who reports directly to Undersecretary of Defense Douglas Feith. And through this line it appears to me that Rumsfeld is culpable, because he was at Abu Ghraib last fall. Indeed, Sy Hersh's *New Yorker* article on Abu Ghraib claims with good substantiation that he was totally aware and even signed off on the use of techniques which are clearly torture. Rumsfeld was given a tour by Brig. General Janet Karpinski, who was supposed to be in charge of the prison—although she said nothing when she was prohibited from accessing certain areas of it—and so she's also accountable. It's important to understand that the Geneva Conventions, the Hague Regulations of 1907, the U.S. Army Field Manual, all mandate that a criminal investigation be opened. And now President Bush, as Commander in Chief would be accountable under *Field Manual 27-10* precisely because he is Commander in Chief of the U.S. armed forces under the U.S. Constitution. We know the White House knows this because if you read White House Counsel Alberto Gonzales's memo, he specifically tries to exempt the U.S. from the Geneva Conventions for Guantanamo and Afghanistan. You can see that Gonzales was afraid of Bush and others being held directly accountable. Moreover, because Powell dissented, we know there was a debate about this, so Bush had to have been aware of the implications of what was being done, which is also backed up by the memos from Ashcroft. These memos have been unearthed by *Newsweek*. So ultimately what we have here are people at the highest levels of the chain of command guilty of ordering or not preventing torture, which is both an international crime against the Geneva Conventions and the Torture Convention and a domestic crime as well. What we have then is a conspiracy among the aforementioned individuals to commit war crimes and crimes against humanity. Let me add one more thing that's very important to remember: The principles set forth in *27-10* of personal criminal accountability for war crimes goes back to the Nuremburg Charter, Judgment and Principles derived from the post–World War II trials of Nazi war criminals. Similar principles of criminal accountability were applied by the United States to the Japanese Imperial Army war criminals.

LEVINE: In fact, President Bush has compared the war on terror to the war against the Nazis.

BOYLE: Then we have even more reason to bring this to people's attention: The Nuremburg Principles were in fact originally the idea of the U.S. Government which then orchestrated the prosecutions in Nuremburg. People need to understand the pedigree and heritage here. These are very grave offenses which the U.S. government a generation ago prosecuted and executed Nazis for committing. And Japanese war criminals too.

LEVINE: How can any of the people you mentioned be prosecuted?

BOYLE: The military could do it, or the Dept. of Justice, which would have default power to do so if the military didn't. But for this of course we'd need a special prosecutor and that law has been allowed to lapse. Attorney General

Ashcroft, who is clearly part of the criminal conspiracy, would never push a war crimes investigation against his colleagues or President Bush.[2]

Despite our best efforts, the military jury sentenced Staff Sergeant Mejia to spend one year in prison. We immediately had him declared a prisoner of conscience by Amnesty International, the highest accolade that this Nobel Peace Prize–winning human rights organization can bestow upon anyone. Staff Sergeant Mejia was the first prisoner of conscience designated by Amnesty International in the United States since President George H. W. Bush's war against Iraq.[3]

The Pentagon's effort to make an example out of Staff Sergeant Mejia with its particularly harsh, vindictive, and punitive persecution of him in the glare of worldwide news media publicity lost sight of that prescient observation by the early Christian apologist Tertullian: "The blood of martyrs is the seed of the Church." Many more U.S. military resisters would follow in the courageous footsteps of Staff Sergeant Mejia.

One such resister was First Lieutenant Ehren Watada, who went public in early June 2006 with his decision not to deploy to Iraq with his Stryker combat brigade:

> It is my conclusion as an officer of the armed forces that the war in Iraq is not only morally wrong but a horrible breach of American law. Although I have tried to resign out of protest, I will be forced to participate in a war that is manifestly illegal. As the order to take part in an illegal act is ultimately unlawful as well, I must, as an officer of honor and integrity, refuse that order.[4]

Because of this act of courage and principle, Lieutenant Watada would bear the distinction of becoming the first commissioned officer in the U.S. armed forces to be referred to a general court-martial for refusing to participate in the war against Iraq. This is analogous to a German officer refusing to participate in the Wehrmacht's 1939 invasion and occupation of Poland, which precipitated World War II. The acts of military resistance by Staff Sergeant Mejia and Lieutenant Watada represented the cutting edge of both military and civilian resistance as well as of public opposition to the war. The American peace movement immediately mobilized in support of them.

When Lieutenant Watada refused to deploy to Iraq with his Stryker combat brigade on June 22, 2006, the U.S. Army responded by filing criminal charges against him on July 6. In accordance with the UCMJ, Lieutenant Watada was charged with one specification under article 87, missing movement. Lieutenant Watada was also charged with two specifications under UCMJ article 88, contempt toward officials, in this case for making public comments critical of President Bush, despite his right to do so under the First

Amendment. Lieutenant Watada was also charged with three specifications for violating UCMJ article 133, conduct unbecoming an officer and a gentleman. If convicted of all these charges, Lieutenant Watada faced a maximum punishment of dishonorable discharge, forfeiture of all pay allowances, and seven years imprisonment.

On August 17, 2006, the U.S. Army conducted an article 32 investigation into the charges at Fort Lewis, Washington. According to the UCMJ, an article 32 investigation is the military's functional equivalent to a grand jury proceeding to inquire into the facts and the law with respect to the charges and determine whether they are reasonably based: "At that investigation full opportunity shall be given to the accused to cross-examine witnesses against him if they are available and to present anything he may desire in his own behalf, either in defense or mitigation, and the investigation officer shall examine available witnesses requested by the accused."

Lieutenant Watada called three expert witnesses: former UN assistant secretary-general Dennis Halliday, who in 1998 had resigned this high office as a matter of principle because of the United Nations' complicity with the genocidal economic sanctions imposed on the people of Iraq by the UN Security Council; retired U.S. Army colonel Ann Wright, who in March 2003 resigned her commission as a foreign service officer in the U.S. State Department while she served as the deputy chief of mission at the U.S. embassy in Mongolia, to protest the Bush administration's criminal war of aggression against Iraq; and myself. Like Staff Sergeant Mejia and Lieutenant Watada, Dennis Halliday and Colonel Wright had paid high prices for acting on their principles.

Excerpts from the transcript (with minor editing and corrections) of the testimony I gave on behalf of Lieutenant Watada at his article 32 hearing on August 17, 2006, are reprinted below. The direct examination of me was conducted by Eric Seitz, Lieutenant Watada's civilian attorney of record. He and I had worked together sixteen years earlier for the successful defense of U.S. Marine Corps corporal Jeff Paterson (see chapter 4). Jeff Paterson publicly supported Lieutenant Watada throughout this ordeal, passing the torch to a new generation of U.S. military resisters.

In a report released by the army on August 22, the article 32 investigating officer found that the army had reasonable grounds to pursue its case against Lieutenant Watada on the charges of missing movement, contempt toward officials, and conduct unbecoming an officer and a gentleman. The investigating officer recommended to his commanding general that all of these charges be referred to a general court-martial, which is the most serious form of criminal proceeding that the military can institute against members of the U.S. armed forces. All efforts by Lieutenant Watada's attorneys to negotiate an alternative assignment or a lesser administrative penalty were rebuffed.

At the hearing, the army introduced into evidence a videotape of Lieutenant Watada's August 12, 2006, remarks to the Veterans for Peace Convention, which was held in Seattle after criminal charges had already been preferred against him. There, Lieutenant Watada most eloquently and courageously spoke: "Today, I speak with you about a radical idea. It is one born from the very concept of the American solider (or service member). It became instrumental in ending the Vietnam War—but it has been long since forgotten. The idea is this: that to stop an illegal and unjust war, the soldiers can choose to stop fighting it."[5] After the article 32 hearing was concluded and its report already submitted, the army preferred another criminal charge against Lieutenant Watada for conduct unbecoming an officer and a gentleman because of this speech, for which he faced an additional year in prison.

On November 9, 2006, Lieutenant Watada's commanding general referred him to a general court-martial on all charges but charge II [*sic*] and its two specifications under UCMJ article 88 for the public use of contemptuous words against President Bush, which were dismissed.[6] No explanation was provided for the dismissed charges. Lieutenant Watada then faced six years in prison.

On January 16, 2007, the military judge assigned to preside at Lieutenant Watada's general court-martial, Lieutenant Colonel John Head, ruled in relevant part that Mr. Seitz could not question the legality of the Bush administration's war against Iraq at the trial. It became obvious that the Pentagon was planning to railroad Lieutenant Watada by means of kangaroo-court proceedings. However, the Pentagon had brought charges against Lieutenant Watada that made it impossible to exclude arguments about the legality of the war at his general court-martial. It was a self-inflicted catch-22 for the Pentagon.

When the court-martial opened on February 5, the Judge Advocate General (JAG) lawyers put on evidence before the military jury that directly raised the issue of the legality of the war—and in a manner favorable to the defense of Lieutenant Watada. In addition, Mr. Seitz did a brilliant job of cross-examining the witnesses produced by the JAG lawyers, demonstrating to the military jury the relevance of those issues to Lieutenant Watada's defense. After the JAG lawyers closed their case for the prosecution, the judge engaged in improper questioning of Lieutenant Watada as to his position on the legality of the war, before he took the witness stand. Lieutenant Watada made it perfectly clear that in his forthcoming testimony before the military jury he was going to state that the reason he did not deploy for Iraq was that he believed the war was illegal. When after repeated badgering Judge Head could not shake Lieutenant Watada from his determination to so testify, the judge then declared a mistrial.

The judge realized that he had lost control of the proceedings, that these legal arguments had already made the jury favorably disposed to Lieutenant Watada, and that Lieutenant Watada would forcefully and credibly explain to the military jury that the Iraq war was illegal and why. Consequently, there was a good chance that the military jury would acquit Lieutenant Watada on one or more—or even all—of the charges. The judge pulled the plug on the JAG prosecution because he realized that if Lieutenant Watada was acquitted on any of these charges, which was quite likely, it would be a great blow to the Pentagon, to the Bush administration, and to the continuation of the Iraq war.

To avoid this debacle, the judge invoked a pretrial factual stipulation as a pretext to declare the mistrial. Judge Head quite disingenuously argued that Lieutenant Watada had somehow stipulated to his own guilt before the opening of the trial—in other words, that Lieutenant Watada and Mr. Seitz did not understand the nature of the pretrial stipulation that they had signed. Of course this argument was preposterous. Lieutenant Watada, Mr. Seitz, the JAG lawyers, and Judge Head knew exactly that he was stipulating to facts only, and not to criminal intent, which remained to be determined by the military jury.

Despite the Pentagon's public protestations to the contrary, under no circumstances was Judge Head motivated to protect the due process rights of Lieutenant Watada when he declared the mistrial; Judge Head had already grievously violated Lieutenant Watada's due process rights when he ruled that all arguments as to the legality of the war would be excluded. Nonetheless, at that point in the court-martial, jeopardy had already attached (since the JAG case was closed and Lieutenant Watada was about to testify on behalf of his own defense), and thus a second prosecution of Lieutenant Watada would be barred by the double jeopardy clause of the Fifth Amendment to the U.S. Constitution, which provides that no person shall be "subject for the same offense to be twice put in jeopardy of life or limb." Unfortunately, the double jeopardy clause has been interpreted to permit the re-prosecution of a defendant in the event a jury is unable to reach a verdict and is then discharged by the judge, which was not the case here. Judge Head was fully aware of these constitutional consequences of declaring a mistrial. But as the Judge undoubtedly saw it, the inability to retry Lieutenant Watada would be a lot better for the army, the Pentagon, the Bush administration, and the continuance of the Iraq War than a defeat for them all if the military jury acquitted Lieutenant Watada on any of the charges.

The mistrial of Lieutenant Watada was a great tribute to his personal courage, integrity, and principles. It was also a great triumph for the courtroom skills of Eric Seitz. And it further demonstrated the power of international law, the U.S. Constitution, the laws of war, and the U.S. Army's *Field Manual 27- 10* (1956) for opposing the Bush administration's ongoing and threatened wars of aggression against Iraq, Afghanistan, Somalia, Iran, Lebanon, Syria, Palestine, and other countries around the world. With minor modifications, the arguments set forth below can be applied to resist and stop them all.

PROCEEDINGS OF AN ARTICLE 32(B) INVESTIGATION
in the case of
United States v. Lt. Ehren K. Watada
Headquarters and Headquarters Company, I Corps
Building 2027B, Fort Lewis, WA 98433
17 August 2006, 9:08 a.m.
Reporter's Transcript of Audio Recording of Proceedings

Persons Present:
LTC Mark Keith, Investigating Officer
CPT Daniel Kuecker, Trial Counsel
CPT Scott Van Sweringen, Assistant Trial Counsel
CPT Mark Kim, Assistant Defense Counsel
Mr. Eric Seitz, Defense Counsel
SSG Richard M. Goldstein, Reporter
1LT Ehren K. Watada, Accused

. . .

LT. COLONEL KEITH: Okay. Mr. Seitz, the trial counselor has completed their witness list and has shown us their video footage for my consideration. Are you prepared at this time to call your first witness?

MR. SEITZ: Yes. At this time, we'll call Professor Francis Boyle.

. . .

Q: Prior to today, have you ever testified in any other judicial proceedings?

A: Well, in terms of military proceedings, the court-martial proceedings of Marine Corps corporal Jeff Paterson; then Captain Dr. Yolanda Huet-Vaughn, the Army; Captain Lawrence Rockwood, 10th Mountain Division; Staff Sergeant Camilo Mejia. And then I testified many times in state and federal court, and also in foreign countries.

Q: And have you on those occasions been qualified as an expert witness?

A: Yes. In international law and especially the laws of war. The *Field Manual 27-10*, the man who drafted this for the United States Army, Professor Richard R. Baxter, was my teacher on the laws of war at Harvard Law School. And I was his top student while I was there.

. . .

Q: Are you knowledgeable about the United States' obligations under international law?

A: Yes. I've studied and written about them repeatedly during the last twenty-eight years as a professor.

Q: And in what manner does international law determine how and when the United States may wage war against another country?

A: Well, Mr. Seitz, it's not just international law, it's the U.S. Army *Field Manual 27-10*. Professor Baxter, who drafted this for the army, incorporated international law directly into *27-10*. And all the rules are here. I'm not going to go through them all.

But, basically, as drafted by Professor Baxter, *27-10* includes the Hague Conventions of 1899 and 1907, the Kellogg-Briand Peace Pact of 1928, the United Nations Charter, the Nuremberg Charter, Judgment, and Principles, as well as the Tokyo War Crimes Tribunal. Again, this was published by the army as of 1956. It was supplemented once. But it is still valid and binding on troops in the field, including Lieutenant Watada.

Q: What kinds of requirements must be met before the United States can enter into a war?

A: Well, again, the *Law of Land Warfare* does have a fairly extensive section on it. But there would be two basic requirements, to boil it down in a nutshell and not get into all of it, relevant here.

One, warfare would have to be authorized by the United States Congress, pursuant to the war powers clause of the Constitution.

And then, secondly, unless the United States itself is attacked militarily, or its troops, it would have to be authorized by the United Nations Security Council.

Otherwise, aggressive warfare would be a Nuremberg crime against peace. And that is stated quite clearly in the *Law of Land Warfare*. . . . So what Professor Baxter did in the *Law of Land Warfare* for the army, he simply incorporated the Nuremberg Charter and Principles directly into the *Law of Land Warfare 27-10*, including its notion of a crime against peace. And you can read it right in there. It is clearly listed as an international crime.

Q: Did the United States comply with the appropriate procedures to obtain authorization before it invaded Iraq in 2003?

CAPTAIN KUECKER: Colonel Keith, just for the record, at this point, I don't think any of this testimony would be relevant to the actual charges against Lieutenant Watada. It's a nonjusticiable question, the question of whether to employ forces, based on a ruling that the witness was a witness to in *Huet-Vaughn*. The Court clearly said that it's a political question whether to employ troops and is nonjusticiable in this forum.

Also, being ordered to go to Iraq in the year 2006 is a separate issue as opposed to going after Iraq is now a sovereign country, is a separate issue as opposed to what did or did not happen in 2003.

. . .

MR. SEITZ: We can certainly argue the relevance if you want to. I understand there's an objection being made. Given the nature of these charges, particularly the missing-movement charge, an order was given to a soldier to engage in some conduct, to participate in an action which could subject him to sanctions under any of the authorities which we've provided you exhibits of or to which Professor Boyle has alluded. Then that individual has not only the right, but an obligation to question those orders and to determine for himself or herself whether, in carrying out those orders, he or she would be compelled to do something which is a violation of law, not just international law, but international law as incorporated, as Professor Boyle has indicated, into domestic law and into rules of engagement for the United States Army.

So it isn't as simple as saying that just because you're given an order, that you have to abide by it. There is an obligation which is legally recognized at various different levels—and we've given you some authorities for that—which requires soldiers to make that determination for themselves. And that really is the relevance.

In addition, in this case, we have a number of statements which you've seen which are attributed to Lieutenant Watada, which are alleged to be contemptuous or disloyal or disrespectful. It's our contention and certainly will be our contention at trial that those statements, if true, and if accurate commentaries as to what took place with respect to this particular war, cannot be punishable. They are absolutely protected. And they constitute political commentary, which is absolutely protected, because, in fact, among other reasons, they are true. And so, for that purpose, we seek to offer evidence to demonstrate that what Lieutenant Watada had to say about the war in Iraq was not contemptuous, it was not disloyal. It was, in fact, an accurate commentary on the history of how this war began and how it's evolved.

And to say that we're in a different position in 2006 than we were in 2003 is also an interesting issue we'd be happy to join at trial with counsel. In our view, the situation is far more serious, worse, knowing now what we know today than what we knew back in 2003.

. . .

LT. COLONEL KEITH: Okay. Continue, please.

Q (*By Mr. Seitz*): So, Professor Boyle, my last question to you was, basically, in connection with the United States invasion of Iraq in 2003, did the United States go through the proper processes and meet its obligations before it engaged in that kind of military action?

A: Unfortunately, the Bush administration did not. There was no authorization by the United Nations Security Council for the United States to wage war against Iraq. And that made it a crime against peace, which is in paragraph 498 of the field manual: "Any person, whether a member of the armed forces or a civilian, who commits an act which constitutes a crime under international law is responsible therefor and liable to punishment. Such offenses in connection with war comprise (a) crimes against peace." Professor Baxter incorporated that directly out of the Nuremberg Charter, Judgment, and Principles.

Second, with respect to congressional authorization, there was a war powers authorization adopted by Congress pursuant to the War Powers Resolution. But, unfortunately, the Bush administration procured that authorization from Congress by means of fraud. First, they lied to Congress that Iraq had weapons of mass destruction. And second, they lied to Congress that Iraq had connections with the terrible tragedy of September 11. Neither were true at the time, and this has been proven by everything in the public record since then.

This, in my opinion, as a professor that taught criminal law, constitutes a conspiracy to defraud the United States government, which is a felony.

Q: Does the fact that Congress was induced to authorize the military exercise which led to the invasion of Iraq, does that act as a substitute for obtaining consent or approval from the United Nations?

A: No. There are two sources of approval you have to get: both the Security Council and Congress. Congress has no authority to authorize a crime against peace or war of aggression. And here I would compare what the Bush Junior administration did, to the Bush Senior administration. The Bush Senior administration first obtained authorization from the Security Council, and then, second, obtained authorization from the United States Congress to enforce that Security Council resolution.

The Bush Junior administration tried to get authorization from the Security Council and failed. I regret to say the president did not even follow his father's precedent.

Q: You heard a little discussion a minute ago about events that have ensued since 2003, and here we are in 2006. Do you have any opinions with respect to the conduct of the war which would raise issues pertaining to whether or not the United States is conducting that war in conformity with its obligations under international and domestic law?

A: Right. Well, under the field manual, the same paragraph 498, also using the same language that I won't bother to repeat, says: "Such offenses in connection with war comprise (a) crimes against peace, (b) crimes against humanity, and (c) war crimes." Those are the three classic Nuremberg crimes, again which Professor Baxter directly incorporated into *Field Manual 27-10*.

And certainly, based on my analysis of the situation since the war started, regretfully, we have seen war crimes committed in Iraq: for example, the Abu Ghraib torture scandal, which, in my opinion, the primary responsibility for this goes to the very top of the chain of command. This was authorized certainly by the secretary of defense and straight on down from the top. And yet, so far, the only soldiers to have been prosecuted are lower-level individuals. And the chain of command, from Lieutenant General Sanchez straight on up, has escaped any responsibility at all.

We also have the use of cluster bombs in civilian areas. If you were to use a cluster bomb on a tank formation or troops or something like that, in my opinion, there really is nothing illegal about that. But if you use a cluster bomb in a city with substantial civilian presence, I think that does not comply with the laws of war.

There's also the use of depleted uranium [DU], which violates the Geneva Protocol of 1925, which is also found in the field manual. It's a war crime.

And the depleted uranium is not only poisoning Iraqis, it is poisoning our own troops.

And this goes back, actually, to Gulf War I. There is extensive documentation on this by Major Doug Rokke, who undertook the DU investigation for the Pentagon in Gulf War I and, a very conscientious soldier, contracted Gulf War syndrome himself.[7]

"Shock and awe" to start the war—of course, that was the air force, not the army—again, a war crime. The wanton devastation of a city, town, or village is a Nuremberg war crime.

So, there are others that we can talk about, but I think those are the four major categories I would look at. You have others: murders, rapes, et cetera. You know, it seems to me the military authorities are attempting to deal with those.

But the top of the chain of command either has authorized or has certainly not dealt with those other major crimes that I see.

Q: You have mentioned several times the Nuremberg Judgment. How is that applicable? How does that become enforceable in the context in which we're dealing with soldiers, and Lieutenant Watada in particular, in this period of time?

A: Yes. The United States government set up the Nuremberg Tribunal. It was our idea. The Nuremberg Charter is an executive agreement concluded by the president in his authority as commander in chief of U.S. forces. You can find it in Statutes at Large.[8]

The Nuremberg Judgment is reported in Federal Rules Decisions.[9] It is a valid, binding decision that applies in U.S. federal courts. It's not a foreign decision, but it is a decision that flows from the president's authority as commander in chief.

And finally, of course, Judge Baxter incorporated the principles of the Nuremberg Charter and Judgment right here in *Field Manual 27-10*. He did not attempt to write a scholarly treatise or anything, but he distilled the essence of the Nuremberg Charter, Judgment, and Principles as well as the Tokyo proceedings, and put them in *27-10*, which is still valid and binding in the field fifty years later, today. And it remains substantially the same except for one revision that has not changed any of the principles I'm discussing here today.

Q: And also, similarly, with respect to the Geneva Conventions, which have been mentioned at various different times, how do the Geneva Conventions become applicable to the factual situation in which we find ourselves in this case?

A: Yes, the four Geneva Conventions of 1949 are treaties to which the Senate has given its advice and consent. They are the supreme law of the land under Article VI of the United States Constitution. And, once again, they are incorporated in *haec verba*, in those words precisely, right here in the *Law of Land Warfare*, where Judge Baxter put them, with some commentary, where necessary, where the exact words needed to be supplemented by further practice. But they are right there in the field manual. You can read the references and citations. So, again, it's made very clear that all members of United States armed forces, especially the army, are bound by the Geneva Conventions.

Q: And are you aware of any recent decisions in which the United States Supreme Court has emphasized the applicability of the Geneva Conventions?

A: Yes. *Hamdan v. Rumsfeld*,[10] that just came down this summer. As you know, the president is not a lawyer. But, unfortunately, he got very terrible, I would say criminal, legal advice from his White House counsel, Alberto Gonzales at that time, and his attorney general, John Ashcroft—Gonzales is now the new attorney general—that the Geneva Conventions did not apply to his so-called war on terrorism.

This advice that he received from these political appointees directly contradicted the advice that was given to him by the professional military lawyers, the JAG lawyers, at the highest level, who were all of the position that the Geneva Conventions must be applied by United States armed forces. It also directly contradicted advice that the president was given by the professional international lawyers at the State Department that the Geneva Conventions should apply.

Indeed, then secretary of state Colin Powell, who, as you know, had been chairman of the Joint Chiefs of Staff, sent a memo directly to the president, argued to the president that the Geneva Conventions should be applied, must be applied.

Unfortunately, he listened to these political appointees, and we had the torture scandal at Guantánamo, which, Major General Miller there, acting pursuant to orders of Secretary of Defense Rumsfeld, then went to Iraq to "Gitmo-ize" Iraq. And then, unfortunately, we have the torture scandal in Iraq.

It is my personal opinion that if these orders had not been given by the secretary of defense and presumably with the approval of the president, none of this scandal would have happened.

The army's current manual for interrogation of prisoners of war is impeccable.[11] It was drawn up by professional JAG Corps lawyers. I have reviewed it. It's perfect. There's nothing wrong with it. And if not for these orders that were given, the army, following standard operating procedures, would have applied the currently existing manual, and none of this gross, widespread torture would have happened.

Obviously, in wartime, abuses happen, but it would have been sporadic and I think immediately repressed. But here we had wholesale torture. Major General Miller went from Guantánamo to Iraq and with the consent of Lieutenant General Sanchez, proceeded to "Gitmo-ize," as he put it, Iraq. And that was the origin of the torture scandal in Iraq.

Torture is a grave breach of the Geneva Conventions. It's a serious war crime. Moreover, the International Committee of the Red Cross, which has supervisory jurisdiction over the Geneva Conventions, determined that the torture, since it appeared to be widespread and systematic in Guantánamo, Iraq, and, as you know, it also unfortunately, gravitated to Afghanistan, the Gitmo practices, since it was widespread and systematic, constituted a crime against humanity. When you have war crimes that are widespread or systematic, they become more serious. They become crimes against humanity.

And that too is found in paragraph 498 of the field manual, paragraph (b): "Such offenses in connection with war comprise crimes against humanity." Again, Professor Baxter took that directly from the Nuremberg Charter, Judgment, and Principles.

LT. COLONEL KEITH: Let me interrupt you for a second. Because I'm struggling with the connection between what we've just discussed in terms of Geneva Convention and Guantánamo and those war crimes that you have discussed, that you have alleged have occurred, and how that relates to Lieutenant Watada and his refusal to deploy.

A: Colonel, let me try to clarify the chain of events here.

That is, before the terrible tragedy of September 11, the army had an interrogation manual, which I had read and reviewed and was impeccable. There were no problems at all. It was drawn up by professional JAG Corps lawyers at the highest level, everything you would expect from JAG Corps lawyers, and no problems at all.

Then, acting pursuant to the advice of Alberto Gonzales and John Ashcroft, and rejecting the advice of Colin Powell and the JAG Corps lawyers, the president determined not to apply the Geneva Conventions to al-Qaeda or Taliban. That decision, then, not to apply the Geneva Conventions was implemented at Guantánamo under Major General Miller.

Then, Secretary of Defense Rumsfeld and his deputies instructed General Miller to go to Iraq and, as he put it, to "Gitmo-ize" Iraq, to apply the same type of abusive and violative procedures in Iraq that were applied in Guantánamo.

Again, I think if not for these orders, the army would have followed the basic interrogation manual, and I don't believe any of these abuses would have occurred. There would have been abuses, but not widespread, systematic, as we have seen, regretfully, in the news media coming out of Abu Ghraib.

Q (*By Lt. Colonel Keith*): But that chain of events would have changed nothing for Lieutenant Watada in his decision not to deploy. I mean, is that what I understand?

. . .

A: Well, in the charge on missing movement, it says [reading]: "Any person subject to this chapter who, through neglect or design, misses the movement of a ship, aircraft, or movement with which he is required in the course of duty to move shall be punished as a court-martial may direct." So it raises the question, what is the course of Lieutenant Watada's duty under these circumstances of widespread crimes against peace, crimes against humanity, and war crimes? And, in any event, under *Mullaney v. Wilbur*,[12] the government must prove beyond a reasonable doubt that Lieutenant Watada had a duty to participate in this war that is based on crimes against peace, war crimes, and crimes against humanity.

Q: Let me ask you one question, and that's, if we're discussing, for sake of argument, a declared war that's been declared legally through Congress and through all of those provisions that you discussed with me earlier, is it still possible, then, to have war crimes occur during those legal wars?

A: Yes. That is correct, Colonel.

Q: So the fact that there are war crimes, in your opinion, occurring in this war, what relevance does that have to Lieutenant Watada's decision not to deploy, and the fact that, from your perspective, this war is illegal and unjust to begin with?

In other words, I'm trying to distill your argument to the basic pieces of it. Which is, I believe, the fact that you believe that this war is unjust or illegal in that, from the beginning, there was no authorization legally to enter into it. All of the remaining arguments in terms of war crimes, what happened at Abu Ghraib, what's been going on in Guantánamo, et cetera, are really ancillary to the fact that you're saying this war was illegal to begin with; correct? I mean, is there any more to it?

A: They're cumulative, all three grounds. That is, under the Nuremberg Charter, Judgment, and Principles, a soldier has a right to absent himself or herself from committing international crimes. Indeed, under certain circumstances, you have an obligation. That was decided at the Tokyo Tribunal, in dealing with high-level military officials and government officials. But it did establish that those in command, not civilians, but those in command, have a right, if not a duty, to absent themselves from committing international crimes, meaning crimes against peace, war crimes, and crimes against humanity.

Q: In this circumstance, if we argue that, from your perspective, the war is illegal, does the addition of war crimes or the addition of further crimes that were conducted in the engagements of this war add anything to Lieutenant Watada's decision?

A: Definitely, yes.

Q: In other words, does it make it worse for him to have made that decision not to go? Does it make it easier for him to have made that decision not to go?

A: I think it would make it easier, Colonel, in the sense that he would be commanding troops in the field, and he would have a special obligation as a commander to make sure that none of his troops committed war crimes. And if they did commit war crimes, in this situation of pervasive, I would say regretfully, war crimes going on here, he could be held criminally accountable for war crimes committed by his own troops. That too is found in the *Law of Land Warfare*.

Q: But that is true for every circumstance of war when in combat; correct?

A: Any commander, yes.

Q: Regardless of the war, he is held responsible—

A: That is correct.

Q: —for the commitment of his troops in their execution of their duties; correct?

A: That is correct. And, unfortunately, if—in a situation like this war, where you have, I would say, pervasive war crimes, it really raises the question of the right, if not the obligation, of Lieutenant Watada to say, "I don't want to participate in this." And the authority for that really goes to the Tokyo War Crimes Tribunal, where we tried the Japanese war criminals and established that rule: commanders, both military and civilian, have an obligation to prevent war crimes.

Q: But, again, I'm trying to understand your argument. You mentioned "pervasive war crimes" several times in terms of the prosecution of this war. Those war crimes are independent actions, are they not? Or are you indicating that just the fact that had Lieutenant Watada decided to deploy to this conflict, anything he did during that conflict would be considered a war crime? Is that the line of reasoning I understand you to be saying?

A: No, I'm not saying anything he did. The problem here—

Q: So is it possible for him to have deployed and not committed a war crime in this circumstance?

A: Well, the problem here is that we have people at the very top of the chain of command, up to and including the secretary of defense, who have been authorizing war crimes. So it would be very difficult, if not impossible, for Lieutenant Watada not to be committing war crimes.

Q: Would it be possible for him to have deployed in this circumstance and not commit war crimes?

A: Under the circumstances of this war, if he had deployed, he would be facilitating a Nuremberg crime against peace for sure.

Q: So just in the sheer fact that he deployed, he would be committing a war crime?

A: He would be facilitating a Nuremberg crime against peace.

Q: So currently, everyone in theater, by this argument, by this reasoning, if you will, everyone in theater, in your opinion, who has deployed in support of this operation has committed a war crime just by the sheer nature of their deployment?

A: No, I'm not saying that. It depends on the extent of your knowledge, judgment, and experience.

Q: Okay.

A: And in the case of Lieutenant Watada, as I understand it—I've only talked to him once before coming here—he made a very extensive study of the facts and the law involved here. And the more you know and the higher your rank, the more your responsibility.

So I'm not saying that everyone over there at all is. Again, we're dealing with questions of criminal intent here. They have to be proven beyond a reasonable doubt. And I'm certainly not saying everyone over there is facilitating a Nuremberg crime against peace.

But certainly that's the way Lieutenant Watada saw it, based on his knowledge, judgment, experience, and study. And I agree with his conclusions.

But, again, it goes to his intent and his knowledge.

Q: So in that line, then, it is possible for a soldier to have deployed in this conflict and not commit a war crime?

A: It is possible if that soldier had not studied anything at all about the origins of the war.

Q: Well, if they were ignorant of the origins of the conflict, in your opinion, is it possible that they could have deployed, could be there currently, and not have committed a war crime?

A: If they had not studied any of the law or any of the facts and simply showed up, I'm not saying they are war criminals themselves, no.

Again, I still practice criminal law. I'm not saying that here for any member of U.S. armed forces. Nuremberg established also, there is no such principle as collective guilt. Every question of guilt or innocence under war crimes is individual. So each soldier would have to be looked at in accordance with his knowledge, judgment, and experience about what was going on.

I suspect that the vast majority of U.S. armed forces might conclude that there are no problems with deployment. I don't know. I haven't talked to them.

But certainly in the case of Lieutenant Watada, he is an officer. He had an obligation to inform himself. He was commanding, and was going to be commanding troops in the field. He did study. He did research the facts and the law. And he reached these conclusions. And he is held accountable to what he knows.

And again, paragraph 501 of the field manual makes that clear: [*reading*] "Such responsibility arises directly when acts in question have been committed. The commander is also responsible if he has actual knowledge or should have knowledge through reports received by him or through other means that troops or other persons subject to his control are about to commit or have committed a war crime," et cetera, et cetera.

So clearly, in this case, Lieutenant Watada had knowledge. He had gone out, he had done his job as a conscientious officer, he had studied the facts and the law, and he had reached the conclusions that he did. There might be other officers who haven't engaged in the type of study that Lieutenant Watada did. I'm not expressing any opinion about that.

Q: And had they not, would they therefore not be guilty of war crimes?

A: Well, they're not here, and I'm not expressing an opinion about them one way or the other. But certainly in the case of Lieutenant Watada, he had studied. And so his knowledge is higher. And as a commander, you're charged with the knowledge that you have.

Q: But in the case of another lieutenant, would it be possible that they would, then, therefore be absolved of guilt for a war crime had they not studied and done the things that Lieutenant Watada had done?

A: Unfortunately, that wasn't what happened with General Yamashita in World War II. General Yamashita was the commandant of the Philippines. And troops subject to his control committed atrocities against United States armed forces. There was no evidence that he had authorized it or approved it or anything else. Indeed, apparently, he had issued instructions that this shouldn't happen. Nevertheless, he was tried by a U.S. military tribunal and sentenced to death. And he petitioned for a writ of certiorari to the United States Supreme Court. And the Supreme Court denied the writ of certiorari on the grounds that commanders must know—if a commander knows or should know that troops or others subject to his control either commit or are about to commit war crimes and fail to do anything about it, they are responsible. And General Yamashita was hanged.[13] And that principle of law was directly incorporated into U.S. *Field Manual 27-10* by Professor Baxter.

MR. SEITZ: I have no further questions of this witness. Thank you.

LT. COLONEL KEITH: Trial counsel?

CROSS-EXAMINATION BY CAPTAIN KUECKER

Q: You commented on your previous proceedings, the *Huet-Vaughn* case, the *Paterson* case, and *Mejia*. Was your role the same in each one of those? Can you describe briefly what your role was as an expert witness?

A: I was an expert witness, and I was not paid. And I have not been paid for my appearance here today.

Q: Was your focus the same as it is here today or did you comment on other aspects? What was the focus of your testimony?

A: Well, I covered much of the same ground here today in *Huet-Vaughn*, *Paterson*. In the court-martial of Captain Rockwood at Fort Drum, we dealt primarily with the laws of belligerent occupation that were applicable in Haiti. So that was somewhat more technical—it didn't get into the origins of the war of Haiti. We dealt with the laws of belligerent occupation.

Q: But all of them were with regard to criminal court-martial proceedings?

A: Yes.

Q: You say the—the current mission in Iraq is illegal. Why hasn't Congress or some other agent, body, taken—Why does Congress continue to fund it if it's illegal?

A: Actually, in today's *New York Times*, Senator Warner, the chair of the Senate Armed Services Committee and a Republican, said that, in his opinion, Congress is going to have to reexamine the War Powers Resolution authorization it has given.

Q: But there is an authorization right now on the table that Congress is operating under?

A: Right. And I've already pointed out, and here I agree with Lieutenant Watada, that was procured by fraud. The Bush administration lied about nonexistent weapons of mass destruction in Iraq and lied about Iraq's nonexistent connection with September 11.

Q: In spite of all that, Congress continues to fund the mission?

A: Well, when you have troops in the field fighting and dying, of course you're going to pay for them.

Q: Who in Congress is stating the same rationale as you are with regard to—

A: Congressman John Conyers. And I believe Mr. Seitz is or will introduce the report prepared by his [Congressman Conyers's] staff. He's the senior ranking member of the House Judiciary Committee. And they have produced a comprehensive report. I read the report, the first version, as of December. I haven't read the current version. It just came out last week.[14] And I've been consulting with Congressman Conyers's office on many of these points and providing him advice and information.

. . .

Q: Lieutenant Watada getting on a plane and going to Iraq, that's facilitating a war crime, just that alone?

A: If he went to Iraq to facilitate a Nuremberg crime against peace, yes.

Q: Any evidence that you have heard that he would be required to do that?

A: To do what?

Q: To facilitate a Nuremberg-type offense?

A: Well, my understanding is that he was going to be commanding troops, that it was a Stryker brigade here.

. . .

Q: So anyone who deployed with a Stryker brigade would be facilitating a war crime?

A: I didn't say that at all. But certainly that was the conclusion that Lieutenant Watada reached, based on his study of both the facts and the law.

Q: And you said earlier that somebody who is well read, has studied the origins of the conflict, who would deploy over there, that alone could be a facilitator or a war crime in itself, by being there?

A: I didn't say that. What I said was that based on his study of both the facts and the law, Lieutenant Watada concluded that he had a right to absent himself from committing a Nuremberg crime against peace. And I agree with him.

Q: Okay. So, in his mind, he would have been required to do a specific act over there that would have been a Nuremberg crime?

A: The war itself is a crime against peace. In addition, again, the field manual makes it clear there are three different types of crimes here: crimes against peace, crimes against humanity, and war crimes. And my understanding — again, I only spoke with Lieutenant Watada once — was the objection to deploying was not participating in a crime against peace.

Second was, again, you have a chain of command here at the highest levels who apparently have either authorized or approved pervasive war crimes.

Q: Let me ask it this way, then, I think I understand. Let's take a hypothetical where Lieutenant Watada, based on his study of the conflict in Iraq, says, "No. It's unlawful. I can't go." Me, on the other hand, I study the same works, and I come to a different conclusion. Is it your position that the military should allow Lieutenant Watada to stay here and not deploy, whereas I would have to deploy, if we just came to different conclusions?

A: The Nuremberg Judgment made it quite clear that where a soldier knows to a moral certainty, as he sees it, that an order is illegal, he has to disobey that order.

Q: And that's subjective for each individual service member?

A: Yes. It's subjective.

Q: Good order and discipline is important for the military, of course. Do you agree with that?

A: Sure. My father, after Pearl Harbor, enlisted in the Marine Corps. He invaded Saipan, Tinian, and Okinawa.

Q: So Congress, and the country as a whole, has a vested interest in maintaining good order and discipline within the ranks of the military?

A: Yes.

Q: Based on your philosophy, where one soldier's subjective mind can say something's illegal, so that soldier doesn't go, you don't think that would affect the good order and discipline of a unit?

A: A soldier has an obligation to disobey illegal orders. That's very clear from *Winthrop*[15] and *Little v. Barreme*,[16] decided by the United States Supreme Court. And you'll find it in *Field Manual 27-10.*

Q: With regard to the Nuremberg defense that you talked about with regard to the obligation to refuse an illegal order, doesn't that apply to individual acts committed in wartime? It does not apply to government's decision to wage war?

A: That's not what the field manual provides. The field manual provides quite clearly that the decision to wage war itself must follow both constitutional procedures in Congress and authorization from the Security Council when the United States itself is not attacked.

Now, if Iraq had actually attacked the United States militarily, that would be a different story. But Iraq never attacked us. We attacked Iraq. And that made it a crime against peace under the Nuremberg Charter, Judgment, and Principles. And Lieutenant Watada, then, was correct to say, "I don't want to have anything to do with a crime against peace."

Q: Isn't there a legal argument where the UN resolution from back in 1990 was still ongoing?

A: Even the Bush administration didn't accept that argument. And that is why, finally, they tried to get a second Security Council resolution at the beginning of 2003, and failed.

Q: Isn't it true that Iraq was in breach, material breach, and there even was a UN resolution on that, they were in material breach of that initial resolution?

A: That was for the Security Council to decide, not any state. They did not authorize the use of military force in that resolution.

If you study Security Council resolutions authorizing use of force—which, by the way, President Bush Senior did get. I ask the question, if President Bush Senior got authorization for war from the Security Council, why didn't President Bush Junior?

And the answer is, he couldn't get it. The President Bush Senior resolution authorized the U.S. government to use all necessary means to expel Iraq from Kuwait.

The Bush Junior administration tried to get a similar authorization, and failed. They tried twice, and failed.

Q: That initial resolution said, "and to restore international peace and security to the area."

. . .

A: That resolution was limited to expelling Iraq from Kuwait, which the Bush Senior administration did. And indeed, at that point, the question was, under Bush Senior should the United States government go all the way to Baghdad and depose Saddam Hussein? And President Bush Senior said publicly, "I did not have authorization from the Security Council to do that, and so I did not do it." And Bush Junior did not have authorization, either, none.

Q: But the 1990 resolution says, legally, he had—though there might be a political reason not to at the time, in 1991 or whatever, but it was a political reason. He had the legal basis for doing it based on that 1990 resolution?

A: Well, he's contradicted by his own father. President Bush Senior specifically said that "that Security Council resolution gave me no authority to send U.S. armed forces to Baghdad."

Q: I just—

A: It was limited.

Q: I just read to you the authority.

A: Right. To expel Iraq from Kuwait. That's it.

Q: And to restore international peace and security to the area.

A: Right. With respect to the Iraqi invasion of Kuwait.

CAPTAIN KUECKER: I have nothing further. Thanks.

Lt. Colonel Keith: Two quick questions, Professor. One, who has the authority to declare this war illegal?

A: Well, of course, the International Court of Justice could do so.

Q: Who in the United States has the authority?

A: A United States federal court could do so as well. Or the U.S. Supreme Court could do so as well.

Q: To declare the war illegal?

A: Yes, they could.

Q: Had weapons of mass destruction existed and/or the tie to 9/11 been founded between Iraq and the 9/11 event, would that change your professional opinion on the conduct of this war and the legality of this war?

. . .

A: It would all go back to the authorization of the Security Council, which was not there, and also authorization by Congress. And Congress was lied to on both accounts, by weapons of mass destruction and by the tie-in to 9/11.

Q: Okay.

A: And, by the way, those—

Q: Congress did authorize action, you allege—

A: They—

Q: —with bad information.

A: They were defrauded; right.

Q: Had 9/11 been tied to the Saddam Hussein regime and Congress authorized action, as they did, and a soldier such as Lieutenant Watada deployed in the early days of 2003, would that change the prospect for you, in your mind?

A: There was still no authorization from the Security Council.

Q: Okay.

A: Which made it a crime against peace.

And again, compare what happened here with what President Bush Senior did, where he did get first authorization from the Security Council and then authorization from the United States Congress.

Q: No, I understand that.

So your point—your perspective is still that even independent of that, if weapons of mass destruction had, in fact, been found or there had been a tie to 9/11, it still would be unlawful in that the UN hadn't resolved to do anything about it?

A: The UN had refused twice to give President Bush Junior authorization to use military force against Iraq. Twice. He tried, and he failed twice.

LT. COLONEL KEITH: Okay.

REDIRECT EXAMINATION BY MR. SEITZ

Q: First of all, if in fact there had been a tie-in between Iraq and the attack on the United States in 9/11, wouldn't that have justified the United States then, on grounds of self-defense, to have unilaterally attacked Iraq?

. . .

A: The United States would have a right, under the Constitution and article 51 of the UN Charter, to defend itself with necessary and proportionate means.

Q: Okay. And secondly, if in fact there had been a determination that Iraq did have weapons of mass destruction that were threatening the United States and/or any other countries, in that situation, at least hypothetically, the United Nations might have been in a different position to act than what subsequently transpired; isn't that also true?

A: Well, there it's useful to compare it to the Cuban Missile Crisis, where Cuba actually had weapons of mass destruction targeted on the United States, unlike Iraq, and on top of missiles. And President Kennedy refused the advice of his top advisors to attack Cuba. And he also refused to invoke article 51, because Cuba had not attacked the United States. So if, under those terrible circumstances, myself having lived through the Cuban Missile Crisis and remembering it quite well, President Kennedy did not attack Cuba, I don't understand what the legal basis was at all for President Bush Junior to have attacked Iraq, even if they had some weapons of mass destruction. He should have gone to the Security Council, which he did twice, and gotten authorization, which he twice failed to do.

Q: Now, going back to your last colloquy with Captain Kuecker, I want to just ask you, you would agree, a decision for an individual soldier under the legal authorities that you've cited is a subjective decision that has to be made individually based upon what that soldier knows?

A: That is correct. And that's true for all criminal law.

Q: But that subjective decision, which goes to intent and state of mind, that occurs within an objective factual situation such as the one we have here, where you have stated that there is a problem under international law with respect to the initiation of this war. And within that objective context, Lieutenant Watada has decided that's something that he cannot participate in?

A: That is correct as well. Indeed, I certainly wouldn't be here if I did not believe that the facts and the law back up the conclusions that Lieutenant Watada, who is not a lawyer, reached of his own accord.

Q: So with respect to some other military action which has been properly authorized, if in that context some individual soldier subjectively decides for himself or herself not to participate, as Captain Kuecker correctly pointed out, that would be a problem for discipline and good order in the military, which could properly be prosecuted; isn't that fair to say?

A: That's correct.

Q: Thank you.

NOTES

1. Suzanne Sataline, *AWOL Soldier Pledges to Wage No More War*, Boston Globe, Mar. 16, 2004.
2. Interview by Mark Levine with Francis Boyle et al., *Torture and International Human Rights*, ZNET, Jan. 9, 2005, http://www.zmag.org/content/showarticle .cfm?ItemID=6987.

3. Amnesty International, *Prisoner of Conscience: Staff Sergeant Camilo Mejia Castillo*, Urgent Action 190/04, June 3, 2004 (AI Index: AMR 51/092/2004).

4. Video: Statement of Lt. Ehren Watada (June 7, 2006), http://www.thankyoult.org/mmedia/statement.html.

5. First Lieutenant Ehren Watada, Speech at the Veterans for Peace Convention (Aug. 12, 2006), *available at* http://www.thankyoult.org/images/stories/watadaaug12_vfp.pdf.

6. Teresa Watanabe, *Dissenting Officer Faces Court-Martial*, L.A. Times, Nov. 12, 2006.

7. *See, e.g.*, Doug Rokke, *Bunker Buster Bombs Containing Depleted Uranium Warheads Used by Israel Against Civilian Targets in Lebanon*, Global Research, Nov. 6, 2006, *available at* http://www.globalresearch.ca/index.php?context=va&aid=3748; *see* International Action Center, *Metal of Dishonor: Depleted Uranium* (2d ed. 1999); Rick Anderson, *Home Front: The Government's War on Soldiers* (2004); *see also* Francis A. Boyle, *A Global Pact Against Depleted Uranium*, N.Y. Transfer News Collective, Sept. 23, 2004.

8. 59 Stat. 1544–1589.

9. *The Nurnberg Trial*, 6 F.R.D. 69 (1946).

10. *Hamdan v. Rumsfeld*, 126 S. Ct. 2749 (2006).

11. Since superseded.

12. *Mullaney v. Wilbur*, 421 U.S. 684 (1975).

13. *In re Yamashita*, 327 U.S. 1 (1946).

14. House Judiciary Committee Democratic Staff, *George W. Bush versus the U.S. Constitution* (2006).

15. William Winthrop, *Military Law and Precedents*, I & II (2d ed. 1920).

16. *Little v. Barreme*, 6 U.S. (2 Cranch) 170 (1804).

Conclusion

In the wake of the stunning victory for international law, the U.S. Constitution, and the laws of war with Lieutenant Watada's mistrial came the February 5, 2007, launch of a massive campaign of civil resistance by the Occupation Project initiated by the Voices for Creative Nonviolence under the leadership of the longtime civil resister and repeated Nobel Peace Prize nominee Kathy Kelly of Chicago.[1] On February 21 and February 22, 2007, members of the Occupation Project occupied the home offices of members of the U.S. Congress in Toledo, Ohio; Portland, Maine; Denver, Colorado; Charlottesville, Virginia; Seattle, Washington; Medford, Massachusetts; Madison, Wisconsin; and Chicago, Illinois, to obtain from their respective senators and representatives a vote against President Bush's supplementary budget request of $93 billion to fund its wars of aggression against Iraq and Afghanistan. Widespread protests and arrests occurred in Fairbanks, Alaska; Chicago, Illinois; Toledo, Ohio; Portland, Maine; and St. Louis, Missouri. In addition to these protests, Veterans for Peace conducted affiliated civil-resistance activities at U.S. congressional offices in Missouri that resulted in more than twenty-five arrests in the preceding month alone.[2] These organized, systematic, and nationwide civil-resistance activities and arrests are the harbinger of a massive campaign of national civil resistance directed against the Bush administration's wars of aggression against Iraq and Afghanistan as well as against its self-styled global war on terrorism.

This latest eruption of American militarism at the start of the twenty-first century is akin to that witnessed at the beginning of the twentieth century, with the U.S.-instigated Spanish-American War in 1898. Republican president William McKinley seized some of Spain's colonial territories—Cuba, Puerto Rico, Guam, and the Philippines—inflicted a near genocidal war against the

Filipino people, and at the same time illegally annexed the kingdom of Hawaii and subjected the native Hawaiians (who call themselves the Kanaka Maoli) to near genocidal conditions. Today, by exploiting the terrible tragedy of September 11, 2001, the administration of Republican president George W. Bush has set forth to steal a hydrocarbon empire from the Muslim states and peoples living in Central Asia and the Persian Gulf under the bogus pretexts of (1) fighting a war against international terrorism; (2) eliminating weapons of mass destruction; and (3) promoting democracy. Only this time, the geopolitical stakes are infinitely greater than they were a century ago: control and domination of two-thirds of the world's hydrocarbon resources. The Bush administration has already targeted the remaining hydrocarbon resources of Africa, Latin America, and Southeast Asia for further conquest.

This current bout of U.S. imperialism is what Hans Morgenthau denominated "unlimited imperialism" in his seminal work *Politics among Nations*:

> The outstanding historic examples of unlimited imperialism are the expansionist policies of Alexander the Great, Rome, the Arabs in the seventh and eighth centuries, Napoleon I, and Hitler. They all have in common an urge toward expansion which knows no rational limits, feeds on its own successes and, if not stopped by a superior force, will go on to the confines of the political world. This urge will not be satisfied so long as there remains anywhere a possible object of domination—a politically organized group of men which by its very independence challenges the conqueror's lust for power. It is, as we shall see, exactly the lack of moderation, the aspiration to conquer all that lends itself to conquest, characteristic of unlimited imperialism, which in the past has been the undoing of the imperialistic policies of this kind. The only exception is Rome, for reasons that will be discussed later.[3]

I visited with Hans Morgenthau at his home in Manhattan on November 10, 1979. It was our last conversation before he died on July 19, 1980. I asked him what he thought about the future of international relations. He responded:

> Future, what future? I am extremely pessimistic. In my opinion the world is moving ineluctably toward a third world war—a strategic nuclear war. I do not believe that anything can be done to prevent it. The international system is simply too unstable to survive for long. The SALT II Treaty is important for the present, but over the long haul it cannot stop the momentum. Fortunately, I do not believe that I will live to see that day. But I am afraid you might.[4]

The factual circumstances surrounding the outbreaks of both the First World War and the Second World War currently hover like the sword of Damocles over the heads of all humanity. The only hope we have to prevent World War III and a nuclear holocaust is civil resistance. Toward that end this book has been written.

NOTES

1. Rebecca Harris, *The Occupation Project Begins*, In These Times, Feb. 26, 2007.
2. Press Release, Institute for Public Accuracy, *Arrests at Congressional Offices*, Feb. 22, 2007.
3. Hans J. Morgenthau, *Politics among Nations* 52–53 (4th ed. 1968).
4. Francis A. Boyle, *World Politics and International Law* 73 (1985).

Index

neutrality, 12, 130, 180
Neutrality Act, 78
Nicaragua. *See* Iran-Contra scandal
nihilism, 4, 15–18
Nixon, Richard (37th president):
administration/government, 13–15,
103, 108, 128, 132, 149. *See also*
impeachment: of Richard Nixon
nonjusticiability. *See* political-question
doctrine
North Atlantic Treaty Organization. *See*
NATO
nuclear freeze movement, 20
nuclear weapons, 2–3, 8–9, 12, 18,
19–20, 28–30, 33, 37–38, 45, 48,
52–54, 56, 62, 70, 75–81, 83–84,
86–97, 100–102, 106–11, 113. *See
also* weapons of mass destruction;
individual names of civil resisters
nuclear winter, 114–15
Nuremberg, 9, 16–17, 47, 66–68, 77,
84–85, 89, 98, 105–6, 113, 170–71,
176, 181–82, 185–86, 205; Charter,
9, 16–17, 18, 22, 42, 46–47, 54, 62,
66–67, 88, 123–24, 163, 169, 203,
209, 215; defense, 46–47, 99, 107;
Judgment, 9–10, 16–17, 18, 22,
46–47, 54, 62, 66–67, 92, 97, 124,
163, 166, 203, 209, 215; Principles,
9, 16–17, 18, 22, 46–47, 54, 62,
66–67, 72n5, 84–88, 91–92, 97, 106,
108, 110–12, 124, 143, 163, 203,
209, 215; privilege, 10; and war
crimes, 16, 21, 28, 53, 66, 85, 89, 91,
116, 202, 204–5, 210–11, 214–15

OAS (Organization of American States),
13, 16–17, 19–20, 28, 104, 118, 163
occupation. *See* belligerent occupation
Occupation Project, 223
oil, 120, 124, 126–27, 190, 201
Omaha, Nebraska, 94, 109, 111
Operation Desert Shield, 147
Operation Imminent Thunder, 139
Organization of American States. *See*
OAS

Orlando v. Laird, 150
Ostensen, George, 76, 79, 80–82,
86–87
"Our jails are filling up with saints," 22

Palestine, 200
Panama, 19–20, 174
Paquete Habana, The, 8, 57, 60–61, 77,
83, 112, 169
Paterson, Jeff (corporal), 21–22,
121–23, 128–29, 143–45, 150–51,
155–57, 197, 200, 213
Pax Christi, 18
Pentagon, 1, 2, 17, 28, 63, 76, 81, 92,
94, 105, 109–10, 114–15, 123,
162–63, 193, 196–97, 205
people power, 22–23
People v. Jarka, 27–29
Pershing II, 101–2, 104, 109, 149
Plato, 36
Platte, Ardeth, 7, 22
Pledge of Resistance: against the
invasion of Nicaragua, 19–21;
against the war on Iraq, 4
Plowshares (Ploughshares), 18, 20, 22,
37–38, 45, 52, 54, 70–71, 79, 80–81
plutonium triggers, 18
Poland, 133, 196
political-question doctrine, 24, 150,
156–57, 202
Politics among Nations (Morgenthau),
11, 224
Powell, Colin (secretary of state), 166,
195, 206–7
power politics, 5, 11–14, 22, 31
president. *See* Constitution, U.S.:
commander-in-chief clause;
individual names of presidents
Presidential Directive 59, 89–90, 95,
101–2, 105, 113
prison, Haitian. *See* Haitian National
Penitentiary
prisoner of conscience, 196
privilege vs. obligation, under
international law, 62
Prize Cases, The, 118–19, 129–30

Made in the USA
Monee, IL
09 September 2021

77686832R00141